The Resurrection Narratives of the Synoptic Gospels

STUDIES IN THE SYNOPTIC GOSPELS

by Herman Hendrickx, CICM

The Infancy Narratives
The Passion Narratives of the Synoptic Gospels
The Resurrection Narratives of the Synoptic Gospels
The Sermon on the Mount

The Resurrection Narratives of the Synoptic Gospels

Herman Hendrickx

Geoffrey Chapman
London

A Geoffrey Chapman book published by
Cassell Ltd
1 Vincent Square, London SW1P 2PN

First edition copyright 1978 by East Asian Pastoral Institute, PO Box 1815,
Manila, Philippines
Revised edition © Geoffrey Chapman, a division of Cassell Ltd. 1984

Cum permissu superiorum

This edition first published 1984

ISBN 0 225 66401 1

British Library Cataloguing in Publication Data

Hendrickx, Herman
  The Resurrection narratives of the Synoptic Gospels.—Rev. ed.—(Studies in the
  Synoptic Gospels)
  1. Jesus Christ—Resurrection—Biblical teaching   2. Bible, N.T.
  Gospel—Criticism, interpretation, etc.
  I. Title   II. Series
  232.9′7   BT481

Typeset in VIP Times by
D.P. Media Ltd, Hitchin, Hertfordshire

Printed and bound in Great Britain by Biddles Limited, Guildford

Contents

Preface

This book had its beginning in a series of lectures on the synoptic resurrection narratives given to several groups of theology students and catechists. The positive reaction to my earlier books on the infancy narratives and passion narratives encouraged me to revise my notes thoroughly in the light of recent publications.

The affirmation, common to all the gospels, that God has raised Jesus from the dead is the foundation of Christian belief and preaching. However, the way in which this affirmation is expressed in the New Testament presents a problem. Circumstantial details vary and the different narratives need to be viewed in their historical contexts. This book looks first at the general problems raised by the synoptic resurrection narratives and then discusses the narratives in detail in a sequence of seven chapters. The final chapter offers considerations for preaching on the resurrection texts, especially in relation to the liturgical readings.

It is impossible to account in detail for every idea or formulation for which I am indebted to New Testament scholarship and such an apparatus would be beyond the scope and format of this book. Notes have therefore been kept to a minimum but a full bibliography is included, together with suggestions for further reading. I am deeply indebted to the work of many biblical scholars and I wish to record here my appreciation and thanks.

I should like to thank all those who had a share in the publication of this book. I am especially indebted to Rev. John Linskens, CICM, for allowing me to make use of some notes on the historicity of the resurrection narratives a.d for the valuable remarks and corrections suggested after the reading of the manuscript; to Rev. John O'Regan, OMI, for reading the manuscript and making a number of stylistic improvements, and last but not least to Sister Victorina de la Paz, SCMM, Publications Director in the East Asian Pastoral Institute, whose kind concern was so obvious at all times.

Note on the revised edition

The first edition of this book was published at the beginning of 1978 and with a few exceptions could take into account the literature on the resurrection only up to 1976.

Therefore the author and the publisher, Geoffrey Chapman, decided to complete and update the bibliography and to expand and revise the book somewhat in the light of some important recent publications. The author wishes to single out for special mention the book by Richard J. Dillon, *From Eye-Witnesses to Ministers of the Word. Tradition and Composition in Luke 24* (Analecta Biblica 82; Rome: Biblical Institute Press, 1978).

We trust that this expansion and other, mostly minor, revisions will make the book more readable and useful for the reading public we have in mind.

I should like here to express my gratitude to Miss Anne Boyd, Chief Editor, without whose interest this second edition would not have been possible, and Miss Fiona McKenzie, Senior House Editor, for her invaluable editorial work.

1 Introduction

Resurrection narratives?

When we turn from the passion narratives to the resurrection narratives we notice a striking difference. While in the passion narratives we are dealing with continuous accounts which relate a more or less convincing development of facts, we face here a fragmentary tradition consisting of relatively isolated accounts.

In the account of the finding of the empty tomb and the announcing of the resurrection, the three synoptic gospels are still parallel, but afterwards Matthew and Luke go their own ways. For the accounts of the appearances of the risen Christ, they apparently did not depend on common Marcan material. Moreover, unlike the passion narratives, the need for a continuous account was no longer felt. Matthew and Luke wanted to establish that Jesus had risen and that he had appeared to his disciples, and single appearance accounts seemed to make this point sufficiently. It was apparently, first of all, particular theological views, but also personal sympathies and local preferences (Galilee or Jerusalem), which determined the choice of the evangelists. Their texts differ so much that most synopses do not try to give any parallelisms after the pericope of the empty tomb. The accounts also defy any attempt at harmonization.

In the previous paragraphs we used the expression 'resurrection narratives'. But can we really speak of resurrection narratives? Certainly not in exactly the same sense as we speak of passion narratives. For while we are told in the latter that 'they brought him (Jesus) to the place called Golgotha . . . and they crucified him. . .' (Mk 15:22, 24), and that 'Jesus uttered a loud cry, and breathed his last' (Mk 15:37), none of the evangelists gives an account of the resurrection itself. Mark, Matthew, and Luke describe the finding of the empty tomb by the women, and Matthew and Luke go on to describe several appearances of the risen Christ to a group of women and to the apostles. But none of them says that anybody saw Jesus come out of the tomb or rise from the dead, for the good reason that the resurrection itself cannot be observed and is beyond description. Indeed, the *appearance* stories are precisely that and not *resurrection* stories as such, since nobody saw the resurrection itself, but only appearances of the (already) risen Christ. Moreover, the appearances of the risen Christ could be narrated as external events only by patterning them on the encounters with Jesus during his public ministry. Nevertheless, the accounts of the events after Jesus' death and burial are usually referred to as 'resurrection narratives', and for convenience we will do the same.

The scope of this book

Anyone who wants to talk or write about the resurrection of Jesus should first of all listen to the Easter message of the New Testament and faithfully interpret it in line with its own intention. But secondly, the contemporary human situation should also be considered. The interpreter should show how true and fruitful the Easter message is for each of us now.

In this present book, we limit ourselves to the Easter message of the synoptic gospels, and ask ourselves what it contains. We will see that it is first of all the proclamation, the affirmation of the reality of Jesus' resurrection, and secondly an explanation of the significance of this event.

Our study is, therefore, limited in a twofold way. First, we realize that a complete study of the Easter message in the New Testament should start with Paul's affirmation of the resurrection, more especially with I Cor 15:3–8, but also with Gal 1:15–16, I Cor 9:1–2, Phil 3:7–11, where Paul speaks of his personal experience of the risen Christ. Because of this, we at no time wish to give the impression that we are intending to present a full account of the New Testament witness concerning the resurrection.

Secondly, this book deals with the Easter message as it appears in the synoptic gospels. Chapters Two to Eight try to give a verse-by-verse exegesis and to discuss the literary form and the historical value of the different pericopes. We do not intend to work out a complete present-day theology of the resurrection. Others have done this very skilfully and their works can be found in the bibliography. Our interest in the present meaning of the resurrection remains limited to its homiletic and catechetical implications, as can be seen in the last chapter.

Having thus clearly indicated the self-imposed limitations of this work, we now turn to the resurrection narratives of the synoptic gospels.

2   The Empty Tomb – I

(Mk 16:1–8)

Mk 16:1–8

Mk 16:1–8 belongs to a group of three closely related accounts (Mk 15:40–41; 15:42–47; 16:1–8) which may be considered as one continuous unit. With the vast majority of present-day New Testament scholars we believe that the gospel of Mark, written by A.D. 70, ended with 16:8. Mk 16:9–20 is a combination of material from the other gospels, and was therefore added to Mark after the composition of these gospels between A.D. 80 and 100. The addition must have taken place close to or after A.D. 100. Arguments drawn from grammatical considerations, e.g., that it is grammatically barbarous to end a sentence with a conjunction (Mk 16:8 ends with *gar*, 'for'), or speculations concerning possible mutilation of the original text, cannot possibly outweigh the evidence of the ancient manuscripts. This evidence shows that the text of Mark when it began to circulate ended with a reference to the fear of the women in what is now Mk 16:8. This means that the gospel did not originally include any appearance narratives, i.e., accounts of the risen Christ appearing to his disciples. While some think that Mark did not yet know any detailed *account* of these appearances, it is also possible that Mark was familiar with the appearance tradition, but deliberately avoided making narrational use of it and limited himself to a mere reference to it in Mk 16:7. This would mean that for Mark the empty tomb story sufficed as an announcement of the Easter message and was considered by him as an adequate conclusion to his gospel. It means also that Mark had an understanding of Jesus' resurrection quite different from those of Paul (I Cor 15:3–7) and the other evangelists.

> **Verse 1:** And when the sabbath was past, Mary Magdalene, and Mary the mother of James, and Salome, bought spices, so that they might go and anoint him.

There are no less than four indications of time in Mk 16:1–2. The clause 'and when the sabbath was past' situates the events mentioned in Mk 16:1–8 on Saturday evening, after 6 p.m. In verse 2 the action begins the next morning. It is not likely that both verses belong to a single pericope moulded by years of oral tradition. Verse 2 has a better chance of being the beginning of the tradition which Mark presumably received. Verse 1 looks like an editorial attempt to attach Mk 16:1–8 more smoothly to the scene of Jesus' burial (Mk 15:42–47) which took place on Friday at sunset, when the sabbath began.

The list of women, 'Mary Magdalene, and Mary the mother of James, and Salome', which does not tally with either Mk 15:40 or 15:47, is considered by many to belong to the pre-Marcan tradition and to be firmly attached to the present pericope. The list of women, therefore, does not share the editorial character of the rest of the verse. It would have been moved up by Mark from verse 2, where it was found between 'the first day of the week' and 'went', to its present place.

That the women 'bought spices' is explained by postulating an incomplete burial in Mk 15:42–47, although there was no indication in that pericope that anything was lacking. In fact, the statement about the motive of the women, 'so that they might go and anoint him', presents several difficulties. Firstly, the embalming of a body was apparently not in accordance with contemporary custom, since there is not a single example available. Secondly, the completion of funeral rites on a Sunday morning after burial on Friday night seems inconceivable in the Palestinian climate, in which decomposition would already have set in. But our concern should not be so much to recover the women's actual historical motive as to determine what Mark, the redactor, could be expected to have accepted as plausible. The real motive for the delay until Sunday morning may well be that the following scene was firmly set on Sunday morning in the tradition. Originally it may have been independent of a burial account or a report about buying spices the night before. Thirdly, the intention of the women seems to be inconsistent with Mk 15:46, according to which Joseph of Arimathea had carefully buried the body, and had apparently done whatever was required by Jewish law and custom. It has also been noted that although the women play an important part in the account up to its conclusion in Mk 16:8, anointing is not mentioned again after the first verse.

By this verse Mark seems to affirm three things: firstly, the reality of Jesus' death; secondly, the attachment of the women to Jesus; thirdly, that they did not expect anything like a resurrection. They are described as fulfilling a duty out of devotion and are not expecting the divine action which, in fact, has already taken place.

Verse 2: And very early on the first day of the week they went to the tomb when the sun had risen.

The time of the women's arrival is stated twice: 'and very early . . .

when the sun had risen'. The first expression, 'very early' (*lian prōi*) seems to imply a time around 4 a.m. It has been thought to clash with the last clause of the verse, 'when the sun had risen'. But it is not unusual for Mark to qualify a vague indication of time with a more precise one (cf. Mk 14:12). The phrase 'very early' of this new beginning seems to recall the similar phrase in Mk 1:35, 'and in the morning, a great while before the day' (*prōi ennucha lian anastas*).

The phrase 'the first day of the week' is also quite important in Mark's redaction. By means of his three indications of time, 'the day before the sabbath' (Mk 15:42), 'and when the sabbath was past' (Mk 16:1), and 'the first day of the week' (Mk 16:2), Mark harmonizes his chronology with the 'three days' of the prophecies of the passion in Mk 8:31; 9:31; 10:33–34. We have indeed three days in this account: before the sabbath, the sabbath, the first day after the sabbath.

The fourth and last temporal indication in Mk 16:1f. is 'when the sun had risen'. The phrase is not in contradiction with 'very early', since it can very naturally be understood as narrowing and specifying the latter vague indication of time. In the present context, the two phrases complement each other and contribute to the vivid character of the account.

Verse 3: And they were saying to one another, 'Who will roll away the stone for us from the door of the tomb?'

This verse is clearly related to the last clause of Mk 15:46, 'and he rolled a stone against the door of the tomb'. There the tomb was closed, and it is now reopened in almost literally the same words in Mk 16:3–4, Mk 15:47 serving as preparation for the present scene.

It has been remarked that one would expect the women to think of this question before setting out, and that the tomb was most probably closed with a cylindrical stone which one man could move, and most certainly three women. But these considerations miss the point. The question is a stylistic means of heightening the tension of the account and is included for its dramatic effect. It is consistent with the women's original intention to anoint the body of Jesus; it prepares for the surprise effect which follows in verse 4, and leads to the women's actual entry into the tomb in verse 5.

Verse 4: And looking up, they saw that the stone was rolled back; for it was very large.

The women had been wondering on the way how the stone would be removed, but now they look up and see that the stone is already removed. Mark makes no attempt to explain *how* the stone was rolled away, but there can be no doubt that he intends to relate an extraordinary event: 'the stone was rolled back'. The passive mood suggests that it had been rolled away by God himself, or by an angel acting as God's agent. Indeed, in biblical language, the passive form of the verb indicates that God is the subject of the action mentioned.

Several scholars have noted the astonishing restraint of the Marcan narrative. It is implied that the tomb is empty, but it is not stated until verse 6. Verse 4 heightens the tension of the account, but there is no trace of faith. Even at the end of the account (verse 8) the women will not yet believe; only 'trembling and astonishment had come upon them'. This shows clearly that, according to the gospel records, *faith in the resurrection does not depend on and does not originate with the finding of the empty tomb.*

> **Verse 5:** And entering the tomb, they saw a young man sitting on the right side, dressed in a white robe; and they were amazed.

Mark now relates that the women enter the tomb and what they see there. There are three significant points: the young man, his position, and his dress.

First, the young man. The 'young man' of Mk 14:51–52 and the one of Mk 16:5 have been linked together as symbolic representations of Jesus himself who leaves the linen burial cloth (*sindōn*; only five or six times in the New Testament: twice in Mk 14:51–52; once or twice in Mk 15:46; Mt 27:59; Lk 23:53), and reappears in glorious white (Mk 16:5). Recently, it has been pointed out that in the two cases the 'young man' indeed represents Jesus, but is at the same time clearly distinguished from him: in Gethsemane by Jesus' simultaneous presence and in the tomb by the reference to Jesus' absent body (cf. Mk 16:6, 'he is not here'). This has led to the conclusion that the 'young man' is a representation of the risen Christ because he represents the believer who through baptism participates in the resurrection of Christ. It has also been said recently that the 'young man', who acts as a messenger, is not just the baptized Christian in general, but the newly baptized Christian in Mark's community, or even that community itself, including Mark. It is the Marcan community, rather than the risen Christ, which delivers the message.

Secondly, the position of the young man now becomes clear. In Mk 12:36 and 14:62 Christ is referred to as sitting at the right hand of God. The same state is promised to the Marcan community by the position of the young man.

Thirdly, the white robe is that worn in heaven (Rev 6:11; 7:9, 13, 14), and the phrase 'clothed' (*peribeblēmenos*) is also repeatedly found in a heavenly context (Rev 7:9, 13).

The women were 'amazed'. Both here and in the following verse, this amazement is expressed with a rare Greek verb (*ekthambeisthai*) used only by Mark in the New Testament (cf. Mk 9:15; 14:33). The verb expresses a strong sense of awe in the face of the divine. In the present verse, it is no longer a question of surprise: the unexpected meeting with the young man provokes fear. Like verse 4, verse 5 displays a certain restraint, so that the term describing the women's reaction (*exethambēthēsan*) is surprisingly strong. It does not leave any doubt that the women are faced here with a supernatural phenomenon. Consequently, the reader is made to look forward to another, even higher climax.

Up to now we have not been told anything about the presence or absence of Jesus' body. Our attention for the moment is drawn to the way the women are more and more disconcerted and are finally confronted with a heavenly messenger. Strictly speaking, they do not find the tomb empty, but give all their attention to the young man. At this point the narrator expects us to listen carefully. The 'young man' is here not to be described, but to be *heard*. We can expect the core of the account in the message which follows.

Verse 6: And he said to them, 'Do not be amazed; you seek Jesus of Nazareth, who was crucified. He has risen, he is not here; see the place where they laid him.'

Verse 6 fulfils our expectations: it contains the heart of the account, the words spoken by the young man constitute its climax.

The young man's words, 'Do not be amazed', echo the last clause of verse 5. Whenever the living God encounters men, his first words dismiss their fears. Men cannot help being *afraid* when they realize that they are in the presence of the awe-inspiring majesty of God. RSV's translation 'amazed' is definitely too weak to render *ekthambeisthe*. The words 'do not be amazed/afraid' prepare the hearers for the announcement to follow.

The decisive statement is formulated in an impressive antithesis: 'You seek Jesus of Nazareth, who was crucified – He has risen'. The latter phrase sheds light on the following clause 'he is not here', again followed by the young man's invitation to them to see for themselves, 'see the place where they laid him'.

The words 'you seek Jesus of Nazareth' are declaratory and not interrogatory, and connect the present statement to the context of the women's visit to the tomb. The name 'Jesus' is accompanied by two attributive adjectives, 'the Nazarene' (*Nazarēnos*) and 'the crucified' (*ton estaurōmenon*). The first is almost exclusively Marcan in the New Testament. Nowhere else is Jesus called 'the Nazarene' in words addressed to his followers. The phrase is used, however, in Peter's proclamation at Jerusalem (Acts 2:22; 3:6; 4:10). When he asserts the divine power of salvation manifested by the name Jesus, he says, 'the name of Jesus Christ of Nazareth, whom you crucified, whom God raised from the dead' (Acts 4:10). The similarity between this text and Mk 16:6 has been pointed out: in both passages we find the same antithetical structure, opposing crucifixion and resurrection by means of the same vocabulary: *stauroun*, 'to crucify', and *egeirein*, 'to rise', 'to raise', and finally the same specification, 'Jesus of Nazareth'. Mk 16:6 recalls Mk 1:9, where Jesus was said to come from 'Nazareth of Galilee', and points forward to the mention of Galilee in Mk 16:7, resulting in a certain emphasis on Jesus as the Galilean (the non-Jerusalemite?).

Both Mk 16:6 and Peter's discourses probably represent the traditional vocabulary which took shape in Jerusalem during the earliest times of Christian reflection and preaching. A common source in the preaching of the Church is the most obvious explanation for the kinship between Mk 16:6 and Acts; and Jerusalem is almost certainly the place of origin for an affirmation of the resurrection in antithesis to the crucifixion. It was here that the message assumed its apologetic and even polemic tone. The Jerusalem Church had to overcome the scandal of the cross and oppose the reactions of its adversaries by showing how God responded to Jesus' rejection by the Jewish leaders. The proclamation of Jesus' resurrection at Jerusalem clearly appears as a rehabilitation, by God's power, of 'the Nazarene, the crucified'.

The second adjective, 'the crucified', serves as a title rather than as an identification of Jesus for the women. It is one of the characteristic titles of the Christian kerygma and is found elsewhere only in Paul's letters (I Cor 1:23; 2:2; Gal 3:1).

The phrase 'he has risen' (*ēgerthē*, literally, 'he was raised') expresses the core of the young man's message. The passive form 'he was raised' is generally considered older than the active 'he has risen' or 'he rose'. The former also points to God as the author of the action. Unlike I Cor 15:4, which by using a perfect passive (*egēgertai*) emphasizes the present state of Christ as the Risen One, Mk 16:6 has the aorist passive, expressing more directly the action performed. It emphasizes more the transition from one state to another than the outcome as such.

The kerygmatic character of Mk 16:6a has long been pointed out. Its formulary, ill-adapted to its immediate hearers, the women, bears witness to the fact that the account was destined for a particular audience. Pronounced by the young man, who is undoubtedly understood to be an angel, it signifies that the paschal message of the apostles is the Word of God. Since this formulary came presumably from the apostolic preaching in Jerusalem, we must look to this place for the community context in which the account took shape. Further indications will point in the same direction.

The phrase 'he is not here' expresses a further consequence: if God had raised Jesus to life, his corpse could not be there. The phrase 'he is not here' belongs to the proclamation: it further explicitates what is expressed by 'he was raised'.

After declaring that Jesus is not there, the young man goes on to draw the women's attention to 'the place where they laid him'. It is apparently part of the young man's task to establish that the tomb is empty. In fact, Mark never says that the women *saw* the empty tomb. The clause 'see the place where they laid him' is certainly not intended as a strict proof of the proclamation 'he was raised'.

The formula 'he is not here; see the place where they laid him' is unique in the gospels. It is not sufficiently explained by referring to the visual, vivid character of Mark's style. The account reveals a tradition or a narrator who is familiar with the places mentioned. We should even say that this way of calling attention to a precise place shows an *interest in the place as such*. In fact, a similar interest is discovered at the end of the burial account, where it is said that the women 'saw where he was laid' (Mk 15:47), with emphasis on the place. In what context or situation could this interest have manifested itself in this form?

A number of texts could easily be cited from accounts of Christian pilgrims in Palestine which are quite similar to Mk 16:6, but there are no ancient Jewish texts of this kind. However, religious and popular interest in tombs of holy persons is well attested in Judaism of the time of Jesus and the origins of Christianity. An impressive list of tombs well known in Jesus' time has been gathered. The monuments erected on or near some of them testify to a collective interest in the tombs of holy men. This seems to have been the case especially with the tombs of prophets or virtuous martyrs. It seems probable, therefore, that Mk 16:1–8 is a kind of account which would suit believers who were interested in the tomb of Jesus. The formulation and orientation of the account can be explained by veneration centred on the tomb of Jesus.

On the basis of the formulation of the text which betrays a particular interest in the place as such, and the other evidence just mentioned, a number of scholars have traced the origin of the text to a liturgical celebration at the tomb of Jesus. Although others have said that the words 'see the place where they laid him' could easily have been written without any connection with the place of the tomb except for remembrance or imagination, we are inclined to attach some weight to the former scholars' arguments.

Re-reading verse 6, we realize now that the order of propositions is intentional. The assertion of the resurrection, 'he is risen', precedes the reference to the absence of the body, 'he is not here'. Mark does not proceed from the physical fact to its supernatural explanation. His order is not that adopted by apologetics. God's revelation, mediated by the young man, affirms the unexpected: 'he has risen'; and this revelation explains the strange fact which, however, is never stated apart from the revelation: 'he is not here'. The invitation to see for themselves is not intended as a proof of the resurrection. It is rather the other aspect of the fact which is explained through divine revelation:

'Since he has risen, he cannot be here; and see for yourselves that he is not' (J. Delorme).

> **Verse 7:** 'But go, tell his disciples and Peter that he is going before you to Galiliee; there you will see him, as he told you.'

The revelation-announcement of the resurrection is followed by a command which – and this should be emphasized – is not directly concerned with the resurrection. In Mt 28:6 Matthew rewrites Mk 16:7 in such a way as to include the message of the resurrection.

Verse 7 is usually taken to be an editorial verse inserted into an already complete pericope. The final phrase, 'as he told you', refers to Mk 14:28, which is also an editorial insertion. The latter verse is most probably derived from Mk 16:7, the origin of which must therefore be sought elsewhere.

'His disciples and Peter' are the recipients of the message. This formulation is very unusual in the New Testament where Peter, if present, is almost always mentioned first: Peter and the disciples. Apparently this formula did not place enough emphasis on Peter for Mark's present purpose. Peter is singled out for special mention. Mark does not want to say just: tell Peter and the others; but: tell the disciples and especially Peter (to whom the Lord will appear first). Thus Peter is not only given the first place, but is also singled out as especially designated to receive this message. There may also be an allusion here to Peter's denial.

The first part of the message is: 'he is going before you to Galilee'. What does the phrase 'going before' (*proagei*) mean? The same verb occurs in Mk 14:28, which reads: 'But after I am raised up, I will *go before* you to Galilee', and to which Mark has provided a cross-reference in Mk 16:7, 'as he told you'. The two passages must, therefore, be taken together, although we should reckon with the possibility that the phrase *proagei* ('going before') does not have exactly the same meaning in the two texts.

In Mk 14:27a, Jesus prophesied that all the disciples would fall away. The fact that Jesus prophesied this should remove the scandal of this defection for the later Christians: Jesus was not taken by surprise; he knew it all beforehand. Moreover, it was all part of God's revealed plan. Therefore, Mk 14:27b cites Zech 13:7, 'for it was written, "I will strike the shepherd, and the sheep will be scattered" '. The shepherd is obviously the leader of the people of God. Then we understand also the function of Mk 14:28, 'But after I am raised up, I will go before you to Galilee'. This verse must be understood as a continuation of the thought expressed in Mk 14:27: after the resurrection, the shepherd will gather the scattered sheep, and lead them to new and better pastures: he will lead the new people of God to Galilee.

The question whether this command to follow Jesus to Galilee is related to the earlier call in Galilee to follow him and to become fishers of men (Mk 1:17) can be answered only after we determine what is supposed to happen in Galilee. To what do Mk 14:28 and 16:7 refer? One thing is clear: the disciples will see Jesus there (Mk 16:7). But what is the meaning and purpose of this encounter? A closer look at Mk 14:27–30 and 16:7 provides an important clue to the solution of this question. Jesus' prophecy that he would go before the disciples to Galilee is pronounced as a counteraction to the apostasy of the disciples. Peter's affirmation of loyalty (Mk 14:29) and Jesus' declaration that Peter will deny him thrice (Mk 14:30) further stress this failure. In this context, Galilee becomes the place where the disciples return to Jesus and the scattered group of disciples is reconstituted: there the scattered sheep (cf. Mk 14:27b) will be gathered together. Jesus' very first act in Galilee was to form a group of disciples (Mk 1:17). The risen Christ will now restore the scattered group of disciples. Galilee is the place of 'the beginning of the gospel' (Mk 1:1), but it is also the place of completion. This means that Jesus is raised for the benefit of his disciples: they are to see him again in Galilee.

Some scholars have shown that the references to Galilee in Mark are primarily references to the Gentile mission of the early Church. Galilee is both place and symbol. This means that Mark is always moving at two different levels: at the historical/physical/geographical level of Jesus' presence in Galilee and at the symbolic level of a series of references to the experience of the early Christians in the Gentile world. These two levels are difficult to sort out, but it means that in both Mk 14:28 and 16:7 the symbolic reference is emphasized. These verses may be taken to say that Jesus is leading his disciples into the Gentile world and that it is first of all in the Gentile world of the Church's mission that they will see him. The verses considered have even been understood as Jesus' call through the Marcan community to the Jerusalem community to inaugurate a mission to the Gentiles.

In the light of Mark's emphasis on Jesus' didactic ministry (cf. Mk 1:21–28; 4:1–34; 8:38; 13:31), the last words of Mk 16:7, 'as he told you', take on a very special meaning. They communicate to the disciples the absolute assurance of the resurrection. Jesus' word is as real as his own presence. The disciples' meeting with the risen Christ will be at the same time the result of their obedience to and the confirmation of this word. It is the word of One who affirms that he will appear to his disciples after his death on the cross. One who keeps this word is One whose word 'will not pass away' (Mk 13:31).

Recently it has been proposed to understand *eis tēn Galilaian* in Mk 16:7 and 14:28 not as '(in)to Galilee', but 'in Galilee'. In the first, commonly accepted translation, Jesus is understood to have left Jerusalem and to be on his way to Galilee. The disciples and Peter are implicitly invited to follow him to Galilee to see him there. Jesus' going to Galilee as well as the meeting with his disciples (at an appearance of the risen Lord or at his parousia as Son of Man?) is seen as a single occurrence. But if one reads 'He is going before you *in* Galilee and you will see him there', Jesus' preceding does not happen on the way from Jerusalem to Galilee, but in Galilee itself. Hence it would not be confined to one single occurrence, but would rather refer to a permanent relationship between Jesus and his followers. While the idiom of Mark does not allow us to choose between 'to Galilee' and 'in Galilee', it is contended that the former causes more problems for the intepretation of Mk 16:7–8 than the latter. Besides, the theme of 'seeing' is said to support the second interpretation. The usual interpretation of 'there you will see him' as referring to one or more appearances of the risen Lord, and the one which understands it as referring to the parousia, are subject to serious objections. Therefore, a third meaning is suggested, related to other places in Mark where the theme of seeing occurs in the context of the misunderstanding of the disciples (Mk 4:11–13; 6:47–52; 8:11–21; 8:22–26; 10:46–52). In contrast with that of the disciples, Bartimaeus' seeing is at the same time understanding. In Mk 16:7, then, 'there you will see him' may very well mean understanding after the blindness of the past has been healed. Accepting that 'he is going before you to/in Galilee' must make sense for both the disciples of Jesus and the readers of Mark, it is to be understood not as a single occurrence but in terms of a continuing relationship. Both the disciples and Mark's readers must 'go back' to what Jesus said and did in Galilee (Mk 1:14 – 8:21) and follow him on his way (Mk 8:27 – 10:52) in order to understand him.

> **Verse 8:** And they went out and fled from the tomb;
> for trembling and astonishment had come upon them;
> and they said nothing to anyone,
> for they were afraid.

This final verse of the pericope is constructed symmetrically: two activities (one negative) are attributed to the women; both are based on a 'for'-clause, the reason being in each case the same in different words – fear.

The effect of the young man's message is to cause 'trembling and astonishment'. The fear which Mark attributes to the disciples (e.g., Mk 4:41; 9:6) is a theological rather than a psychological phenomenon. It brings to the fore the disciples' lack of faith, their incapability of grasping the messianic import of the words and deeds of Jesus. The fear of the women too seems to express their failure to understand what has happened.

The clause 'they said nothing to anyone' has been associated with the Marcan theory of the messianic secret. The phrase 'nothing to anyone' (*oudeni ouden*) recalls Jesus' words to the leper who was cured, 'see that you say nothing to anyone' (*mēdeni mēden*; Mk 1:44).

As is often the case with his secrecy materials, Mark probably did not create this notice, but rather re-interpreted the silence of the women, which in the tradition constituted their reaction to the appearance of the young man, in the sense of his messianic secret. As Mk 9:9 indicates, it is not until after the resurrection that the messianic secret is completely lifted, and then it is to be proclaimed by the disciples. The women, therefore, should not proclaim it and should not say anything to anyone. Thus Mk 16:7 seems to refer not only to Jesus' appearance to his disciples, but also to the proclamation of the messianic secret and the inauguration of the mission.

Recently, some scholars have gone beyond this interpretation. They point to Mk 10:32, '. . . and they were amazed (*ethambounto*), and those who followed were afraid (*ephobounto*)'. There the disciples' reaction to Jesus' leading them toward Jerusalem was amazement and fear, and ultimately 'they all forsook him, and fled' (Mk 14:50), after which they disappear from Mark's gospel, except Peter, who still 'followed him at a distance' (Mk 14:54), but then similarly disappears after his denial of Jesus. Of all people, it is a centurion responsible for his execution who confesses that Jesus was the Son of God (Mk 15:39). At this point the women appear in the gospel and seem to take over the role of the disciples. But now the reaction of the women is described in practically the same terms as those found in Mk 10:32. 'They were amazed' (Mk 16:5, *exethambēthēsan*) and 'they were afraid' (Mk 16:8, *ephobounto*). Mark concludes this gospel with a reference to flight, fear and silence. Like the disciples, the women are both historical figures and symbolic figures representing Christian communities which Mark knew and for which he wrote. The women fail to communicate the message entrusted to them by the 'young man'. The Jerusalem community, led by 'his disciples and (especially) Peter', never really accepted the call of the risen Christ communicated to it by the Marcan community, symbolized by the young man. They never really inaugurated a mission to the Gentiles, and thus failed the risen Christ.

The historicity of the account of the empty tomb

For our present purpose it is sufficient to speak of the historicity of the Marcan account, for, as we will see in the following chapters, Matthew and Luke depend on Mark and do not have much, if any, additional information. The question to be answered for the Marcan account is then: which part of the account should be ascribed to the editor and what was the extant tradition which he used?

There is no doubt that Mk 16:1 is altogether Marcan in wording and composition. Nor in our opinion, can the editorial character of Mk 16:8b be doubted. Here too the structure and the theological theme (the messianic secret) are to be ascribed to Mark. Further,

Mk 16:7 is also to be attributed to Mark, for it expresses his Galilean theme, no matter in what sense we interpret it. In this verse Mark apparently sticks to this theme to the extent of creating the embarrassing anomaly that the women are told to take the message to the disciples and especially Peter, but do not say anything to anybody. Then, Mk 16:3–4 should also be considered redactional. The accounts of the burial and of the resurrection were originally independent of each other. It was only when they were combined in Mark's redaction of the gospel that the problem of the great stone before the entrance of the tomb had to be faced, for, according to Mk 16:5, the women entered the tomb. The editor had to clarify this, and to do so he used the latter part of Mk 15:46 to compose Mk 16:3. Besides, the expressions 'to one another' (*pros heautas*) and 'for it was' (*ēn gar*) in verse 4b are typically Marcan. This leaves verse 4a, which may very well have belonged to the extant tradition. Because of Jn 20:1 it is considered possible that the tradition mentioned a visit by Mary Magdalene alone.

(2)　　And (very early) on the first day of the week, Mary Magdalene (and Mary the mother of James, and Salome) went to the tomb when the sun had risen.

(4a)　And she (they) saw that the stone was rolled back.

(5)　　And entering the tomb she (they) saw a young man sitting on the right side, dressed in a white robe (and they were amazed).

(6)　　And he said to them, 'Do not be amazed; you seek Jesus of Nazareth, who was crucified. He has risen, he is not here; see the place where they laid him.'

(8a)　And they went out and fled from the tomb; for trembling and astonishment had come upon them.

According to some scholars this extant tradition was already composite. They distinguish two parts in the text. Firstly, women discovered the empty tomb on the morning of the first day of the week. Secondly, an angel revealed to them that Jesus had been raised from the dead. The first part deals with an observable earthly event, whereas the second part speaks of a revelation from heaven in the form of an appearance and the words of an angel. The latter is a technical literary device already used in the Old Testament and in Jewish literature to express that the meaning of a particular fact or earthly situation cannot be understood as such by man, and has to be revealed by God himself, through an angel. These scholars then study these two parts separately.

A. *The finding of the empty tomb*

This narrative would have run approximately as follows:

(2)   And on the first day of the week, Mary Magdalene (and Mary the mother of James, and Salome) went to the tomb when the sun had risen.

(4a)   And she (they) saw that the stone was rolled back.

(5)   And entering [they saw that the tomb was empty].

(8a)   And they went out and fled from the tomb; for trembling and astonishment had come upon them.

What can be said about the *origin* and *historicity* of such a story?

(a)   This story would certainly be considerably older than our present gospel of Mark. In the Fourth Gospel we have something very similar, even more loosely connected with the angel motif (Jn 20:1).

(b)   That a group of women went to the tomb is in perfect agreement with the customs of the time. They apparently went there to mourn. Besides, the early Church would hardly have invented a story about *women* witnessing this fact; there were apparently no men around. The men left for Galilee after the tragedy of the day of Preparation, and there is no indication that they left with any knowledge of an empty tomb. The question has often been raised as to why the disciples left Jerusalem for Galilee. The most acceptable answer seems to be: because the feastdays for which they had come to Jerusalem were over. As far as their connection with Jesus was concerned, no matter how much they may have been still personally attached to him, it was all over now. They returned to Galilee where the risen Christ appeared to them. The theme of the empty tomb was not at once connected with these appearances, since the empty tomb tradition was connected with Jerusalem.

(c)   The *fact* of the empty tomb was never disputed by Jesus' adversaries. They only tried to give a *different explanation* of this fact, e.g., tomb robbery. Besides, in the Jerusalem setting it would have been difficult for the disciples to preach the resurrection, understood in Jewish categories, if they could not point to an empty tomb. But it should immediately be added that the empty tomb as such does not clarify the Christian meaning of the resurrection in which a *transformation* of the body is essential (cf. I Cor 15:35–50). The resurrection belief, or rather the exaltation belief in its earliest forms, does not seem to refer to the empty tomb. The earliest texts emphasize the different character of the bodily existence of the risen Christ, the *discontinuity* of his earthly and exalted bodily existence. But they uphold also the historical *continuity* of the person. If either of these essential aspects is omitted, the resurrection mystery as a *saving* mystery would lose its meaning for *us*.

The *continuity*: if the risen Christ was not the same person as the Jesus who suffered and died, he would not have delivered us from the old existence of flesh, sin and death – to use Paul's terminology. But we have to concede to scholars like M. Brändle that Jesus' tomb did not have to be empty to maintain this continuity. In I Cor 15, Paul upholds this continuity, although he shows no interest in the empty tomb. The tomb did not have to be empty. But another question is what, historically, happened. After all, if at a fairly early date there was in Jerusalem a cult of the (empty) tomb, the only possible source of this cult seems to be a tradition of an empty tomb.

The *discontinuity*: if the resurrection of Christ did not mean that he entered into an entirely different existence, an existence which cannot be localized and dated, it would be meaningless *for us* as a saving mystery, for we would never enter into a new existence either. To give too much attention to the empty tomb could easily obscure this essential aspect of the mystery of Jesus' resurrection, because we would give the impression that it was nothing more than the resuscitation of a corpse from the tomb. The early Christians certainly did not want to say this. Even the account of the empty tomb itself never goes so far as to describe the event as a resuscitation of Jesus. So, we may say that the empty tomb story *could* obscure the essential aspect of the resurrection kerygma, but it *need not* necessarily do so. M. Brändle answered the question whether the tomb of Jesus had to be empty negatively, and correctly so. But the question remains whether Jesus' tomb was *actually* empty or not. This question is not easy to answer. The only thing we can say with certainty is that there was a fairly early tradition in Jerusalem that the tomb was empty.

We may draw the following conclusions from these considerations: Firstly, we should not capitalize on the empty tomb and certainly never say that we believe in the empty tomb. It is clear that the first Christians did not look upon the empty tomb as a proof of the resurrection. On the one hand, they realized that an empty tomb could be explained in different ways and, on the other hand, they knew that the reality of the resurrection as saving mystery can be known only by revelation, expressed in the announcement by an angel. Secondly, faith in the resurrection does not necessarily imply the idea of a material body being taken up again. We should not lose sight of the fact that Jesus' resurrection was unique, quite different from, e.g., the raising of Lazarus, but also different from the resurrection of the dead on the last day. Neither Paul nor the evangelists actually suppose that Jesus took up a material body after three days. They do believe that Jesus had been raised and glorified all the time after his death. The idea of his 'soul' being somewhere separated from the rest of his person apparently never occurred to the early Christians. In biblical times, people did not think in terms of body and soul as two separate or separable entities. Bodily existence means in the Bible a relationship and a presence. In this sense Jesus' life after death was bodily from the very beginning. If the gospels still speak of a burial, it is not because the corpse was so important to them. It was certainly not as important to them as it was and is to later dichotomized thinking.

B. The angelophany

A study of this part of the text shows that the evangelists display great freedom in remodelling this feature according to their own views. The place and time of the appearance and the number of the angels is different in the three synoptic gospels. So is the content of the message. The angels seem to say quite different things, and these differences apparently reflect the respective concerns of the different evangelists. They are not so much concerned with what the angel(s) exactly said as with what they themselves have to say to get the Easter message across in the situation which they are facing.

What then can one say about the *historicity* of this feature?

(a)   The traditional view holds that an angel or angels actually appeared to the women at the tomb. This would make this account unique in Jewish literature, for everywhere else, references to appearances of angels are apocalyptic literary devices intended to express and interpret other-worldly events. The reference to angels is an 'interpretament', that is, a literary means of interpretation. Apocalyptic writers, writing books while quietly sitting in a chair, can at the same time speak of angels flying around!

(b)   Another interpretation holds that the appearance of angels is indeed a literary device to indicate that the women received special enlightenment at the tomb. This opinion is more acceptable than the traditional view, but it is not without difficulties. The resurrection faith seems to have risen from an original experience of the Eleven, not in Jerusalem but in Galilee. Besides, the message of the angels is expressed in the forms of the later kerygma or proclamation of faith. Moreover, Jn 20:1–2, which has a good chance of containing an older tradition, does not mention a revelation at the tomb, at least not in the first instance.

(c)   The best interpretation seems to be the following: The women discovered the empty tomb in Jerusalem. They fled in fear. The Eleven experienced an apparition of the risen Christ in Galilee. Their message, 'He has been raised', was connected with the account of the empty tomb when they came back to Jerusalem. Their revelation experience in Galilee was the true explanation of the empty tomb which the women had found. The interpretation given (by the angels) is, in fact, the expression of the revelation the Eleven received in Galilee. When the kerygma 'He has been raised' was converted into story-form and combined with the account of the empty tomb, this was quite naturally done by means of the classical apocalyptic literary devices of appearances and announcement by angels.

The considerations above were developed on the supposition that in the extant account which Mark received a more ancient tradition can be discovered which referred neither to an angel nor to the Easter message. But this hypothesis has recently been rejected by a number of scholars. They ask whether it is imaginable that there ever were traditional narratives which were limited to the neutral statement of a material fact, i.e., the empty tomb, or whether there ever was a single narrative about the empty tomb with no reference to a divine revelation of its meaning and thus without any illumination by faith in the resurrection.

It seems that these questions can be answered only negatively, and we therefore share the opinion of those who hold that the account of the women's visit to the tomb contained an Easter message from the beginning of its existence.

As to the *origin* of this extant tradition, a number of scholars writing over the past twenty years or so have argued that the account of the empty tomb had its origin in an annual liturgical gathering at the tomb. Their first argument is drawn from the stress the text lays on a *determined time*, meaningful for Christian worship and referring to a feast commemorating the resurrection on Easter at sunrise (cf. Mk 16:2). The second argument is drawn from a similar stress on the *place* where the body was laid (Mk 15:47; 16:6). The quasi-liturgical character of Mk 16:6 indicates that it does not record an historical manifestation but is rather to be situated in the liturgical celebration of the Jerusalem community. The mention of the going to the tomb is also to be related to this celebration, more specifically to a procession to the tomb.

Therefore, the contemporary situation giving rise to the account was a liturgical celebration of the Jerusalem community, and its literary form is that of a 'cultic aetiological legend'. By 'legend' nothing depreciatory is meant. The story is so called because it involves a breakthrough from heaven to earth with the appearance and speaking of an angel. It is called a 'cultic' legend because it was presumably used for a yearly Christian celebration at the tomb. And finally, it is called 'aetiological' because it explains why this tomb was the object of such a cult.

It has been said that the emphasis on both place and time can easily be explained in another way, but the alternative explanations are not very convincing. We conclude, then, that the arguments given by the above-mentioned scholars are quite impressive and that their hypothesis is worth further consideration.

As to the *historicity* of the extant tradition, it has often been said that the proclamation of the resurrection in a Jewish Palestinian context presupposed knowledge of the empty tomb. But in fact there is no reference to the empty tomb in the earliest resurrection preaching. Why this silence? The usual answer is that it did not need to be made explicit because it was not questioned either by Christians or by Jews. However, this reply is unsatisfactory. If, from the beginning, the Jews had been faced with a reference to the empty tomb, they would have needed and actually have given some explanation of their own. They would have said from the beginning: 'You went to the wrong tomb' or 'you stole the body of Jesus'. And the early Christians would have been forced from the beginning to develop explicitly some apologetics concerning the tomb.

But now it is established that such apologetics came into being only much later in reply to Jewish calumny, which in turn was an answer to a Christian preaching which did explicitly speak of the empty tomb.

It seems, therefore, that at first the Christians did not know, or at least did not speak, of an empty tomb. This was most probably so because on the basis of their Easter experience they realized that the resurrection of Jesus was altogether different from the resuscitation of a corpse from a tomb. Neither for the Christians who believed in the resurrection nor for the Jews who understood but rejected their message had an empty tomb any relevance. This seems to be the only reasonable explanation of the total silence of the earliest tradition.

The whole issue, therefore, boils down to the question why certain Christians who already believed in the risen Christ would have celebrated his resurrection in a sacred, empty tomb about the year A.D. 60. Was the finding of the empty tomb an historical tradition? In that case the initial silence of friend and foe is hard to explain.

3   The Empty Tomb – II

(Mt 27:62 – 28:15)

The two features which change the inner direction of Mt 28:1–10 are found largely outside the pericope proper: the tradition of the guard at the tomb (Mt 27:62–66; 28:11–15) and the commission of the disciples (Mt 28:16–20). The combination of the account of the guard at the tomb and Mk 16:1–8 bends the latter to the ends of the former. Mt 27:62 – 28:15 shows that the events at the tomb were due not to a fraud but to supernatural intervention. In Matthew, the commission of the disciples by the risen Christ (Mt 28:16–20) is the climax of the gospel. The words of the angel of the Lord (Mt 28:6–7) and of the risen Christ himself (Mt 28:9–10) are subordinate to that final scene.

Because Mt 28:1–10 is, as it were, framed by Mt 27:62–66 and 28:11–15, we will first deal with these pericopes and then with the account of the empty tomb proper. The final pericope of the gospel (Mt 28:16–20) will be studied in Chapter Five.

The guard at the tomb (Mt 27:62–66)

The account of the guard at the tomb and the ensuing bribing of the soldiers is a remarkable tradition which is found in Matthew alone. The aim of these two pericopes is not to prove the resurrection of Jesus objectively, but rather to affirm that his body was not stolen. This nuance is important for our understanding of Matthew's ideas concerning the resurrection. The resurrection will not be established by the guards. It is only with the women that the angel (Mt 28:5–7) and the risen Christ converse (Mt 28:9–10). It seems rather improbable, therefore, that Matthew intended this story of the guard at the tomb as a preparation for the resurrection narrative, as if he wanted to place 'objective' guards at the tomb. Rather, he remains faithful to the general idea of primitive Christianity which understood the resurrection as an event *revealed* to the disciples, but *not objectively imposed* on enemies and indifferent people.

> **Verse 62:** Next day, that is, after the day of Preparation, the chief priests and the Pharisees gathered before Pilate

Matthew's time indication, 'next day, that is, after the day of Preparation', is surprising since he could have said 'on the sabbath' or simply 'the next day'. It is possible that we have here an example of Matthew's well-known fidelity to his sources. He found the expression 'the day of Preparation' in Mk 15:42. Since he omitted this time indication in the parallel verse, Mt 27:57, he may have made up for it in the present verse. The evangelist may also have wanted to suggest that the Jewish authorities were in a hurry to stave off the dangers which they will mention in the ensuing conversation with Pilate. We could paraphrase the clause: 'Next day, that is, right after the day of Preparation'.

It seems, however, that Matthew accords also special importance to the phrase 'the day of Preparation'. It indicates the day of Jesus' death which, for Matthew and his community, was much more important than the Jewish sabbath. The whole pericope is coloured by specifically Christian interests, and Mt 28:15, 'this story has been spread *among the Jews* to this day', points to a situation and a time in which Christians spoke of 'the Jews' as outsiders.

'The chief priests and the Pharisees' are the official representatives of the people. In the present composition of his gospel Matthew certainly refers to Mt 21:45, which is his own conclusion to the parable of the wicked tenants where, at least implicitly, 'the chief priests and the Pharisees' are made responsible for the passion and death of Jesus. They consider themselves responsible for the people of God. In fact, they will express their concern for 'the people' in Mt 27:64.

They 'gathered before Pilate'. The verb 'to come together' (*sunagesthai*) suggests a unity of purpose of the Jewish and Roman authorities: they plot together. Matthew uses the same verb to describe the gathering of Herod and the chief priests in the story of the Magi (Mt 2:4; see also Mt 22:34, 41; 26:3, 57; 28:12). It always implies a conspiracy of those opposed to Jesus. The origin of this expression may be found in Acts 4:5, 'On the morrow their rulers and elders and scribes were gathered together (*sunachthēnai*) in Jerusalem . . .'. This is followed by an explanation from scripture in Acts 4:25–26 which quotes Ps 2:1, 2, 'Why did the Gentiles rage, and the peoples imagine vain things? The kings of the earth set themselves in array, and the rulers were gathered together (*sunēchthēsan*), against the Lord and against his Anointed.' In Acts 4 these combined forces try to prevent the preaching of Jesus' message. Here in Mt 27:62–66, they try to stop the message of the resurrection by ascribing it to deceit on the part of the disciples.

Verse 63: and said 'Sir, we remember how that impostor said, while he was still alive, "After three days I will rise again."'

The Jewish leaders call Jesus an 'impostor'. This is a man who leads the people astray by deceiving them in the field of doctrine. We think here of *Testamentum Levi* 16:3 where a man who changes the Law in the name of the Most High is called an 'impostor' (*planos*). The same expression is found in Justin's *Dialogue with Trypho* 108: 'a godless, lawless sect was founded by a certain Jesus, a Galilean impostor. When we crucified him, his disciples stole him during the night from the tomb . . . and so they *deceive* the people.'

The chief priests and the Pharisees recall a prediction made by Jesus himself about his resurrection 'after three days'. Whatever predictions about his passion and resurrection Jesus may have uttered during his public ministry, there is no doubt that they were considerably less explicit than the predictions which we now find in the gospel (Mt 16:21; 17:22–23; 20:18–19). The present formulation of these predictions is influenced by the post-Easter faith of the early Christians. It should also be noted that these predictions belonged to the instruction of the disciples and were not pronounced in the presence of 'outsiders' like the Jewish authorities. Matthew is apparently more interested in the overall theological and apologetic impact of the narrative than in historical accuracy.

Unlike Mark, who uses the expression 'after three days' (Mk 8:31; 9:31; 10:34), Matthew has 'on the third day' in the parallel texts. Most probably 'after three days' is the older expression. Matthew changed it into 'on the third day' in Mt 16:21; 17:23; 20:19.

In what is generally considered the oldest written kerygmatic formula we read:

> . . . that Christ died for our sins
>   in accordance with the scriptures,
> that he was buried,
> that he was raised on the third day
>   in accordance with the scriptures and
> that he appeared . . . (I Cor 15:3–5).

There cannot be any doubt that in the first part of this statement the phrase 'in accordance with the scriptures' refers to 'for our sins'. Similarly, in the second part of the formula, the phrase 'in accordance with the scriptures' refers to 'on the third day'. The latter phrase apparently expresses the salvific meaning of the resurrection, just as 'for our sins' expresses the salvific meaning of Jesus' death. The early Christians expressed the salvific meaning of the events by means of references or allusions to the Old Testament. This is exactly the import of the twice-repeated 'in accordance with the scriptures' in I Cor 15:3–5. For the first part of the kerygmatic formula almost all exegetes agree that the allusion is to Isa 53:6, 'and the Lord has laid on him the iniquity of us all' and Isa 53:12, 'yet he bore the sin of many, and made intercession for the transgressors'. Similarly, 'on the third day' seems to be a reference to Hos 6:2, 'After two days he will revive us; on the third day he will raise us up, that we may live before him'. If in the predictions of the passion Matthew and Luke independently changed Mark's 'after three days', they did so most probably under the influence of a credal formula which we find in I Cor 15:3–5. Anyway, for Matthew the two phrases have apparently the same meaning, since in the present verse he uses 'after three days', but in the following verse the Jewish authorities are referred to as asking that 'the sepulchre be made secure until the third day'.

The meaning of the expression 'on the third day' has also been clarified by referring to the meaning which the third day often has in *targum* and *midrash* literature: God never leaves the just one in danger for more than three days; on the third day he intervenes to save him. 'On the third day', therefore, would not be an historical indication, but a theological affirmation of the certainty of God's saving intervention. The resurrection thus becomes the supreme achievement of all the marvellous interventions of God in salvation history.

Verse 64: 'Therefore, order the sepulchre to be made secure until the third day, lest his disciples go and steal him away, and tell the people, "He has risen from the dead," and the last fraud will be worse than the first.'

The Jewish authorities request Pilate to 'order' the sepulchre secured, and Matthew seems to suggest that they were in a position to make such a request. He apparently refers to Mt 27:58, 'He went to Pilate and asked for the body of Jesus. Then Pilate *ordered* it to be given to him.' By granting a private burial, Pilate himself had created the situation which could give rise to the dangers just mentioned.

The verb 'to secure' (*asphalizein*) is used three times in this pericope (Mt 27:64, 65, 66) and should therefore be given due attention. The only other instance in the New Testament is found in Acts 16:24, stating that Paul's and Silas' feet were 'fastened' or 'secured' in the stocks. It is part of a 'liberation miracle' (Acts 16:22–35) narrating Paul's imprisonment and miraculous liberation at Philippi. No matter how well the authorities 'secured' Paul and Silas, God's powerful intervention set them free. So here, no matter how much the authorities made the sepulchre secure, God's intervention would not be foiled. If the disciples preached that 'he was risen from the dead', it was certainly not because the authorities did not take the necessary precautions.

In their concern for 'the people' the scribes and Pharisees feared that the theft of Jesus' body would be followed by the disciples' proclamation that 'he was risen from the dead'. This supposes a situation other and later than that prevailing within twenty-four hours after Jesus' death. The disciples were scattered and hardly constituted a danger at that time. The phrase 'the disciples' is used here in the sense of 'the Christians', and the whole situation clearly presupposes the Christian proclamation of the resurrection. The authorities fear the effects of the Christian proclamation which they call a 'fraud' (*planē*; see Mt 27:63, *planos*, 'impostor').

This 'fraud will be worse than the first', because it would affect not just a few persons but 'the people' (*laos*), the whole holy Jewish nation. The first fraud must refer to Jesus' alleged claim to be the Messiah. 'The last fraud' is then the Christian community's kerygma of Jesus' resurrection from the dead. This second fraud would become possible if the disciples succeeded in stealing the body of Jesus.

The authorities request Pilate to secure the tomb 'until the third day'. This detail obviously presupposes the specific Christian message: 'He was raised on the third day'. The phrases 'on the third day' and 'after three days' are certainly to be traced to the post-Easter Christian tradition. Jesus himself most probably announced his victory after seeming defeat in terms of the fourth song of the Suffering Servant (Isa 52:13 – 53:12). He certainly did not prophesy in so many words that he was going to be raised 'after three days' or 'on the third day'. The phrase 'after three days' seems to refer to an experience of the disciples after three days or a short interval, while the phrase 'on the third day' seems to be a later soteriological expression inspired by Hos 6:2. The present story, however, takes the two expressions in a precise chronological sense: after three days there will no longer be any reason for fear.

Verse 65: Pilate said to them, 'You have a guard of soldiers; go, make it as secure as you can.'

Pilate grants the request: 'You have your guard', i.e., I now put one at your disposal. Indeed, as the continuation indicates, we should read: 'have your guard' (an imperative). The word 'guard' (*koustōdia*), which is found in the New Testament only in this pericope (Mt 27:65, 66) and in Mt 28:11, may indicate the official character of this scene. The reference to a guard is a common feature of the so-called 'liberation miracles'.

Some scholars say that the phrase 'as you can' implies a certain sarcasm on the part of Pilate. But this seems out of place in a narrative which shows fairly close co-operation between Pilate and the Jewish authorities, to the extent that this Pilate looks somewhat different from the one presented in the passion narrative proper. Should it not rather be said, therefore, that the phrase, which is ambiguous in itself, is used in such a way as to express the sarcasm or irony of the Christians who composed the narrative? After all, Mt 27:62–66 and 28:11–15 are attempting to refute a Jewish objection against Christian apologetics based on the empty tomb.

Verse 66: So they went and made the sepulchre secure by sealing the stone and setting a guard.

After receiving the go-ahead from Pilate, the Jewish authorities took all necessary steps: the stone was sealed and the guard was set. The entrance of rock tombs was closed by a great round stone. It was sealed by putting slime or wax on and into the joint between the stone and the rock and impressing a seal in the wax. The scene reminds us of Dan 6:17, 'A stone was brought and laid upon the mouth of the den, and the king sealed it with his signet and with the signet of his lords, that nothing might be changed concerning Daniel'. In the early Church, Daniel's escape from the den of lions was considered a type of Jesus' resurrection, but we cannot determine with certainty whether Matthew already thought of it in this way.

The scene is all set for the events of 'the first day of the week'. This passage has strongly influenced Matthew's version of the account of the empty tomb. Matthew, as it were, capitalizes on the passage's apologetic value.

But since Mt 27:62–66 and 28:11–15 are closely related and probably come from the same (oral) source, we will deal now with the latter pericope.

The bribing of the soldiers (Mt 28:11–15)

Verse 11: While they were going, behold, some of the guard went into the city and told the chief priests all that had taken place.

While Mary Magdalene and the other Mary (cf. Mt 28:1–10) were going, some of the guard reported back to the chief priests. It is rather surprising that the soldiers report not to Pilate but to the chief priests – perhaps because Pilate had commanded the chief priests to set the guard at the tomb (Mt 27:65). 'All that had taken place' (cf. 27:54, 'what took place') is a very general expression: the soldiers could not give any precise information since at the crucial moment they 'became like dead men' (Mt 28:4).

Verse 12: And when they had assembled with the elders and taken counsel, they gave a sum of money to the soldiers

'When they had assembled' (*sunachthentes*) clearly refers back to Mt 27:62, 'the chief priests and the Pharisees gathered (*sunēchthē-san*)'. As at the very beginning of the passion narrative (Mt 26:4; cf. 27:1, 7), the chief priests and the elders again 'take counsel'. Once more they try to solve their problems by spending a sum of money. Apart from its use in the parable of the talents (Mt 25:14–30; cf.

25:18, 27) the expression for 'money' is found only in the accounts of Judas' betrayal (Mt 26:15; 27:3–10). Just as money was used to betray Jesus into the hands of the Jewish authorities, so now it is used to silence the news of the resurrection.

> **Verses 13–14:** and said, 'Tell people, "His disciples came by night and stole him away while we were asleep." (14) And if this comes to the governor's ears, we will satisfy him and keep you out of trouble.'

Previously we were told that the Jewish authorities requested Pilate to take some measures for fear that the disciples would 'tell the people . . .' (Mt 27:64). Now when all precautions have proved useless, they give their own version, 'Tell the people . . .'. Thus the Jewish authorities make use of the fraud which they had expected the disciples to commit. The disciples who preach to the people that 'he has risen from the dead' (Mt 27:64) are here contrasted with the chief priests who *teach* (cf. Mt 28:15!) that the disciples stole him away.

The combination of the phrase 'by night' with a reference to sleeping soldiers makes us think of Acts 12, where we are told that Peter was liberated from prison at night, while sleeping between two (sleeping) soldiers and later on passing two (sleeping) guards (Acts 12:6–11). The reference to the stealing of the body reminds us of Mt 27:64. The verb for sleeping (*koimaomai*) is found in several epiphany texts (I Kgs 19:5; Dan 8:18). The word is used in Greek for the sleep of death. If the evangelist had this in mind, we have here a case of unprecedented irony. In Mt 28:4 he says, 'for fear of him the guards trembled and became like dead men'. Now they should 'tell people' that they had been overcome by a heavy sleep, whereas in reality the vision of the angel left them 'like dead'. In fact, their story lacks all logic. Indeed, at first sight the emergency seems to be dealt with prudently. But on closer scrutiny much of the story is not very clear. How can the guards admit that they slept on duty? And how could the Jewish authorities and the soldiers think that Pilate, once he had heard of the matter, would simply suppress the story of the guards' misconduct? Instead of punishment they get a reward. Thus Matthew parodies another feature of so-called 'liberation miracles': the punishment of the inattentive soldiers (cf. Acts 12:19).

> **Verse 15:** So they took the money and did as they were directed; and this story has been spread among the Jews to this day.

The soldiers accepted the bribe and did as they were directed (literally, 'taught', *edidachthēsan*): they circulated the concocted story so widely that it was still being propagated 'among the Jews to this day', i.e., at the time the evangelist was writing. Thus Matthew explains how it was that they did not believe in the resurrection. He does so in a sentence which is clearly apologetic in nature.

The conclusion of this pericope seems to be consciously patterned according to the conclusion of the gospel: 'teaching (*didaskontes*) them to observe all that I have commanded you' (Mt 28:20). Jesus' true teaching is contrasted with the 'teaching of the Jews' which originates from cunning and corruption. The true disciple does the will of Christ, the Jews rely upon gossip and rumours.

The historicity of Mt 27:62–66; 28:11–15

The following observations should be made:

(1) The text contains several expressions which have a definitely Christian, post-Easter ring: 'after the day of Preparation'; 'they gathered' (allusion to Ps 2:1–2); 'after three days I will rise again'; 'until the third day'; 'his disciples . . . tell the people, "He has risen from the dead" '. All these expressions show that the account is secondary to the preaching of Christ's resurrection to the Jews, using the story of the empty tomb as apologetic evidence.

(2) There seem to be a number of historical improbabilities in the account:

  (a) The authorities are said to take several steps which are almost unthinkable on a sabbath, though it has been pointed out that exceptions from the sabbath law were possible.

  (b) The soldiers do not report to Pilate but to the chief priests. The latter promise that, if necessary, they will persuade Pilate not to take any action against the soldiers.

  (c) Although the soldiers are bribed into presenting a false story, the Christians – or at least Matthew – know all about their real experience.

(3) The literary form of the account is unique in the gospel tradition. It is a lively dialogue introduced and concluded by a narrative section. The narrator skilfully succeeds in getting the reader involved in the story while at the same time revealing his own feelings and reactions. This literary form undoubtedly supposes a certain degree of literary sophistication which is unknown in the earliest gospel tradition. This literary sophistication becomes more predominant in the later apocryphal gospels.

(4) The other gospels do not mention this incident. This does not necessarily prove that the narrative is entirely legendary. Matthew may have been the first to put an oral tradition down in writing in Mt 27:62–66; 28:11–15. It seems impossible, on the basis of literary analysis, to separate tradition from redaction and thus to distinguish different layers in the narrative of Mt 27:62–66; 28:11–15.

In conclusion, we subscribe to the opinion of those scholars who say that when we speak of the historical reliability of Mt 27:62–66; 28:11–15, we are facing insurmountable riddles. On account of the obvious apologetic tendencies of the narrative, the many improbable features and the fact that the other gospels do not mention the incident, it is very difficult to reach any degree of historical certainty concerning the sealing of the tomb and the bribing of the soldiers. Perhaps we are dealing here with a contemporary mode of speaking accepted in the Near East which, in the form of a story, ridicules Jewish talk about the theft of Jesus' body by the disciples.

The place of the account in the gospel of Matthew

Much more important than the question of historicity is that of the place of Mt 27:62–66; 28:11–15 in the overall theological outlook of the gospel of Matthew. After all, the author speaks of 'this (i.e., his) day' (Mt 28:15), and we have seen that the account should indeed be read and interpreted on this level. The account reflects the experience of the massive rejection of the Christian message by 'the Jews'. This is one of the fundamental issues of Matthew's gospel.

The gospel emphasizes that during his earthly ministry Jesus 'was sent only to the lost sheep of the house of Israel' (Mt 15:24). During Jesus' public ministry the same thing was said to the disciples: 'Go nowhere among the Gentiles . . . but go rather to the lost sheep of the house of Israel' (Mt 10:5–6; compare Mt 28:16–20, applicable to the time after the resurrection). At the same time the gospel exposes the massive opposition of the Jewish leaders to Jesus' message. In this context Matthew repeatedly uses the very significant verb 'to withdraw' (*anachōrein*; cf. Mt 2:14, 22; 4:12; 12:15; 14:13; 15:21), meaning not only that Jesus withdraws *from* the Jews, but also that he withdraws *to* the Gentiles. This is a sign of the tragedy to come: Christianity withdrawing to the Gentiles after Israel as such has rejected the Christian message. For Matthew this drama culminates in the exclamation 'His blood be on us and on our children!' (Mt 27:25).

In the present pericopes (Mt 27:62–66 and 28:11–15) the evangelist wants to show that their hatred went beyond the tomb. By means of bribery they manage to characterize the central message of Christianity as a mere deception. This story stands 'to this day' as a monument of Israel's total opposition. From now on they are no longer God's people, Israel. They have become 'the Jews', just one nation among the others.

The bridges between Christianity and Israel were certainly not broken down during the first decades after the death of Jesus. For a long time the Christian mission was mainly directed to Israel. Even Paul, the 'apostle of the Gentiles', fully respected the special place of Israel. For Matthew, the bridges were apparently burned after the destruction of Jerusalem in A.D. 70. This appears clearly from Matthew's version of the parable of the wedding feast (cf. especially Mt 22:6–7, 8–10) and his own interpretation of the parable of the wicked tenants in Mt 21:41, 43: '. . . Therefore I tell you, the kingdom of God will be taken away from you and given to a nation producing the fruits of it'. In its present function of culmination of the Matthean theme of Israel's rejection, and introduction to the Gentile mission (cf. Mt 28:16–20), Mt 27:62–66; 28:11–15 came into being after the destruction of Jerusalem in A.D. 70.

Mt 28:1–10

Verse 1: Now after the sabbath, toward the dawn of the first day of the week, Mary Magdalene and the other Mary went to see the sepulchre.

RSV's translation of Matthew's indication of time is probably not correct. It has been shown that equivalent expressions found in Mishnaic Hebrew ('after the sabbath, the light of the first day of the week') mean: in the twilight of Saturday evening. In fact, in Lk 23:54, we find the same expression used in that sense for Friday evening. It seems, therefore, that translations like 'on the evening after the sabbath had drawn to a close' (W. C. Allen) or 'late on the sabbath, when the first day of the week was beginning' are preferable. For Matthew, therefore, the women arrived at the tomb after the sabbath, i.e., Saturday after 6 p.m., when it was dark. One may wonder whether the darkness, which Matthew seems to imply, is already an element of the apocalyptic picture which he is going to develop.

Matthew reduces the number of women at the grave to two, omitting Salome so as to remove the Marcan discrepancy between the names of the women at the burial (Mk 15:47; Mt 27:61) and those of the women at the tomb. He also changes the motive of the women's visit. In Mark they come to complete the burial rites (Mk 16:1, 'so that they might go and anoint him'). In Matthew they simply come 'to see the sepulchre'. Matthew can easily omit the anointing since he does not say that the women enter the tomb (compare Mk 16:5). Moreover, Matthew evidently felt the difficulty inherent in Mark's account, according to which Joseph of Arimathea had apparently completed the burial rites. He has also said that the chief priests 'made the sepulchre secure by sealing the stone and setting a guard' (Mt 27:66), so that the women could not possibly enter the tomb. Matthew says now that they went there 'to see the sepulchre', or *to watch*, apparently doing the same as they were said to do in Mt 27:61, 'Mary Magdalene and the other Mary were there, sitting opposite the sepulchre'. Matthew may be suggesting that the women expected something to happen. And indeed, in the following verses we will get an 'apocalyptic show'.

Verses 2–4: And behold, there was a great earthquake; for an angel of the Lord descended from heaven and rolled back the stone, and sat upon it. (3) His appearance was like lightning, and his raiment white as snow. (4) And for fear of him the guards trembled and became like dead men.

As is clear from verse 1, Matthew had Mk 16:1–8 before him. But he omitted Mk 16:3–5, which was formulated in relation to the women's intention to enter the tomb and anoint the body of Jesus. Matthew had to omit this passage because his version of the empty tomb is framed by the story of the guards (Mt 27:62–66 and 28:11–15) which made it impossible to let the women enter the tomb. But we cannot speak of a simple omission because, in fact, he *replaces* Mk 16:3–5 by Mt 28:2–4, which has its function within the context of the story of the guards. Matthew's concern to give an answer to Jewish allegations that the preaching of the resurrection was based on deceit could no longer be served by Mk 16:3–5. Instead Matthew told his readers who really removed the stone, etc. The women were mere spectators watching the tomb, and the soldiers were paid to spread the story of the theft, but knew what really happened.

Besides, Mt 28:2–4 shows apocalyptic interests typical of the gospel of Matthew. For instance, the text is very similar to another apocalyptic passage which we find in Mt 27:51–54.

Mt 27:51–54	Mt 28:2–4
(51) And behold the curtain of the temple was torn . . . and the earth shook	(2) And behold, an angel descended there was a great earthquake
(52) The rocks were split the tombs were opened	the stone was rolled away (the tomb was opened)
(53) Many bodies were raised	(in verses 6–7 the angel announces that he is raised, but here in verses 2–4 the resurrection is not mentioned).
(54) Those who guarded Jesus, having seen the earthquake and the other happenings, were filled with awe.	(4) Those who guarded the tomb trembled for fear and became like dead men.

From these findings we can conclude that verses 2–4 have to be read on the level of and completely in line with Matthew's editorial concerns. And since the passage is so closely related to the story of the guards, we should say the same about Mt 28:2–4 as we said about that pericope. This means, among other things, that the text has to be assigned to the time after the destruction of Jerusalem in A.D. 70. But the question should still be asked whether Matthew made use of an existing tradition or whether he composed it himself from materials which he found in Mark and in previous parts of his own gospel. The following analysis of the passage supports the latter possibility.

The phrase 'and behold' emphasizes the events that follow. The 'great earthquake' recalls the theophany of Ex 19:18 and I Kgs 19:11–12 (cf. Mt 27:51). In our present text, too, it is the appearance of an 'angel of the Lord' which causes the earthquake (cf. the causal 'for').

Let us now have a closer look at the following three points: (1) the tomb; (2) the presentation of the angel; (3) the reaction of the women.

(1) *The tomb.* According to Mark's account, the women found the tomb open; they entered, saw the young man in white, and were amazed. In Matthew, the two motifs of the removal of the stone and the apparition are combined. The apparition does not take place inside the tomb, and it is the angel himself who removes the stone, thus answering the question raised in Mk 16:3, 'who will roll away the stone for us?' (*tis apokulisei ton lithon?*). Matthew writes: 'the angel . . . rolled back the stone' (*apekulisen ton lithon*). Mark still added in Mk 16:4b, 'for it was large', which is intended to explain the reflection but which, in typical Marcan way, comes at the end of the verse. The powerful intervention suggested by Matthew is prepared for in the burial account, where 'he (Joseph of Arimathea) rolled a great stone to the door of the tomb' (Mt 27:60).

(2) *The presentation of the angel.* Matthew is again guided by Mark: 'a young man sitting on the right side, dressed in a white robe' (Mk 16:5). 'Sitting on the right side', an expression which marks the dignity of the young man, easily evokes the image of a throne. Matthew seems to underline this same glorious aspect of what one would almost call an 'enthronement': he sat upon the stone (cf. Mt 28:2). As in Mark, the 'sitting' of the angel is followed by the description of his garment. The differences are of the same kind as other editorial changes made elsewhere by Matthew (compare, e.g., Mt 3:4 and Mk 1:6). Where Mk 16:5 speaks of 'a young man . . . dressed in a white robe', Mt 28:3 has: 'his appearance was like lightning, and his raiment white as snow'. This redoubling may very well be redactional, as in the account of the transfiguration where Matthew adds 'his face shone like the sun' before the description of the garment (compare Mk 9:2–3 and Mt 17:2; the same construction and the same redoubling face–garment as in Mt 28:3).

(3) *The reaction of the women.* In the description of this third motif Matthew is rather different from Mark, but we find similar re-writings of the Marcan source in other parts of Matthew, and the expressions used here by Matthew can be found elsewhere in his gospel. As we

already noted, Mt 28:2–4 is particularly closely related to Matthew's description of the apocalyptic signs which accompanied the death of Jesus (Mt 27:51–54).

We may conclude, then, that the particularities by which Mt 28:2–4 is distinguished from Mark can be explained by other passages in the gospel of Matthew. The account is, therefore, very Matthean in character, but it remains nevertheless so close to Mark that we cannot speak of a Matthean insertion. The present passage does not presuppose any source different from Mk 16:1–8. The Marcan source, however, has been thoroughly edited by Matthew with the help of previous, especially traditional apocalyptic passages of the gospel (cf. the earthquake, the descent of the angel, his appearance like lightning). This means that the details found in Matthew but not in Mark are not to be attributed to additional information about the events, but rather to the particular way in which Matthew edited the tradition he found in Mark.

> **Verses 5–7:** But the angel said to the women, 'Do not be afraid; for I know that you seek Jesus who was crucified. (6) He is not here; for he has risen, as he said. Come, see the place where he lay. (7) Then go quickly and tell his disciples that he has risen from the dead, and behold, he is going before you to Galilee; there you will see him. Lo, I have told you.'

Here Matthew follows Mark with only minor alterations. The clause 'but the angel said to the women, "Do not be afraid" ', is clearly a new beginning which constitutes a contrast with verse 4. Mt 28:1, 5 presuppose that the women have also seen the event. But unlike the guards' reaction (they 'trembled and became like dead men'), *theirs* should not be a paralysing terror. *They* should not be afraid (the Greek text adds explicitly *humeis*, 'you'). We could paraphrase: Unlike the guards, you should not be afraid.

Then the angel goes on to say in words which are very similar to Mark's text: 'I know that you seek Jesus who was crucified'. The only striking difference is the phrase 'I know' (cf. Mt 28:7, 'I have told you') by which the angel seems to attract attention to himself. He speaks as God or the risen Christ would speak. In fact, this is the only instance in which this phrase is attributed to an angel. He knows that whatever the women did was inspired by a loving seeking of Jesus.

However, the women are told that their seeking was in vain, since 'he is not here'. Matthew places this phrase before 'for he has risen', and thus the empty tomb may appear as a *proof* of the resurrection. In Mark 'he has risen' comes first and is part of what follows, i.e., the *confirmation* of the proclamation of the resurrection in the fact that he is not here and that the tomb is empty. It is also possible that Matthew places the phrase 'he is not here' first in order to emphasize how much the seeking of the women is in vain, thus building up the tension towards the positive announcement: 'for he is risen'. It is a very meaningful absence indeed.

This is immediately followed by the phrase 'as he said' (*kathōs eipen*). In Mark we read further on, '. . . he is going before you to Galilee; there you will see him, as he told you' (Mk 16:7), which refers to Mk 14:28, 'But after I am raised up, I will go before you to Galilee'. Matthew anticipates this 'as he told you' (*kathōs eipen humin*) and connects it with 'for he has risen'. It is no longer a reference to a prophecy of Jesus' appearance in Galilee (Mk 14:28; Mt 26:32), but a reference to the prophecies of the passion and especially of the resurrection, which is mentioned every time (Mt 16:21; 17:23; 20:19). For Matthew this prophetic evidence seems to be very important and is, therefore, mentioned before the evidence of the empty tomb ('come, see the place where he lay').

'Come, see the place where he lay' is only a slight but not unimportant change of the Marcan source (Mk 16:6, 'see the place where they laid him'). First, with the imperative 'come' the angel seems to invite the women to enter the tomb; the women did not previously have this intention (cf. Mt 28:1, 'to see the sepulchre'). Or perhaps the angel invites them to come closer to the tomb without entering it (cf. Mt 28:8, where Mark's 'and they went out' is changed into 'they departed'). Secondly, Matthew makes Jesus the subject of the verb and thereby emphasizes the identity of the One who was buried and has now risen. The One who was buried is the same as the One who has risen. Mk 16:6 refers back to Mk 15:47, 'Mary Magdalene and Mary the mother of Joses saw where he was laid'. The parallel verse Mt 27:61 says only that they 'were there, sitting opposite the sepulchre'. In Mark the seeing of 'the place where they laid him' seems to have more importance than in Matthew, where the emphasis is on Jesus' prophecy ('as he said').

'Then go quickly and tell his disciples.' Matthew adds the adverb 'quickly' and omits the phrase 'and Peter'. In Matthew the expression 'his disciples' always indicates a larger group than the Twelve. Whenever the evangelist refers to the Twelve, Peter is always explicitly mentioned in the context as the head of the Twelve, but whenever he uses the expression 'his disciples', Peter is not mentioned, and is even eliminated from the text if he was mentioned in the parallel text of Mark.

The first part of the message is 'he has risen from the dead', which are exactly the same words as those used by the chief priests in Mt 27:64. Those who want to denounce the apostles as deceivers have thus made themselves unconscious announcers of the true message. In line with Matthew's editing of verse 6, where he made the resurrection the object of 'as he said', the resurrection itself becomes more explicitly the centre of the message which they have to bring to the disciples: 'He has risen, as he said. . . . Go quickly and tell his disciples that he has risen.'

The second part of the angel's message is again almost identical with that of Mark: 'and behold, he is going before you to Galilee; there you will see him' (Mt 28:7b). These words still belong to the message which the women have to bring to his disciples (cf. Mt 28:10, 16–20).

But then the angel continues, 'Lo, I have told you'. Matthew had already anticipated Mark's 'as he told you' in Mt 28:6 ('as he said'). Now in the parallel text the words are attributed to the angel and become his prophecy about Jesus' future appearance in Galilee. The angel's words are so solemn and Jesus-like that it seems as if the figure of the angel and the risen Christ flow into each other. This impression is reinforced by the fact that the immediately following appearance of the risen Christ to the women at the tomb (Mt 28:9–10) looks like a doublet of the angel's appearance. Practically speaking, we now get a development with two peaks: (1) 'He has risen, as he said' and (2) 'you will see him (= he will appear), as I have told you'.

> **Verse 8:** So they departed quickly from the tomb with fear and great joy, and ran to tell his disciples.

Unlike Mark, Matthew does not say that the women 'went out (of the tomb)'; but in line with the angel's command to 'go quickly' (Mt 28:7), 'they departed quickly from the tomb'. Their reaction is not 'trembling and astonishment' but 'fear and great joy'. Omitting that 'they said nothing to any one, for they were afraid' (Mk 16:8), Matthew says that the women hurried away in excitement and joy 'to tell (literally, to announce) his disciples', a phrase which refers to Mt 28:10. Matthew, who throughout his gospel has shown little interest in the messianic secret, does not want to point now to its final unveiling, as Mark does, but rather leads straight from the account of the empty tomb to the final appearance and commission (Mt 28:16–20). Therefore, the women do not remain silent, but tell the disciples so that the latter may proceed to Galilee for the great commission.

> **Verses 9–10:** And behold, Jesus met them and said, 'Hail!' And they came up and took hold of his feet and worshipped him. (10) Then Jesus said to them, 'Do not be afraid, go and tell my brethren to go to Galilee, and there they will see me.'

Compared with Mark, this is a wholly new element in the narrative. The intention of the women to carry out the angel's command to 'tell his disciples' is interrupted by an appearance of the risen Christ himself. Most scholars think that Matthew inserted here a tradition of which we find an expanded version in Jn 20:11–18, and an abbreviated version in the longer ending of Mark, more precisely in Mk 16:9–11. They point to the fact that Matthew did not manage to harmonize this insertion perfectly, for in Mt 28:7 it had been announced that the risen Christ was (already) going ahead to them to Galilee, and now he suddenly appears to the women near Jerusalem. Morever, the message given to the women does not contain anything new, and verse 10 seems to be a mere repetition of verse 7, except, of course, for the omission of the mention that he is going ahead of them (= actually on the way), because the risen Christ is actually here in Jerusalem. The only remarkable difference is that the disciples are here referred to as 'my brethren'. But did Matthew really have any special information which he inserted here, or is this passage constructed by Matthew from materials which he found in Mark or in previous parts of his own gospel?

'And behold, Jesus met them and said, "Hail!"' (Mt 28:9a). The phrase 'and behold' (*kai idou*) is certainly Matthean. It is found thirty-three times in his gospel and is very apporpariate for introducing an appearance (see Matthew's infancy narrative: Mt 1:20; 2:13, 19; see also the baptism and transfiguration accounts: Mt 3:16 and 17:3, 5). Then the risen Christ greets the women: 'Hail' (*Chairete*). This is a habitual Greek salutation, but nothing prevents us from attributing it to the redactor because, in Matthew's passion narrative, the greeting has been addressed to Jesus twice (Mt 26:49; 27:29), and in the first instance it has been added to the text of Mark (compare Mt 26:49 and Mk 14:45).

Next, Mt 28:9b describes the reaction of the women: 'And they came up and took hold of his feet and worshipped him' (literally, 'And they approaching held his feet and worshipped him'). The participle 'approaching' before a finite verb (here 'took hold') is very character-istic of the Matthean redaction. It is found fifty-one times in Matthew and almost always points to a solemn moment. It is often followed by an important statement. Here it obviously introduces the women's worshipping Jesus. The verb 'to worship' (*proskunein*) is also very Matthean. It is typical for the description of encounters with the risen Christ (cf. Mt 28:17), and is often used in the gospel of Matthew, in which the features of the risen Lord break through more clearly, especially in the miracle stories (cf. Mt 8:2; 9:18; 14:33; 15:25). It has been convincingly argued that the phrase 'took hold of his feet' should not be understood in line with the risen Christ's invitation to touch his body (cf. Lk 24:39; Jn 20:27) or with Jn 20:17, 'Do not hold me'. It describes a gesture of respectful greeting and is in reality nothing more than a way of developing the simple expression 'and worshipped him'. It serves to emphasize the act of worshipping. The women react to an epiphany of the Lord.

In the light of this explanation the following words also become clear: 'Then Jesus said to them, "Do not be afraid" ' (Mt 28:10a). The introductory phrase, 'Then Jesus said to them', is entirely Matthean. The same should be said of the reassurance, 'Do not be afraid'. It is very appropriate since the women have just expressed their reverential fear. And so the whole structure appears perfectly parallel to two other passages where the same reverential fear is expressed, i.e., Mt 28:16–18 and 17:6–7.

Mt 28:16–18	*Mt 17:6–7*
Now the eleven disciples . . .	
And when they saw him	When the disciples heard this
they worshipped him;	they fell on their faces,
but some doubted.	and were filled with awe.
And Jesus came	But Jesus came
and said to them, (saying),	and touched them, saying,
'All authority in heaven. . . .	'Rise, and have no fear.'
I am with you always.'	

The really difficult part of the text is Mt 28:10b c, 'Go and tell my brethren to go to Galilee, and there they will see me'. The women seem to be given once more the same message as in verse 7. Why should Matthew add this after telling us in verse 8 that the women were on their way to deliver the message? And is there no contradiction between verse 7, where it was said that the Lord would be seen in Galilee, and verse 9–10, where he appears to the women in Jerusalem?

To the latter question we should answer that verse 7 spoke of an appearance *to the disciples* and that in the present composition of Matthew this refers undoubtedly to Mt 28:16–20. Jesus' appearance to the women is not in contradiction with Mt 28:7. We would even add that this appearance is in line with the words of the angel as Matthew understood them. The special insistence on the Easter message, indicated above, brings us closer to an appearance of Jesus himself *to the women*, who are not sent to Galilee.

To the former question whether or not verse 10 is an unnecessary redoubling of verse 7, we should answer negatively. The fact that the command is now given by the risen Christ himself is a new element. Already in Mark the angel referred to a word of Jesus; this is now made explicit by Matthew. It is true that in Matthew's redaction a greater insistence appears on the proclamation of the resurrection (cf. 'as he said' in Mt 28:6) and on the concern to emphasize the authority of the angel who proclaimed it (cf. 'Lo, I have told you' in Mt 28:7). But the change can be explained fully only in the light of verses 9–10, where the previous promise ('as he said') is surpassed by the words which Jesus himself addresses to the women. Moreover, Jesus' words are no longer a simple *promise* but an *order* (compare 'he is going before you to Galilee' and 'tell my brethren to go to Galilee').

No doubt this is the reason for the appearance to the women. It prepares for the appearance in Galilee in a much more direct way than the announcement by the angel. In Matthew, the correspondence between order and execution is underlined with particular care. This tendency is especially manifest in the final chapter of the gospel. In preparation for the appearance to the eleven disciples (Mt 28:16–20), Matthew omits the special mention of Peter in the angel's words (compare Mt 28:7 and Mk 16:7), and adds a formal order, given by Jesus personally, 'to go to Galilee'. The disciples will obey: 'Now the eleven disciples went to Galilee' (Mt 28:16), just as the women previously obeyed the order of the angel, 'Then go quickly' (Mt 28:7), and 'departed quickly' (Mt 28:8), and Jesus' own order, 'go and tell' (Mt 28:10), as we can gather from 'while they were going' (Mt 28:11).

The only element which has not yet been explained is the rather unexpected occurrence of the phrase 'my brethren'. However, this term should not be surprising in the gospel of Matthew, which repeatedly calls attention to the fact that Jesus' followers and disciples are his brethren. We refer here, e.g., to Mt 12:49, 'and stretching out his hand toward his disciples, he said, "Here are my mother and my brothers!"' which is much more explicit than the parallel text in Mk 3:34. At the end of Matthew's description of Jesus' Galilean activity and before he formally starts a new section with Mt 13, the parable chapter, the disciples appear as those who, unlike the rest of the people, obey the will of the Father and are, therefore, called 'brothers' by Jesus. That the risen Christ now speaks of 'my brethren' and orders them to go to Galilee means a new foundation of the discipleship, which is related to what happened before in Galilee and now appears as a final commission which will consist in making disciples of all nations (cf. Mt 28:19).

We should also refer to Mt 25:40, 'And the King will answer them, "Truly I say to you, as you did it to one of the least of these my brethren, you did it to me."' Against the previously fairly generally accepted opinion that 'my brethren' refers to all the hungry, thirsty, naked, imprisoned people of the world, there is a growing consensus among scholars that Matthew refers here to the disciples who have been sent to all nations. This interpretation fits well into the current interpretation of a series of other Matthean texts (Mt 10:40ff.; 12:48ff.; 24:9, 14; 25:32; 28:18b–20). We should also note that in Mt 18:15, 21, 35 the title 'brother' refers to the members of the Christian community.

The use of the phrase 'brethren' has been related to Ps 22(21), which plays an important role in the passion narrative (cf. Mt 27:35, 39, 43, 46). Ps 22(21):22 reads: 'I will tell of your name to my brethren'. We may also think of Rom 8:29, 'in order that he might be the first-born among many brethren'.

Summing up, we would say that Mt 28:9–10 is composed by

Matthew to serve as transition between the account of the tomb and the appearance and commission in Galilee (Mt 28:16–20). Our study of verses 9–10 confirms that Matthew's version of the empty tomb narrative does not presuppose any source other than Mark. Matthew has developed his Marcan source in two directions which may have been suggested by the text of Mark itself. On the one hand, the establishment of the empty tomb becomes an announcement of the resurrection which is more autonomous and detachable from the motif of the appearances. This development allows Matthew to insert Mt 28:1–10 between the two 'panels' of the story of the guards (Mt 27:62–66 and 28:11–15). On the other hand, another line of development starts from the angel's message and, according to the schema order–execution, directs the story of the women more strictly to the appearance in Galilee.

4 The Empty Tomb – III

(Lk 24:1–12)

Luke's development of the Marcan source is not unlike Matthew's in that his version of the story of the empty tomb is also followed by appearances. But the inner changes in Lk 24:1–12 are greater than in Mt 28:1–10. The connection with the burial narrative has become closer, especially in the matter of anointing; Lk 23:56 has already mentioned that the women 'returned, and prepared spices and ointments', and now we are told that 'they went to the tomb taking the spices which they had prepared' (Lk 24:1). Luke solves the problem posed by Mark's three lists of women (Mk 15:40, 47; 16:1) by mentioning no names at all. Only in Lk 24:10 are we given three names and the text suggests that at least five women were involved. The most significant change is that Luke lets the women enter the tomb directly, where 'they did not find the body' (Lk 24:3), thus turning the pericope for the first time into what its title usually indicates: the finding of the empty tomb (in Mark the women find a young man inside the tomb, and in both Mark and Matthew it is pointed out to them by the young man/angel that Jesus is not there).

> **Verse 1:** But on the first day of the week, at early dawn, they went to the tomb, taking the spices which they had prepared.

This verse is a direct continuation of the burial account. Neither in Lk 23:55–56 nor here does Luke mention the names of the women (but see Lk 24:10). The women prepared spices on Friday evening, but because of the sabbath law they could not go to the tomb before Sunday morning. What is the meaning of these Lucan alterations? It should first be noted that in Luke the women participate more closely in the burial than in Mark and Matthew: 'The women . . . saw the tomb, and how his body was laid' (Lk 23:55). Apparently Luke was embarrassed by the fact that the women, who had followed Jesus from Galilee and ministered to him (Lk 8:3), had not embalmed Jesus' body on the occasion of the burial itself. As it was now, the burial was not complete, but the women could not help it because the spices had not only to be bought but also to be prepared. They did this the very same evening. But then they did nothing for twenty-four hours because of the sabbath.

Luke's note on the preparation of spices (Lk 23:56a; 24:1) replaces Mark's 'bought spices' (Mk 16:1c). The mention of the 'ointment' (*mura*) reminds us of the story of the forgiven woman sinner (Lk 7:37) and of the anointing at Bethany (cf. Mk 14:3), omitted by Luke but probably alluded to here.

As soon as they could, that is, 'on the first day of the week, at early dawn', they went to the tomb to anoint the corpse with 'the spices which they (themselves) had prepared' on Friday evening. In this way Luke expresses the women's love and concern for Jesus. However, it is also clear that they expect to find a corpse. Thus verse 1 expresses at the same time the women's love for Jesus and the limitations of their (faith-)insight.

Verses 2–3: And they found the stone rolled away from the tomb, (3) but when they went in they did not find the body.

At the end of verse 3 the so-called Western Text (Codex Bezae and Old Latin; followed by RSV) omits the phrase 'of the Lord Jesus', but because of the evidence of the majority of the manuscripts and the use of the same title in Acts 1:21; 4:33; 8:16, more and more scholars are in favour of its authenticity.

Luke drastically shortens and modifies the text of Mark. He omits altogether the women's questioning as to 'who will roll away the stone' (Mk 16:3). He can easily do so since he has not mentioned that a stone had been rolled against the door of the tomb (compare Mk 15:46 and Lk 23:53). He limits himself to a note which is parallel with Mk 16:4, but divests the event of the miraculous character which Mark seems to attribute to it. The women's perplexity is transferred from Mark's query about the stone to the discovery inside the tomb. Thus the evangelist gets straight to the point: 'they found the stone rolled away ... but ... they did not find the body'. Luke, therefore, explicitly records the women's failure to find the corpse. In fact, he seems to contrast the discovery they made ('they found the stone rolled away') with the discovery they failed to make ('they did not find the body').

According to Mark, the women noticed that the stone was rolled away, and were then intercepted by an angel and invited to inspect the tomb. According to Luke, it was only after they had discovered for themselves that the tomb was empty that their perplexity began. The body was gone: this undeniable, prosaic fact is mentioned before anything else. Here we get a true empty tomb apologetic, *starting* from the empty tomb. This approach was very important for Greek readers who, unlike Jewish readers, might possibly think of a merely *subjective* vision of Jesus' soul being in heaven. No wonder that Luke reduces the visionary elements of the account.

. . . the counterpoint drama which Mk had built into the narrative of the women's experience at the empty tomb has been shifted in Lk's editing. Now the contrast is not between the women's project and the angelic Easter tidings but between *the whole experience at the tomb and the subsequent birth of the Easter faith!* The tomb experience seems to conclude an observation of all the material *facta paschalia*, but after it faith is yet to be born. The final word from the witnesses' standpoint is Lk 24, 24: *auton de ouk eidon* [him they did not see]. . . . If the whole tomb experience is now to become a contrasting episode to the risen Lord's own instilling of the Easter faith (24, 25ff.), then the painstaking establishment of all the *bruta facta* of the experience will serve only as the foil *ex parte hominis* to the risen One's activity! . . . The *fact* of the empty tomb begets *perplexity* and requires the *interpreting word* of the angels. Here we encounter the first of three combinations of *unintelligible facts* versus *elucidating word* which will constitute the controlling pattern of this chapter's design (vv. 2–3 *vs*. 5–7; 19–24 *vs*. 25–27; 36–43 *vs*. 44–49).[1]

Verses 4–5: While they were perplexed about this, behold, two men stood by them in dazzling apparel; (5) and as they were frightened and bowed their faces to the ground, the men said to them, 'Why do you seek the living among the dead?'

Mark's 'young man dressed in a white robe' has become 'two men in dazzling apparel'. There can be no doubt that for Luke these 'two men' are angels, as can be seen from the later mention 'that they had even seen a vision of angels, who said that he was alive' (Lk 24:23). The verb 'to stand by' (*ephistamai*) is also found in Lk 2:9, literally, 'and the angel of the Lord stood by (*epestē*) them'. Acts 10:30 is an even closer parallel: 'and behold, a man stood before me in bright apparel' (cf. also Acts 11:13, 'And he told us how he had seen the angel standing in his house'). The model for all these texts seems to be Dan 8:15, 'When I, Daniel had seen the vision, I sought to understand it; and behold, there stood before me one having the appearance of a man'.

We should also note the parallel between this passage and the account of the ascension, where we are told that 'behold, two men stood by them in white robes' (Acts 1:10). In both cases the two men serve the function of interpreting an event after it has occurred, and their presence underlines the eschatological significance of the events witnessed. That there are *two* men instead of one is most probably due to the tendencies of popular story-telling, not to the requirements in Jewish law for witnesses (Deut 19:15), since the two men do not really function as witnesses.

The language of verse 4 is also similar to that of Lk 9:30, 'And behold, two men talked with him . . . who appeared in glory'. Luke's account of the transfiguration is preceded by statements about the Son of man: he will come 'in his glory and the glory of the Father and of the holy angels' (Lk 9:26), and 'there are some standing here who will not taste death before they see the kingdom of God' (Lk 9:27). The immediately following transfiguration (Lk 9:28–36) was not the inauguration of the kingdom, but a preparation for the understanding of Jesus' suffering. Now, after his suffering, the glory with which he will return is inaugurated: 'Was it not necessary that the Christ should suffer these things and enter into his glory?' (Lk 24:26). However, whereas in the transfiguration Jesus' 'raiment became dazzling white', and Moses and Elijah appeared with him 'in glory' (Lk 9:29–30), here the two men wear 'dazzling apparel', and Jesus' glory receives only an indirect confirmation. Throughout chapter 24 Luke remains consistent with his eschatological doctrine. Jesus never appears in glory, since this is reserved for his final coming, when 'they will see the Son of man coming in a cloud with power and great glory' (Lk 21:27). But Luke associated the resurrection with the transfiguration to emphasize that the kingdom was a present reality although the popular apocalyptic expectations were not met. It has been well said, therefore, that in verses 4–5 Luke has remodelled Mark's text giving it an apocalyptic form.

As could be expected, the reaction of the women is not faith, but awe and fear: they do not dare to look up. The whole address to the women has been thoroughly re-written. The question 'Why do you seek the living (one) among the dead?' contains a note of rebuke: If they had listened to the words of Jesus they would know that the tomb is not the proper place to look for him. Unlike Mark and Matthew, the crucifixion is not mentioned (but see Lk 24:7). Similarly in Acts, Luke concentrates on the resurrection, or rather on the Lord living and working through the Spirit: 'after he had given commandment through the Holy Spirit to the apostles whom he had chosen. To them he presented himself alive (literally, the living one) after his passion' (Acts 1:2b–3a). The proper antonym for *pneuma*, 'spirit', in Lk 24:37, 39 is not 'physical one', 'material one', or 'palpable one', but *living one*.

> **Verses 6–8:** 'He is not here, but has risen. (6) Remember how he told you while he was still in Galilee, (7) that the Son of man must be delivered into the hands of sinful men, and be crucified, and on the third day rise.' (8) And they remembered his words,

The clause 'he is not here, but has risen', is absent from Codex Bezae and the Itala form of the Old Latin translation, and is considered by many an insertion from Mt 28:6 (cf. Mk 16:6), but the manuscript evidence seems to be in its favour. Its presence in the recently discovered second-century papyrus [P⁷⁵] made many reconsider their stand, and recent critical editions of the Greek New Testament (the second edition of the United Bible Societies and the twenty-sixth edition of Nestle) have accepted it as part of the authentic text of Luke's gospel.

Luke evidently had Mark before him, but he has completely re-written the Marcan text. Let us compare the two passages:

Mark 16:7	*Luke 24:6–8*
Go, tell his disciples and Peter *that he is going before you to Galilee*; there you will see him, as he told you.	Remember how he told you, *while he was still in Galilee*, that the Son of man. . . . And they remembered his words.

In Luke's overall theological plan (from Galilee to Jerusalem in the gospel, and from Jerusalem to Rome in Acts), the climax of the gospel must be in Jerusalem. Therefore, he cannot record any appearances of the risen Christ in Galilee without producing an anti-climax. Luke preserved the mention of Galilee found in Mk 16:7, but gave it an entirely new meaning: instead of pointing forward to Galilee as the place where the appearance(s) will take place, he refers back to Galilee as the place where Jesus prophesied his passion and resurrection. In line with this editorial change he has previously omitted Mk 14:27–28. Thus Luke has simply obliterated all reference to an appearance of the risen Christ in Galilee. Instead he refers to passion prophecies such as are found in Lk 9:22, 44 and 18:32–33. The women should 're-member' these prophecies; they should realize that it was all planned by God and that in the context of this plan everything is perfectly intelligible.

In verse 7 Luke quotes a resume of passion prophecies:

Luke 24:7	*Passion prophecies*
saying that the Son of man must	9:22 saying 'The Son of man must. . .' (parallel Mk 8:31)
be delivered into the hands of men	9:44 to be delivered into the hands of men
and be crucified	(parallel Mk 9:31)
and on the third day rise	18:33 and on the third day he will rise (different Mk 10:34)

It is clear that with one exception (*staurōthēnai*, 'to be crucified') every word or phrase in verse 7 can be traced to Mark or to Luke's editing of Mark. Unlike Mark and Matthew, Luke uses the title 'Son of man' in his account of the risen Lord. Concerned with the identity of the risen

One, Luke points out that Jesus spoke of the fate of the Son of man: he must suffer, die, and rise on the third day. This Son of man must be identified with Jesus and makes his appearance on the third day. The word 'must' (*dei*) plays an important role in Lucan theology and occurs more often in Luke than in any other New Testament writing (about forty times in Luke-Acts), especially in the context of the suffering of Jesus as the necessary way to glory (cf. Lk 9:22; 17:25; 24:26; Acts 1:16; 3:21; 17:3). It denotes the plan of God in saving history as expressed in the scriptures. The phrase 'delivered into the hands of sinful men' seems to be a combination of 'to be delivered into the hands of men' (Mk 9:31; Lk 9:44) and 'betrayed into the hands of sinners' (Mk 14:41; no parallel in Luke). By the phrase 'sinful men' Luke states that this central event of salvation history has a bearing upon all people, an idea which is of the first importance in Lucan theology.

The statement of the angels is not so much the breaking of a joyous news (as in Mark), as a reproach implying that a proper understanding of past experiences should have prevented surprise and perplexity at the empty tomb. In this respect the angels' reproach may be compared with the risen Lord's words to the disciples at Emmaus (Lk 24:25f.). The reality of Easter has still to take hold of them, although they have observed all the material facts of Easter.

> Uniquely Lucan is the three-fold association of the passion prophecies with the Easter narratives, following a planned allotment of one restatement of the prophecies to each of the three narratives (cf. 24, 7.26.46; also v. 20). By thus forming the structural mainstays of Lk's Easter story, the restated passion formulas seem to suggest that *Easter revelation is essentially unlocking of the mystery of the messiah's passion*, which his followers were prevented from understanding until this point.[2]

The women 'remembered his words', and began to understand and believe. Here the empty tomb has become something entirely comprehensible, the outcome of what God had planned from the beginning.

> **Verse 9:** and returning from the tomb they told all this to the eleven and to all the rest.

Luke changes Mark's 'and they went out and fled' into 'and returning . . . they'. Though in Luke the women are not given any order to 'go and tell' (compare Mk 16:7), they return from the tomb and report their experience ('all this') to the Eleven (the Twelve minus Judas) and 'to all the rest' of the disciples, a phrase which prepares the way for Lk 24:22–23 by including others with the Eleven. Like Matthew, Luke considers it necessary for the women to tell the disciples, in order to lead into the resurrection appearances which he has added to his Marcan source; but, unlike Matthew, he has no account of a resurrection appearance to the women themselves.

Verse 10: Now it was Mary Magdalene and Joanna and Mary the mother of James and the other women with them who told this to the apostles;

The names of the women who have seen the tomb empty, and thereby become witnesses, are now given: Mary Magdalene (found in all lists), Joanna (taken from Lk 8:3), and Mary the mother (or wife?) of James (from Mk 16:1). But Luke indicates that he gives only a few names and that more women were involved. They kept on telling (*elegon*) 'the apostles'. The use of the term 'apostles' for the disciples prior to their post-resurrection commission is characteristic of Luke (cf. Lk 17:5, 22:14). For Luke, an 'apostle' is a witness to the whole of Jesus' life from his baptism by John the Baptist until his ascension (cf. Acts 1:22). Here the word may have been chosen in order to emphasize the purpose for which the women tell the news, namely proclamation to the whole world (cf. Lk 24:47–49).

Verse 11: but these words seemed to them an idle tale, and they did not believe them.

This verse apparently intends to preserve the independence of the apostles' witness: if the apostles proclaimed the resurrection, it was not on the basis of the women's testimony. Luke certainly suggests that the fact that the witnesses were women played a role here. The point is made once more in Lk 24:22–23. This feature would be perfectly understandable to Greek readers. Note that Paul does not mention any women in I Cor 15:5–8. Luke seems to be suggesting to his readers: I know how you feel about women as witnesses; so did the apostles, and they were mistaken! In Lk 24:24 we read that some disciples went to the tomb and confirmed the report of the women.

The phrase 'these words' refers first of all to the report of the women, but if we look at verses 8–9 ('and they remembered *his words* . . . they told all this to the eleven'), Lk 24:11 seems also to suggest that they considered Jesus' own words idle talk! At the same time Luke tells his readers that the apostles were not exactly credulous and that, if they finally believed, it was on the ground of other, personal experiences.

Verse 12: But Peter rose and ran to the tomb; stooping and looking in, he saw the linen cloths by themselves; and he went home wondering at what had happened.

This verse is missing from the so-called Western Text. Many consider it an interpolation based on Jn 20:3–10, but the external evidence against the verse is very weak. It has often been said that Lk 24:12 'interrupts' the text since verses 11 and 13 form a natural unity. But the phrase 'two of them' probably refers to 'the eleven and to all the rest' in Lk 24:9 rather than to verse 11. In fact verse 11 describes the reaction of the 'apostles' (cf. Lk 24:10), followed by the reaction of Peter, emphatically introduced in Lk 24:12, 'But Peter . . .'. The link between verses 11 and 12 is confirmed by the use of the phrases 'they did not believe' (*ēpistoun*, verse 11) and 'wondering' (*thaumazōn*, verse 12) which will be associated in Lk 24:41, 'And while they disbelieved (*apistountōn*) for joy, and wondered (*thaumazontōn*)'.

Lk 24:12 seems to be in perfect accordance with Luke's presentation: Peter goes to check the report of the women. Lk 24:24 alludes to such action, and from Lk 24:34 we gather that Christ appeared first to Peter. It is true that our present verse does not perfectly agree with Lk 24:24, 34 and that the vocabulary shows a striking similarity to Jn 20:3–10, but this proves only that Luke is here using an independent tradition, which was expanded by John into a full story (Jn 20:3–10).

On second thoughts Luke apparently could not accept the implication of verse 11 that the disciples did not even care to verify the story of the women. Peter 'saw the linen cloths' in which Jesus' body had been wrapped, yet 'he went home wondering at what had happened'. This 'wondering' is not faith but the opposite. Observing the empty tomb does not lead Peter to faith. Only the risen Christ himself can overcome the unbelief of the disciples by manifesting himself to them (Lk 24:32, 45). Once more the empty tomb is not sufficient.

It is therefore impossible to see in Lk 24:8–12 anything like the birth of Easter faith. This does not mean that verse 8 does not record any progress towards faith. In fact, 'remembering' will be an important element of the Easter revelation's comprehensive view of salvation history.

Summing up, we would say that, although some scholars tend to reduce Luke's dependence on Mark to secondary reminiscences, the opinion of those who hold that Mk 16:1–8 is the basic account which by itself sufficiently explains the Lucan exposition enjoys a higher degree of probability.

5 The Revelation and Mission of the Risen Christ (*Mt 28:16–20*)

Exegetes have long recognized that the final pericope of the gospel of Matthew (Mt 28:16–20) brings together several dominant themes in the evangelist's theological perspective. The well-known remark that Mt 28:18–20 is the key to the whole gospel of Matthew underlines the importance of the pericope we are going to study and we are not surprised to find this remark quoted in the introduction to several recent studies on the gospel as a whole or on the passage under consideration.

> The well ordered advance of action and ideas in a literary work is an indication of clear thinking and literary sophistication. In Matthew's gospel, the action and the ideas (theology) progress steadily to the climactic missionary mandate of Mt 28:18–20, which provides not only a summary of the central themes of the gospel but a clue to its movement as well.[3]

Peter Ellis

Exegesis of the text

Verse 16: Now the eleven disciples went to Galilee, to the mountain to which Jesus had directed them.

The reference to the 'eleven disciples' is redactional. It depends on Mt 28:7. Although both the angel (Mt 28:7) and Jesus himself (Mt 28:10) had told the women to inform the disciples that they should meet Jesus in Galilee, we are now informed that they actually meet him on a mountain.

Throughout his gospel, Matthew is not primarily concerned with identifying the disciples and the Twelve (or Eleven), or with depicting them only as the companions of the historical Jesus. Rather he tries to show that they hear and understand Jesus' teaching (cf., e.g., Mt 13:11, 51) and to provide a model for the Christian. By avoiding the term 'apostle' and by equating the disciple with 'brother' (cf. Mt 18:15, 21; 23:8; 25:40) and 'little one' (*mikros*, Mt 18:10; 25:40,

45), Matthew fosters the identification of the disciples with the members of his own community. In Matthew's community 'disciple' is an ecclesiological term. Throughout the gospel, and especially in its last paragraph, Matthew tries to combine two perspectives: firstly, the disciple shares in the power of the risen Lord (cf. Matthew's treatment of the miracle stories), and secondly, the disciple faithfully transmits the teaching of the earthly Jesus. For Matthew, the 'Twelve' are not so important as 'Twelve' or as 'apostles'. They play the part of exemplary disciples. They therefore appear at the end of the gospel, not as the 'Twelve' or as 'apostles', but as 'the eleven disciples', whose task is to 'make disciples'.

The use of the verb 'to go' (*poreuesthai*) is almost certainly Matthean. Matthew uses it in twenty-nine instances of which only six have a synoptic parallel, and often it is clearly redactional (e.g., Mt 9:13; 10:6–7; 11:7; 21:2, 6; 28:7).

The disciples went to 'Galilee', which in Matthew symbolizes the place of exile in which Israel forced Jesus to live (Mt 2:22), but which is at the same time the place of the opening to the Gentiles (Mt 4:15, 'Galilee of the Gentiles'). Galilee was the neglected part of Israel and its population was partly Gentile. During his public ministry Jesus occupied himself mainly with Israel, but he had also occasional encounters with Gentiles which meant great hopes for them (Mt 8:10–12; 15:28) and left no hope for Israel. After having left Galilee and confronted Israel in Jerusalem, Jesus now again orders the disciples, 'his brothers', to go to Galilee to which he will go ahead of them, not to occupy himself there again with Israel, but to leave Israel definitively and to commission his disciples to call the Gentile nations.

The place where the disciples meet Jesus is further specified as 'the mountain'. In Matthew, 'mountain' used in the absolute sense is the place for a specific relevant action of Jesus.

We think here first of all of the mountain of the temptation story (Mt 4:8) which definitely plays an important role in the understanding of the final scene of the gospel (cf. Mt 28:18).

Next we should refer to the mountain on which Matthew situates the Sermon (Mt 5:1), in which he depicts Jesus as the Messiah powerful in word. He deals here with Jesus' powerful teaching to which Mt 28:20, 'all that I have commanded you', certainly refers. Jesus' teaching and its *exousia* ('power', 'authority'), and the disciples who come to Jesus are all elements closely associated with the mountain setting in Mt 5:1.

Thirdly, in the context of the walking on the water (Mt 14:22–33), we are told that Jesus 'went up the mountain' (Mt 14:23; RSV: 'he went up into the hills'). Jesus' saving intervention (Mt 14:31–32) exemplifies his saving presence which Mt 28:20b promises to the disciples for 'always, to the close of the age'.

Fourthly, we have a summary of healings which Jesus performed

(Mt 15:30f.) after he 'went up the mountain' (Mt 15:29; RSV: 'he went up into the hills'). Matthew is concerned with striking a balance between Jesus as the Messiah of the word and as the Messiah of the deed. Having given us a programmatic representation of Jesus' teaching on the mountain (Mt 5:1 – 7:29), he now presents Jesus' healing activity in a similar programmatic way, on the mountain.

Finally, we should pay attention to the transfiguration scene (Mt 17:1–8) which takes place on the mountain (Mt 17:1). In Matthew, as in Mark, this scene is embedded in a context in which 'Son of man' is the leading Christological title (cf. Mt 16:13, 27, 28; 17:9, 12). But, whereas in Mark this title is closely related to the 'teaching' that the Son of man 'must' die, in Matthew the title is closely related to the Church to be founded. Nevertheless, it is also related to the 'teaching' of Jesus, but to the 'teaching' as Matthew understands it. For Matthew, Jesus' teaching is his authoritative interpretation of God's will, founded on the nearness of the kingdom and Jesus' closeness to the Father; this teaching is found in an exemplary way in the Sermon on the Mount (Mt 5:1 – 7:29). For Matthew there is a close connection between this teaching and the Son of man title as well as the Church of the Son of man with which the evangelist deals in the pericope which precedes the transfiguration (Mt 16:13–28). The transfiguration associates Jesus with 'the law and the prophets' (note that Matthew changes Mark's 'Elijah with Moses' into 'Moses and Elijah'!) which the Son of man came to fulfil. The disciples should 'listen to him' (Mt 17:5) as to the one to whom 'the law and the prophets' and God himself bear witness. The mountain scene of Mt 17:1–8 is found at the end of the Galilean activity of Jesus, at the beginning of which we found the Sermon on the Mount in which Jesus programmatically declared: 'Think not that I have come to abolish the law and the prophets; I have come not to abolish them but to fulfil them' (Mt 5:17).

There is a far-reaching correspondence between the proclamation 'This is my beloved Son, with whom I am well pleased' (Mt 17:5) and 'All authority in heaven and on earth has been given to me' (Mt 28:18b), as also between the command 'listen to him' (Mt 17:5) and 'make disciples of all nations . . . teaching them to observe all that I have commanded you' (Mt 28:19a, 20a). These strong correspondences between the two scenes may indicate that in Matthew's understanding the final mission appearance completes the transfiguration.

In view of the fact that Matthew situated Jesus' programmatic Sermon on a mountain and that he created another parallel mountain scene (Mt 15:29), it is probable that it was Matthew himself who conceived the concluding scene of his gospel as a mountain scene. Qualifying this mountain from the Christological point of view, we should say that it is the 'place' of the Son of man, whom Israel thought of as Messiah and who in reality is the Son of God. From the ecclesiological point of view, this mountain is at the same time the 'place' where the circle of disciples is gathered and obtains its form (Mt 5:1) and the 'place' where the disciples receive their definitive authority and mission (Mt 28:16). On the same mountain on which Jesus had proclaimed his teaching (Mt 5:1 – 7:29) he now gives his disciples full authority to spread his teaching among all nations.

Among the remaining references to a mountain we should refer to the saying about the city on the mountain (RSV: 'a city set on a hill') which is found in Matthew only (Mt 5:14), and which he has related to discipleship and its function in the world.

Summing up, we can say that the location of the great commission on the mountain in Galilee has a relevance which fits in with other mountain themes in Matthew.

The clause 'to which Jesus had directed them' is redactional. Firstly, it refers to Mt 28:10c, 'go and tell my brethren to go to Galilee'. Secondly, it is an integral part of verses 16–17 which were almost certainly drafted by Matthew. Thirdly, in all three instances where the adverb *hou* ('where' or 'to which') occurs in Matthew, it is probably redactional in nature (Mt 2:9; 18:20; 28:16). When we read the clause in the light of passages like Mt 1:24; 21:6; 26:19; 28:15, it is clear that Matthew intends to depict Jesus as one who gives a divine command, and the disciples as men who obey Jesus as they would obey God.

Verse 17: And when they saw him they worshipped him; but some doubted.

The circumstantial clause 'when they saw him' is redactional, as can be seen from the fact that it refers to Mt 28:7c, 'there you will see him', and Mt 28:10d, 'and there they will see me'. It is a matter of dispute among scholars in what sense 'seeing' should be understood here, but the clause does not constitute any real difficulty, since all through the gospel the form *idou/idontes* with accusative is used to refer to the person or the thing one is going to deal with. The emphasis is not on seeing but on the action or reaction expressed in the following main clause, here 'they worshipped him'.

The verb 'to worship' (*proskunein*) is a favourite word of Matthew (thirteen times in Matthew, against twice in both Mark and Luke). Matthew has previously stated that the Magi worshipped Jesus (Mt 2:11) and has altered or expanded his Marcan source in five places so as to describe the gesture of those who approach Jesus as *proskunēsis* (Mt 8:2; 9:18; 14:33; 15:25; 20:20, all except the last in miracle stories). But the most relevant parallel for our present passage is the way the women at the tomb are described as worshipping Jesus (Mt 28:9). In all instances mentioned this worship originates in faith, and expresses faith and trustful surrender, devotion, entreaty and submission. It concerns only Jesus, the 'king of the Jews' (Mt 2:2) and 'Christ' (Mt 2:4), the 'Lord' (Mt 8:21; 15:25) and 'Son of God' (Mt 14:33).

The phrase 'but some doubted' has been the object of much discussion and its sense remains unclear. Only a few scholars maintain that 'some' refers to a group distinct from the eleven disciples. Some are of the opinion that all eleven disciples see Jesus, all worship and all doubt, and translate: 'but they', referring to those who saw Jesus, namely the eleven. Other scholars argue that only some among the eleven doubt, and translate: 'but some'. The third opinion seems to have the best grammatical support, although recently it has been proposed to end the sentence after *prosekunēsan* ('worshipped') and to understand *hoi de* as referring to the eleven. Thus the sentence *hoi de edistasan* should be translated: 'But they doubted'.

In Matthew and in the whole New Testament the verb *distazein* is found only here and in Mt 14:31, and the episode of Peter walking on the water (Mt 14:28–31) has been considered the key to the meaning of this verb in our present passage. The verb expresses the difficulty of discerning the divine dimension of Jesus and totally submitting oneself to him in worship. It ought to be interpreted as part of Matthew's motif of 'little faith' (cf. Mt 6:30; 8:26; 14:31; 16:8; 17:20) and is different from the doubt motif of the resurrection accounts in Luke and John. In Matthew, the disciples' doubt should not be understood as positive disbelief or refusal to worship. It seems better not to press the question of the motivation for this doubt. It is generally characteristic of disciples as Matthew presents them.

An allusion has rightly been seen in the repeated reference to 'little faith' to the condition of the disciples at the time of the composition of Matthew's gospel. The community referred to in the gospel is a community in crisis and there are even indications that Matthew holds the leaders of the community at least partly responsible for this situation.

'Little faith' is indeed a failing typical of disciples. In our present text, however, unlike many Matthean passages in which 'little faith' is expressly used, there is no trace of rebuke. Instead, we find a note of reassurance, introducing Jesus' final instruction and commission.

While in other New Testament passages (Mk 16:14; Lk 24:41) the mention of doubt may serve apologetic interests by providing an occasion for demonstrating the physical reality of the risen Lord's body, these interests are entirely absent from Mt 28:17, where the doubt is not followed by any demonstration. Nevertheless, the mention of the doubt in Matthew probably also serves the purpose of overcoming this doubt through what is recorded in the following verses. But these verses do not provide any clearer seeing or any other proof of the reality of the risen Christ, but the *word* of Jesus. It seems, therefore, that here the doubt is overcome by that word. Some have seen here an allusion to the problem of the later Church, which seeks a new certainty about the risen Christ beyond the Easter appearance, since this appearance belongs to tradition and to an event of the past. They refer to Jn 20:29, 'Have you believed because you have seen me? Blessed are those who have not seen and yet believe.' In John the hearer or reader of the gospel message is directed to the understanding of faith itself, which can and may do without appearance. In Matthew the *word* of the risen Christ and the disciples' *obedience* to it is the way to the overcoming of doubt. Faith always remains a decision; it is never the result of a syllogism. Nothing can force people to believe, neither appearances nor an empty tomb.

Verse 18a: And Jesus came and said to them,

The literal translation of this clause reads: 'And approaching Jesus spoke to them saying'. The stylistic figure 'he spoke . . . saying' (*elalēsen . . . legōn*) is found here and in three other passages in Matthew. It is always more (Mt 13:3; 23:1) or less (Mt 14:27) redactional. Before Jesus begins to speak, he approaches the disciples.

> Jesus is at this inception of the appearance tradition not merely the One who is alive again, but it is the Lord who in eschatological power confronts and sends his disciples. . . . Jesus comes and encounters the disciples. Prior to his initiative here he has been absent from them. According to the representations he comes from outside of their experience into a present reality.[4]

The verb 'to approach' (*proserchesthai*) is a favourite Matthean term (fifty-three times in Matthew, against six times in Mark and ten times in Luke). But only twice in Matthew's gospel is the term applied to Jesus: here and in Mt 17:6f., another text proper to Matthew which is part of his redaction of the Marcan transfiguration account (Mk 9:2–8). In both texts we are told that Jesus approaches the disciples who are prostrate before him and reassures them. A comparison of our present passage with Mt 17:6–7 confirms a number of things already said about Mt 28:16–20.

Mt 17:6–7	*Mt 28:16–20*
When the disciples heard this,	Now the disciples. . . .
	And when they saw him
they fell on their faces,	they worshipped him;
and were filled with awe.	but some doubted.
But Jesus came	And Jesus came
and touched them, saying,	and said to them,
'Rise, and have no fear.'	'All authority. . . .
	I am with you always. . . .'

Note that the expressions 'they worshipped' and 'they fell on their faces' seem to be equivalent. The phrases 'doubted' and 'feared greatly' (RSV: 'were filled with awe') are also parallel. This confirms what has been said about the ambivalent character of *distazein* (belief mixed with unbelief). The comparison of Jesus' words confirms also what we have said of the reassuring character of these words in Mt 28:18–20 and their function of overcoming the doubt mentioned in Mt 28:17. Indeed, the term 'approaching' (RSV: 'came') seems to describe Jesus' reassuring reaction to the disciples' doubt. In fact, Jesus' address (Mt 28:18b–20) seems to confirm this note of reassurance and to clarify it theologically, although there is no explicit encouragement formula, but we definitely have an assistance formula in Mt 28:20b, 'I am with you always', especially since it recalls Mt 1:23, '. . . Emmanuel (which means, God with us)', thus forming an inclusion of almost the whole gospel.

Verse 18b: 'All authority in heaven and on earth has been given to me.'

The theme of the 'authority' (*exousia*) of Jesus is rooted in the tradition. The term is frequently used by Mark to describe the quality of Jesus' teaching and work (Mk 1:22, 27; 2:10; 6:7; 11:28, 29, 33). Matthew reproduces all but one of these verses (Mt 7:29, the conclusion of the Sermon on the Mount which represents Jesus as the Messiah powerful in word; Mt 9:6; 10:1; 21:23, 24, 27). Mk 1:27 is omitted together with the whole pericope of the cure of the demoniac at Capernaum (Mk 1:23–28; however, it is also possible that Matthew telescopes this account with the story of the Gadarene demoniac in Mt 8:28–34). Matthew adds *exousia* to his Marcan source at one point: '. . . they glorified God, who had given such authority to men' (Mt 9:8; compare Mk 2:12, 'so that they were all amazed and glorified God, saying, "We never saw anything like this!" '). Finally, he takes over the term *exousia* from the source in Mt 8:9 (compare Lk 7:8) within the pericope of the centurion's servant which Matthew inserts in his series of ten miracles (Mt 8:1 – 9:34) in which he represents Jesus as the Messiah powerful in deed.

All this indicates that Matthew intends to highlight the traditional theme of Jesus' authority. For Matthew it implies the definitive or eschatological interpretation by the Son of man of God's will, and is based on Jesus' teaching of the approaching kingdom and on his oneness with the Father (cf. Mt 11:25–27).

The meaning of 'authority' is further specified by the addition of the phrase 'in heaven and on earth'. We find a number of interesting parallels in Mt 16:19b; 18:18, 19, but the only exact parallel is found in Mt 6:10 where the core request of the Lord's prayer, 'Your kingdom come', receives an interpretative addition: 'your will be done on earth as it is in heaven (*hōs en ouranōi kai epi gēs*)'. This has been understood to indicate that the redactor is suggesting that Jesus is the definitive expression of the will of God. Jesus' presence constitutes the eschaton, God's final and decisive intervention. Jesus, who knows the definitive divine reality and lives it, is already making this reality valid on earth in his 'teaching'.

Jesus' authority is further qualified by 'all' (*pasa*). This qualification echoes the 'all' (*panta*) of Mt 4:9, 'All these (i.e., all the kingdoms of the world and the glory of them) I will give you, if you will fall down and worship me', and Mt 11:27, 'All things have been delivered (*paredothē*) to me by my Father'. In both texts the verb (*para-*)*didomai* also appears. Matthew's 'all authority' seems to correspond to and explain 'all things' (Mt 11:27/Lk 10:22; both believed to derive from the hypothetical common non-Marcan source referred to as Q, the first letter of the German word *Quelle*, 'source'). In both Mt 11:27 and 28:18 Jesus is designated as one with the Father and entrusted with the eschaton; the world is faced with salvation and judgment in Jesus.

A comparison of Mt 11:27 and Mt 28:18 reveals several verbal parallels:

Mt 11:27a	*Mt 28:18b*
All things (*panta*)	All authority (*pasa exousia*)
	in heaven and on earth
have been delivered (*paredothē*)	has been given (*edothē*)
to me (*moi*)	to me (*moi*).
by my Father.	

Although Mt 28:18b does not explicitly mention God, the passive 'has been given' suggests divine action, so that we may interpret: 'All authority . . . has been given to me by God', or 'God has given me all authority'. It is not surprising, then, that Mt 28:16–20 has been called a 'new edition' of the central articulation of the Easter experience by the people behind Q (Mt 11:27/Lk 10:22) – their existence, self-understanding and missionary activity.

The Q-saying reflected in Mt 11:27a was certainly influenced by Dan 7:14 in the Septuagint Greek (LXX). In turn, Mt 11:27a affected the composition of Mt 28:18b. The further question whether Dan 7:14LXX more directly influenced the composition of Mt 28:18b, though disputed, is answered in the affirmative by a good number of scholars. A comparison of the two texts literally translated will allow us to evaluate the verbal parallels:

Dan 7:14a	*Mt 28:18b–19b*
and to him has been given	to me has been given
authority	all authority

Dan 7:14a	*Mt 28:18b–19b*
and all the peoples	in heaven and
of the earth according to tongue	on the earth;
and all glory	going, therefore, teach
worshipping him.	all the peoples.

The least we can say is that Matthew seems to have drawn freely upon language from Dan 7:14LXX to frame Jesus' statement of authority. But this statement goes beyond that of Dan 7:14: *all* authority . . . *in heaven and on earth*, i.e., in the whole universe. As we saw, in other Matthean texts speaking of Jesus' earthly ministry, authority or power is also ascribed to him with relation to his teaching (Mt 7:29) as well as to his miracle-working (Mt 8:9, 9:6, 8). But here in Mt 28:18b it is all power in heaven and on earth. This is ascribed to the exalted Lord alone. In fact, the tense of the verb indicates an event which has just occurred and by which this total power has been given to him. This event can be none other than the full glorification of his resurrection.

Summing up, we may say that Mt 28:18b depicts Jesus as the eschatological teacher and judge, the Son of man, in accordance with the thought of Mt 6:10; 8:9; 9:6, 8; 12:8; 16:19; 18:18, 19; 21:23, 24, 27 and 13:36–43.

Indeed, the interpretation of the parable of the weeds (Mt 13:36–43) contains the key to Matthew's understanding of the Son of man. The connections between this parable found in what is often considered the central chapter of the gospel and the concluding pericope allow us to conclude that 'Son of man' is the title in which the presence and work of Jesus in all its phases (before/after Easter; towards Israel/towards the nations) and forms (in his earthly person/as the exalted Lord through the medium of his disciples on earth) are brought under a common and finally decisive denominator. The 'field' on which the Son of man sows the 'good seed', i.e., 'the sons of the kingdom', is, according to Matthew, the 'world' (*kosmos*), or the 'kingdom of the Son of man' (Mt 13:41; cf. 16:28; 20:21). The explicit universalism of the identification of the 'field' with the 'world' (Mt 13:38) is reflected in the fact that the mission of the disciples (Mt 28:19) is directed towards 'all nations'.

Verse 19a: 'Go therefore and make disciples of all nations,

Scholars debate how much emphasis is placed on 'go' ('going'). The phrase 'go' is an expression characteristic of Old Testament commissionings (cf. Gen 12:1; 24:4; Ex 3:16; 6:11, etc.). In our present passage, *poreuthentes* ('going') is undoubtedly understood by the redactor as taking the place of the 'go' in Mt 10:6–7, 'but go (*poreuesthe*) rather to the lost sheep of the house of Israel. And preach as you go (*poreuomenoi*) . . .', and as fulfilment of Mt 22:9, 'Go (*poreuesthe*) therefore to the thoroughfares, and invite to the marriage feast as many as you find'. However, as in the Old Testament commissionings, the emphasis does not fall on the participle *poreuthentes* ('going'), but on the following imperative 'make disciples'. It could even be said that the participle is essentially an auxiliary, with no 'commission' force of its own. It serves to reinforce the action of the main verb 'make disciples'. In other words, the core of the command is to 'make disciples', not to 'go'. The command is a commission to form disciples.

The conjunction 'therefore' (*oun*) is typically Matthean (cf. Mt 5:48; 6:8f., 31, 34; 7:12, etc.). It links the command with what precedes it, namely the basis for the obligation which the command entails, 'All authority in heaven and on earth has been given to me' (Mt 28:18b). The 'therefore' has further been related to and understood as a consequence of Mt 21:41b, 43b, '. . . and let out the vineyard to other tenants . . . the kingdom of God will be taken away from you and given to a nation (*ethnei*) producing the fruits of it' and Mt 22:9 cited above. The announcement of Mt 24:14, 'And this gospel of the kingdom will be preached throughout the whole world, as a testimony to all nations (*pasin tois ethnesin*; cf. *panta ta ethnē*)', is now carried through. The word of Isa 42:1-4 previously quoted by Matthew, 'Behold my servant whom I have chosen . . . and he shall proclaim justice to the Gentiles (*tois ethnesin*) . . . and in his name will the Gentiles (*ethnē*) hope' (Mt 12:18–21), is thereby fulfilled.

Although the word 'disciple' (*mathētēs*) is found seventy-three times in Matthew and 262 times in the New Testament, the verb 'to make disciples' (*mathēteuein*) occurs only in Mt 13:52; 27:57; 28:19; Acts 14:21. The active sense of 'making disciples' is found only in the last two passages. The meaning of 'making disciples' in Matthew is related to the meaning he gives to 'disciples' (see above under Mt 28:16). One suspects that the pre-Matthean tradition of the mission charge, like Ps-Mk 16:15, read: 'preach the gospel', and that Matthew has substituted his own word, 'make disciples'. For Matthew, 'to make disciples' is related to the kingdom of God in as far as it is concretely present in the person of Jesus. In our present text it is further specified by the participles 'baptizing them' and 'teaching them.'

The Eleven must make disciples 'of all nations'. There is dispute among scholars whether this phrase means 'Gentiles and Jews' or whether it refers to the Gentiles only, expressing a universalism without any special consideration for Israel, which had ceased to be a factor with the destruction of Jerusalem in A.D. 70.

The defenders of the first opinion show, e.g., that a truly universalistic dimension appears in seven mission accounts in the Old Testament (Gen 12:1–4; 17:1–14; 17:15–22; 26:1–6; 28:10–22; Jer 1:1–10; Isa 49:1–6) and consequently interpret 'all nations' as including both Gentiles and Jews.

Supporters of the second opinion analyse the attitude of Matthew towards Israel and conclude that Matthew's universalism seems to be a universalism without Israel and contrasted with Israel, which has betrayed and so lost its role and function among the nations.

Others confirm this on the basis of a study of the term *ethnē* ('nations', 'Gentiles'), which, they say, in Matthew almost exclusively means 'all the Gentiles', i.e., only non-Jews. The clause *mathēteusate panta ta ethnē* would mean 'make disciples of all the Gentiles'. It would not include the nation of Israel. The following arguments are given:

(1)   In Matthew's time *gôyîm* and *ethnē* referred to that whole collective of nations (the Gentile nations) other than Israel and to those individual non-Jews (Gentiles) who made up the collective.

(2)   (a)   In the five instances of *ethnos/ethnē* where Matthew depends on the Marcan or Q traditions, there are three (Mt 20:19, 25; 6:32) where it definitely means Gentiles, and two (Mt 24:7, 9) where it may possibly (though this is unlikely) include Israel.

(b)   For eight uses of *ethnos/ethnē* in material peculiar to Matthew the obvious meaning in six (Mt 4:15; 10:5, 18; 12:18, 21; 21:43) is Gentiles; in Mt 24:14 and 25:32 *ethnē* could include Israel, but in both cases it seems preferable to interpret it as meaning Gentiles.

(3)   In no case of *panta ta ethnē* in Matthew (Mt 25:32; 24:9, 14; 28:19) can it be persuasively argued that the phrase includes Israel. Rather it designates non-Jewish mankind in its entirety.

(4)   Although the divine plan required that the gospel be preached first to the Jews (Mt 10:5; cf. 15:24, 26), for Matthew the time of the mission to Israel as Israel is over. Henceforth the mission is to the Gentiles.

(5)   Origen, Eusebius, and John Chrysostom all assume that *panta ta ethnē* in Mt 28:19 excludes Israel.

But this conclusion has been challenged because, it is said, the occurrences of *ethnos/ethnē* in Matthew can be divided into three types:

(1)   cases where the word clearly refers only to Gentiles (Mt 4:15; 6:32; 10:5, 18; 12:18, 21; 20:19);

(2)   cases where it is unclear whether the word refers only to Gentiles (Mt 20:25; 24:9);

(3)   cases where it is clear or highly probable that the word does not refer only to Gentiles (Mt 21:43; 24:7, 14; 25:32).

On this basis it is said that *panta ta ethnē* in Mt 28:19 means 'all the nations' or better 'all (the) peoples'.

Israel, the unique chosen people of God, is indeed an entity of the past for Matt; it had its hour of critical choice, and failed to choose rightly. But the *Ioudaioi* remain a present reality for Matt's church (28:15: *para Ioudaiois mechri tēs sēmeron* ['among the Jews to this day']). In Matt's eyes they no longer enjoy the former privileged status of the chosen people of God (21:43). But they do qualify in Matt's vocabulary as an *ethnos* (24:7). And so they do fall under the mandate of the risen Jesus to make disciples of *panta ta ethnē* (28:19).[5]

Verse 19b: 'baptizing them in the name of the Father and of the Son and of the Holy Spirit,

Some scholars have suggested that the triad in Mt 28:19b was shaped from an earlier triadic formula found in the *Similitudes of I Enoch* (39:5–7; 51:3–4; 61:8–10). But the dating of the *Similitudes* poses a problem and some exegetes hold that the work may draw on Christian ideas of the Son of man. Recently it has been maintained that

> . . . the triadic phrase in Matt. 28:19b, naming the Father, the Son and the Holy Spirit, is a development of the triad found in Daniel 7: Ancient of Days, one like a son of man and angels. It is not to be traced to the triad found in the Similitudes, although evidence has been found of the use of common Danielic traditions. The New Testament development is more than an adjustment and alteration of titles; it is the process of 'organic growth' from the original Danielic vision, which is transmuted and kept alive by adaptation. The Matthean triad and Matthew's understanding of it are integral parts of an interpretation of Daniel which emphasizes the wisdom and apocalyptic elements of that work, highlighting the theme of transcendence of death on the part of authentic Israel and highlighting the importance for all nations of Israel's exaltation. . . . Joined to the commission to make disciples, it is presented as inspiration and impetus for the renewal of history by means of the formation of a new community of the Son of Man.[6]

The disciples are to baptize 'in the name of the Father and of the Son and of the Holy Spirit'. Nowhere else are Father, Son and Spirit associated in so formal a way. Elsewhere baptism is spoken of as being in or through the name of Jesus (Acts 2:38; 8:16; 10:48; Rom 6:3; I Cor 1:13, 15; 6:11) and the triadic baptismal formula is absent from the citation of this verse in the writings of Eusebius of Caesarea. He quotes the verse sixteen times without the triadic baptismal formula as follows: 'go and make disciples of all nations in my name'. But it has been convincingly proven that this absence cannot be considered a serious argument against the authenticity of the formula. It can hardly be doubted that Matthew himself wrote the text as it is found in all the manuscripts. Thus he probably bears witness here to the baptismal practice of his community, which was not necessarily that of other communities.

The way has already been paved for the use of the triadic baptismal formula through passages such as I Cor 12:4–6 and II Cor 13:14. The expression 'in the name of' has already been used in Mt 18:20. If the formula depends on Palestinian tradition, it is possible that it should be understood in the sense of the rabbinic expression *leshem*, i.e., 'with regard to', 'thinking of', 'because of'. It would then refer to the disciples' ultimate motivation for baptism rather than to a personal belonging to the one whose name is mentioned during the administration of baptism. Jesus' disciples receive and administer the baptism of repentance (as it came from John the Baptist) 'with regard to' or 'in consideration of' 'the Father and of the Son and of the Holy Spirit'. They carry out the eschatological conversion in consideration of the Father as only the Son knows him and has revealed him (Mt 11:27/Lk 10:22); and because of the Son as only the Father knows him and as the Father has delivered everything to him (Mt 11:27; Lk 10:22); and on account of the Spirit who speaks in the community and in situations where witness has to be given (Lk 12:10, 11f.).

Accounts like the announcement of the birth of Jesus, especially Mt 1:18–20, '. . . she was found to be with child of the Holy Spirit. . . . for that which is conceived in her is of the Holy Spirit', Mt 3:11, '. . . he will baptize you with the Holy Spirit', and the narrative of Jesus' baptism (Mt 3:13–17), in which God sends the Holy Spirit to his Son, and which prefigures the baptism of Christians in the name of the 'Father, Son and Holy Spirit', should help us to explain the presence of the Spirit in this formula.

The triadic baptismal formula expresses the conviction that in the Son as well as in the Spirit God himself becomes present. Thus the Christian community sought to say that God is never an isolated, lifeless God, some kind of ultimate principle of being. From all eternity God opens himself to us by seeking us out and loving us.

This leads us to the communitarian dimension implicitly present in the initiation rite. Indeed, Matthew exhibits in Mt 28:19b(–20a) an interest in the Church or community. The passage has been form-critically classified as a 'regulation of the community' (in German, *Gemeindeordnung*) and related to Mt 16:17–19, designating Peter as the 'rock' and giving him the power of the keys, and Mt 18:15–17, describing the procedure by which one brother was to correct another who had sinned against him. Both texts are found in Matthew only and contain the only uses of the term *ekklēsia* in the four gospels (Mt 16:18; 18:17). These two passages with their emphasis on the regulation of the community seem to have a counterpart in Mt 28:19b–20a: the disciples are initiated in the *ekklēsia* by baptism and by being taught to observe the commands of Jesus which are the core of the community life.

Verse 20a: 'teaching them to observe all that I have commanded you;

For Matthew, the verb 'to teach' (*didaskein*) has a specified meaning: it means explanation of Torah, the way of life revealed by God to his people, and presentation of *Halachah*,[7] as it is done by Jesus in the light of the approaching kingdom and on the basis of his nearness to the Father. Because of this specific meaning Matthew can take over only six of Mark's seventeen uses of *didaskein*. The parables do not belong to what Matthew understands by 'teaching' (compare Mk 4:1, 2 and Mt 13:1ff.); neither do the passion and resurrection prophecies (compare Mk 8:31; 9:31 and Mt 16:21; 17:22). During Jesus' time on earth the apostles do not teach (Mk 6:30 is omitted by Matthew). On the other hand, in the three summaries of Jesus' ministry to Israel (Mt 4:23; 9:35; 11:1) the emphasis in each case is on the 'teaching' of Jesus (see also Mt 5:2; 7:28, 29). Hence, it could be expected that Matthew would emphasize this same theme in his description of the continuing ministry of the post-Easter Church. The use of 'teaching' should be considered typically Matthean.

In Mt 28:20a *didaskein* is used for the last time in the gospel and for the first and only time the verb refers to the 'teaching' of the disciples. But they will teach 'to observe all that I have commanded you'. So even here (especially here) we are concerned solely with Jesus' 'teaching'. It is promulgated in the authority resulting from the approaching kingdom and Jesus' unique relationship with God. The 'teaching' of Jesus is accepted and carried out by those who recognize and accept Jesus' authority, and in it Jesus and God himself, i.e., by those who 'believe'.

We should note especially that Matthew begins the Sermon on the Mount with 'And he opened his mouth and taught (*edidasken*) them . . .' (Mt 5:2, no parallel in Luke). And a few verses later we read: 'whoever then relaxes one of the least of these commandments (*entolōn*; cf. *eneteilamēn*, 'I have commanded', in Mt 28:20a), and teaches (*didaxēi*) men so, shall be called least in the kingdom of heaven; but he who does them and teaches (*didaxēi*) them shall be called great in the kingdom of heaven' (Mt 5:19, no parallel). The Sermon ends with the summary statement, 'and when Jesus finished these sayings, the crowds were astonished at his teaching (*didachēi*), for he taught (*didaskōn*) them as one who had authority (*exousian*), and not as their scribes' (Mt 7:28, 29; compare Mk 1:21–22). The use of *didaskein* in Mt 28:20a certainly refers to the Sermon on the Mount which is the first and most important example of Jesus' teaching. We should also note that there too the disciples are in Jesus' presence and that the whole scene is situated on the mountain (Mt 5:1).

It is then practically certain that 'all that I have commanded you' refers to the programmatic discourse of Mt 5:1 – 7:29, and most probably to the other four discourses in Matthew which end with a summary statement very similar to the one just cited (Mt 7:28, 29; 11:1; 13:53; 19:1; 26:1). But it should also be noted that in the story of the rich young man, Matthew has edited his Marcan source so as to produce the expression 'If you would enter life, keep (*tērei*, 'observe') the commandments' (*tas entolas*; Mt 19:17). This suggests the Matthean origin of the expression in Mt 28:20a. The verb 'to observe' (*tērein*) is another favourite term of Matthew (six times, against once in Mark and none in Luke). Its use in Matthew is always redactional in nature.

> *Entellesthai* in the basic religious sense, of the proclamation of Jesus to the disciples, is found in the Synoptists only in Mt 28:20. . . . Here the content of all that Jesus has said to the disciples is described as *entolē*, with no singling out of the commandment of love as in Jn. In their missionary work the disciples are to teach what Jesus has commanded. . . . But since it is the present Christ who charges the community to do this, and since it is the baptised who are to render this obedience, it is hardly possible to think of this *tērein* ['observe'] of what is commanded in legalistic isolation from Christ Himself in His effective rule among His believing people. In this context the word *entellesthai* simply expresses the unconditional obligation to obedience which, grounded christologically, is the obedience of faith.[8]

The verb *entellesthai* ('to command') is found five times in Matthew, and three times it is redactional in character. The subject of the verb is God (Mt 4:6; 15:4) or Moses (Mt 19:7/Mk 10:3), but once it is Jesus (Mt 17:9). The latter passage seems to be the transition to the final passage of the gospel where the risen Christ is presented as telling the Church of the binding character of 'all that I have commanded you'.

The phrase 'all that I have commanded you' is often found in the Pentateuch (e.g., Ex 7:2; 23:22; 29:35; 31:11; 34:11), where Yahweh is the subject, and it has been concluded from this that Matthew's use of the verb 'to command' aims at placing Jesus on the same level as God and suggesting that they have the same right to be obeyed.

The related phrases 'everyone who' (*pas hostis*) and 'all that' (*panta hosa*) are typically Matthean. They occur nine times in this gospel, but only once with a synoptic parallel (Mt 21:22/Mk 11:24).

Verse 20b: 'and lo, I am with you always, to the close of the age.'

The phrase 'and lo' (*kai idou*, 'and behold') is found seventeen times in Matthew and is almost always redactional. The final clause 'I am with you (*meth' humōn*) always' is the definitive response to the 'doubt' of the disciples (Mt 28:19). In the Old Testament, the clause 'Behold I am (my covenant is) with you' is found in Gen 17:4; 28:15, and 'I am (will be) with you' is found another thirteen times (e.g., Gen 17:19, 21; 26:3; Ex 3:12; 4:15; Judg 6:12, 16). It is an expression of divine reassurance through the promise of divine presence. In Mt 28:20 Jesus is pictured as giving the same reassurance through his active presence.

Within this gospel of Matthew, 'I am with you always' is a conscious reference to Mt 1:23, 'and his name shall be called Emmanuel (which means, God with us)', thus framing most of the gospel by an inclusion which has been said to give the spirit of the whole work. But in between these two passages there are a number of instances where Matthew uses the phrase 'with you' (*meth' humōn*) in a characteristic way. We think, e.g., of Mt 17:17, where Matthew changes Mark's *pros humas* ('with you', Mk 9:19) into *meth' humōn*: 'O faithless and perverse generation, how long am I to be with you?' A little later Jesus says to the disciples that they could not heal the epileptic boy 'because of your little faith' (Mt 17:20; note what we said about 'little faith' above under Mt 28:17). 'I am with you always' is Jesus' final answer to the question 'how long am I to be with you?' (Mt 17:17).

The effect of this presence of Jesus can be clarified by means of the accounts of the stilling of the storm (Mt 8:23–27; note 'O men of little faith', Mt 8:26) and the walking on the water (Mt 14:22–33; note 'O man of little faith, why did you doubt?', Mt 14:31). Only the saving presence of Jesus is capable of overcoming the danger which confronts the disciples and the execution of their mission because of their little faith. Only when the *exousia* ('authority', 'power') of Jesus is permanently with them can they really 'make disciples of all nations'. Their experience of his presence will give them faith, 'and nothing will be impossible to you' (Mt 17:20).

If we take into account that both miracle stories (Mt 8:23–27; 14:22–23) have a strongly communitarian dimension and that the boat is a symbol of the Church, we should also take into account Mt 18:20, 'For where two or three are gathered in my name, there am I in the midst of them', which can be considered as a variant of the God-with-us theme, and where Jesus' presence in the community is described as analogous to the Shekhinah or presence of God.[9]

Moreover, it has been pointed out that the adjective 'all' (*pas*) occurs four times in Mt 28:18b–20: Jesus has been given *all* authority; he wants the Eleven to make disciples of *all* nations and to teach them *all* that he has commanded; and he promises to be with them *all* days. The phrase 'all the days' (*pasas tas hēmeras*; RSV: 'always') is typically Matthean. He uses the word 'day' (*hēmera*) forty-five times, often redactionally (e.g., Mt 3:1; 6:34; 7:22; 10:15, etc.). Moreover, it appears in a number of idiomatic expressions several of which occur in the Synoptics only in Matthew (see Mt 2:1; 4:2; 10:15; 11:12, 22, 24; 12:36; 13:1, etc.). Besides stylistically tying together Mt 28:18b–20, this feature further emphasizes the universal extent and significance of the missionary charge. True, we find a similar use of 'all' in Mt 3:15; 5:18; 7:12; 23:3, but none of these instances can be compared to the emphatic use of 'all' in the final pericope of the gospel.

The phrase 'to the close of the age' is, with one exception, found in Matthew only (Mt 13:39, 40, 49; 24:3; 28:20; Heb 9:26) and is always redactional. It expresses the strong faith of the Church in the enduring presence of the risen Christ.

Summing up, we would say first of all that the preceding analysis shows that the final pericope of the Gospel was probably entirely composed by Matthew himself. This would explain why so far scholars who are of another opinion have not succeeded in determining with any degree of certainty the extent of the alleged piece(s) of tradition which, according to them, underlie these verses.

Secondly, our study confirms the opinion of those scholars who hold that Mt 28:16–20 is a summary of the entire gospel. Indeed, Matthew's final paragraph recapitulates the following themes or ideas: the mountain as a place of Jesus' powerful teaching and revelation (verse 16); emphasis on the need for faith (verse 17); the extent of Jesus' authority (verse 18); the importance of discipleship, and its universal character (verse 19a); the need to 'regulate' the community (*Gemeindeordnung*; verse 19b), in this instance by means of baptism (verse 19b) and teaching (verse 20a); Jesus' permanent presence (verse 20b).

The literary form of Mt 28:16–20

There is no consensus among scholars concerning the literary form of Mt 28:16–20. Some have described it as a 'word of revelation' from a divine figure (here, the risen Christ), placed in a mythological framework (M. Dibelius), or expanded to bring the passage into harmony with Matthew's theological position (G. Strecker), while others show that the passage exhibits a threefold pattern of revelatory word, command and promise (W. Trilling and E. Lohmeyer). Others classify it as a sort of cult legend (because of the appended instruction to baptize; R. Bultmann). Still others have tried to explain the final pericope of Matthew as an 'enthronement hymn' based on Dan 7:13–14 (O. Michel and J. Jeremias). Again others call it a 'concise resurrection narrative' (compare Mt 28:8–10 and Jn 20:19–21), distinguishing it from the more developed 'resurrection tales' (e.g., Lk 24:13–35; Jn 21:1–14; C. H. Dodd). It has also been compared to farewell speeches found in the Old Testament and in post-biblical Jewish literature (J. Munck).

The attempt has also been made to explain Mt 28:16–20 as an 'official decree' as found in II Chron 36:23, 'Thus says Cyrus of Persia, "The Lord, the God of heaven, has given me all the kingdoms of the earth and he has charged me to build him a house at Jerusalem, which is in Judah. Whoever is among you of all his people, may the Lord his God be with him. Let him go up." ' With some support from Gen 45:9–11, it has been argued that the literary form of II Chron 36:23 is very similar to that of Mt 28:16–20 and that the latter text is patterned on the former one. This literary form contains the following elements: messenger formula, narrative, command, and motivation. It is also noted that just as II Chron 36:23 closes the Jewish scriptures, so Mt 28:16–20 closes the work of Matthew (B. Malina).

Recently, in a long series of Old Testament texts, twenty-seven in all,[10] a literary form has been identified which is defined as a divine delegation of power or a 'divine commissioning', composed of the following elements: introduction, confrontation, reaction, commission, protest, reassurance, and a conclusion (B. J. Hubbard). All these elements are found in practically all of the twenty-seven texts mentioned, except the reaction and the protest. Only five commissioning accounts have both. But either the reaction or the protest is found in seventeen of them. It seems that generally the accounts have the individual respond either to the presence of the one who commissions (= reaction) or to the commission itself (= protest). In the critical evaluation of this analysis it has been pointed out that three elements (confrontation, commission, and reassurance) seem to be the essential elements of the form and that the rest seem to be optional. The three elements are found in all of the twenty-seven examples, except three (Gen 35:9–15; 41:37–45; Num 22:22–35), where the element of reassurance is lacking (T. Y. Mullins).

In the next step, B. J. Hubbard shows that Mt 28:16–20 is a New Testament example of the form discovered in the Old Testament. Applying the results of the analysis to this text, he gets the following results:

introduction:	Now the eleven disciples went to Galilee to the mountain to which Jesus had directed them (verse 16).
confrontation:	And when they saw him . . . (verse 17a)
reaction:	. . . they worshipped him; but some doubted (verse 17b).
confirmation:	And Jesus came and said to them, 'All authority in heaven and on earth has been given to me (verse 18).
commission:	'Go therefore and make disciples of all nations, baptizing them in the name of the Father and of the Son and of the Holy Spirit, teaching them to observe all that I have commanded you (verses 19–20a);

reassurance: '. . . and lo, I am with you always, to the close of the
                    age' (verse 20b).

As can be seen from the breakdown of the text, the protest and the
conclusion are lacking, but all the other elements are present. The
conclusion in the form of a statement that the disciples acted as they
had been told is omitted (as in Isa 6; 49:1–6; Jer 1:1–10) because the
affirmation of the permanent presence of Jesus (cf. Gen 17:4; 26:3;
28:15; 46:4; Deut 31:23; Judg 6:16; Jer 1:8) is a more appropriate
conclusion to the gospel as a whole, from both the dramatic and the
theological points of view.

   We prefer Hubbard's opinion to Malina's for two reasons. First,
Hubbard establishes a wide base of examples from the Old Testament,
whereas Malina relies practically on one example, II Chron 36:23,
with some support from Gen 45:9–11. Secondly, Hubbard's analysis is
able to accept Mt 28:16–20 as it is and compare it with the Old
Testament examples. Malina, on the other hand, has to manoeuvre
skilfully in order to overcome a lack of correspondence at a crucial
point (the messenger formula), saying that in Mt 28:16–20 it is
'refashioned as narrative introduction to Jesus' decree'.

   It is difficult to see how Hubbard's arguments to support the view
that the literary form of Mt 28:16–20 is that of a 'divine commissioning' could be improved.

   Lately, however, it has been pointed out that the commission form
is a remarkably common form in the New Testament and that it is used
in non-resurrection texts much more often than in resurrection texts. In
fact, the commission form is more abundant in the New Testament
than in the Old. There are thirty-seven instances of the commission
form in the New Testament.[11] Nine of these have all seven elements of
the commission form: introduction, confrontation, reaction, commission, protest, reassurance, conclusion (T. Y. Mullins). These considerations confirm that in Mt 28:16–20 we are dealing with a 'divine
commissioning'.

6   The Disciples at Emmaus

(Lk 24:13–35)

The Emmaus account occupies a unique place among the resurrection narratives: with its twenty-three verses it is not only the longest resurrection story, but it also constitutes almost half of Luke's resurrection chapter. The Lucan character of the account cannot be doubted. In fact, it is the most Lucan Easter story in chapter 24.

The present text is a *private* Christophany, i.e., not to official witnesses. Such Christophanies evoke signs which bring about recognition of the presence of the risen Lord. They clarify the subjective condition, the adaptation of the internal vision, necessary to recognize the risen Lord in his new condition. The sign given is not a real proof. Only faith can interpret it when the interior vision is prepared for it. The sign reaches only those who are capable of reading it in the light of faith. Lk 24:13–35 is a recognition story with the additional motif of remembrance of both Jesus' meals with his disciples and his words concerning his passion and death. As no other resurrection account, the Emmaus pericope shows the conquest of the enigma of the cross in the Easter faith. The heart of Luke's concern in this account, as in the whole of Lk 24, is his proof-from-prophecy theology.

It is more or less generally accepted that the Emmaus account existed before its insertion into the context of the gospel of Luke and that in its present form it is a complete whole. However, Luke thoroughly overhauled an existing account in order to insert it into his gospel, so much so that no verse or even a complete turn of phrase is without characteristics of Lucan usage or words of Luke's preference.

Exegesis of the text

Introduction (Lk 24:13–16)

> **Verses 13–14:** That very day two of them were going to a village named Emmaus, about seven miles from Jerusalem, (14) and talking with each other about all these things that had happened.

The indication of time, 'that very day', acts as the redactional link with the preceding account. In the context of Lk 24 it can refer only to Lk 24:1. Hereby it strongly connects the account with the day of Easter. Lk 24:29b will complete this time indication: the travellers reach their destination when 'it is toward evening and the day is now far spent'.

The phrase 'two of them', which maintains the continuity of persons in the Easter experiences, introduces the two travellers. Their initial anonymity is surprising. In the present context the phrase 'of them' can only refer to the wider circle of disciples around the Eleven (Lk 24:9). Theoretically, a reference to the apostles (Lk 24:10) is possible, but Lk 24:33, 'and they found the eleven gathered', makes clear that the two did not belong to the Eleven. This may explain why the disciples are introduced as 'two of them': their belonging to the circle of disciples is more important than their name. The phrase 'two of them' prepares for their return to that circle (Lk 24:33). Since the phrase is understandable only in the light of Lk 24:9, it is considered redactional. Furthermore, their return probably did not belong to the original account.

One of the two was Cleopas (cf. Lk 24:18). But who was the other disciple? Various proposals have been made. A rather influential hypothesis holds that Peter was the other disciple, and some have even said that we have here a Galilean Peter-tradition from which Luke (or the tradition?) removed the references to both Galilee and Peter. But this hypothesis has been rejected as fantastic. It is hard to see how a Peter-tradition could lose its reference to Peter, and there is nothing suggesting a previous localization in Galilee.

It should also be noted that nothing in the account indicates that Luke would reckon Cleopas and his companion among the seventy or seventy-two disciples mentioned in Lk 10:1ff.

There are two places which claim the right to be the 'village of Emmaus': Amwas and El-Kubebe. Decision in this matter is made difficult by the fact that (1) the manuscript tradition is not clear; (2) Amwas, which is favoured by the ancient tradition, is too far from Jerusalem to do justice to the data of Lk 24. The real solution should be sought in the redactional work of the evangelist rather than in the answer to the questions about manuscript tradition and geographical indications. In view of Luke's use of the word, one should not depend too much on the description of the place as a 'village'.

It is possible that Luke gave the Emmaus pericope a chronological and geographical framework determined by the whole of Lk 24 and its understanding by the evangelist. The indication 'seven miles' or 'six stadia' is then to be attributed to Luke. Anyway, it can be noticed in other passages that he was not too familiar with the geography of Palestine.

The expression 'from Jerusalem' indicates that the following event should be read in a 'Jerusalem perspective', and also prepares for the travellers' return to the city. But it should also be noted that, although there are many travel accounts in Luke-Acts, there are only two exact indications of distance: Lk 24:13 and Acts 1:12. It has been shown that in Acts 1:12 the ultimate farewell of Jesus should be related to Jerusalem. In Lk 24:13 too the emphasis is not on the exact distance but on Jerusalem. It is as if Luke were saying: Emmaus was at most seven miles from Jerusalem, as he says in Acts 1:12, 'near Jerusalem, (only) a sabbath day's journey away'. The indication of distance may also help to explain how the disciples could return to Jerusalem on the same day (cf. Lk 24:33–35). To Luke Jerusalem is the site of Jesus' appearances. From here the Church will expand and grow.

> **Verses 15–16:** While they were talking and discussing together, Jesus himself drew near and went with them. (16) But their eyes were kept from recognizing him.

These verses introduce the risen Christ as an unknown companion on the road. However, the narrator tells the reader from the beginning that this companion is Jesus. Thus he creates a literary tension – the reader knows what the disciples do not – which is solved only in Lk 24:31. Whereas Jesus' appearance in Lk 24:36ff. causes fear, because they 'supposed that they saw a spirit', here Jesus' coming is as ordinary as a traveller joining others along the road. It has been suggested that 'Luke may be teaching us that the mysterious stranger is Christ himself, manifesting himself through the traveling apostle, the stranger who meets new people in new places' (J. A. Grassi).

The use of the name 'Jesus' is important, establishing the continuity between the Christ of faith and Jesus of Nazareth. The phrase 'drew near' recalls the term used of the kingdom of God (Lk 10:9–11), of Jesus' earlier approach to Jerusalem (Lk 18:35; 19:29, 37, 41), and the apocalyptic redemption (Lk 21:28). The fact that he 'went with them' further suggests the continuity between the activity of the resurrected Christ and Jesus' earthly ministry.

To Jesus' 'drawing near' and 'going with' corresponds his remaining unknown. Ultimately, the incapability to recognize the risen Christ is ascribed to God himself, as the passive 'were kept' (compare 'were opened' in Lk 24:31) suggests. But we should say more: the disciples' incapability to recognize the Lord corresponds to their incapability to believe. The theme of faith is a basic element throughout chapter 24. Luke seems to emphasize that recognition, viz. the Easter faith, is made possible through the personal intervention of the risen One (Lk 24:27, 30). There is no suggestion here of disguise or 'altered appearance'. The two disciples do not recognize the risen Christ not because of his appearance 'in another form' (see Mk 16:12) but because of the 'divinely determined economy of concealment and revelation' whereby the mystery of the person and destiny of the Christ was ultimately to be revealed.

The theme of non-recognition is also found in Jn 20:14, 'but she did not know that it was Jesus', and Jn 21:4, 'yet the disciples did not know that it was Jesus'. They saw a man who walked with them, but they did not see him as the risen One. That was beyond the reach of natural seeing and was not observable by the unaided eye. Jesus had to be revealed to them as the Risen One by way of internal enlightenment. As in similar appearances, a word or a sign is necessary before he is recognized (Lk 24:30–31). At present they lack the understanding, the faith, to see him as the risen One.

For Luke to believe in the risen One, i.e., to recognize him as the One actually living and acting here and now, means first of all to remember the prophecies of the passion and resurrection, which are the fulfilment of the prophecies of the Old Testament; next, the spiritual understanding of the scriptures through the grace of internal enlightenment of which Jesus is the source; and finally, perceiving his presence through the signs he gives of it. We can already discover this Lucan theme in the second (Lk 9:44–45) and the third prophecy of the passion (Lk 18:31–34). Then there was still a veil over the disciples' eyes. It is so even now, when they see this man travelling with them. But Jesus is going to open their eyes (Lk 24:31, 32, 45).

NB Divided into 3 parts

First part of the conversation (Lk 24:17–21a)

Verses 17–18: And he said to them, 'What is this conversation which you are holding with each other as you walk?' And they stood still, looking sad. (18) Then one of them, named Cleopas, answered him, 'Are you the only visitor to Jerusalem who does not know the things that have happened there in these days?'

Jesus is going to prepare the two disciples for his self-revelation. He asks them what they are discussing in such a heated way. The question of the risen Christ interrupts the hopeless discussion of the travellers: 'What is this conversation (literally, 'what are these words') . . .'. The expression reminds us of Lk 4:36, 'What is this word?' The travellers react with astonishment. RSV renders 'sad', but misses the point of the adjective, used only one other time in the New Testament (Mt 6:16, where RSV renders it 'dismal'). The adjective describes the reaction of one who frowns indignantly: 'Are you the only visitor to Jerusalem. . .'. You are putting us on. Every other visitor to Jerusalem knows what happened there, but you don't? Once more the disciples' total lack of faith-recognition is emphasized. They look upon Jesus as a complete outsider who does not even know what every visitor to Jerusalem was supposed to know.

Verse 19: And he said to them, 'What things?' And they said to him, 'Concerning Jesus of Nazareth, who was a prophet mighty in deed and word before God and all the people,

In reply to Jesus' inquiry the two disciples give him a three-point representation of the events: (1) a characterization of the ministry of Jesus up to and including his trial and crucifixion, (2) a statement on the messianic hopes of those who had followed him from Galilee, and (3) a report that the tomb had been found empty by both the women and some of the disciples and that, although the women claimed to have seen a vision of angels and were told that Jesus was alive, the disciples had not seen him.

The second question of the risen Christ, 'What things?', introduces the conversation proper. The attempt to express the work and person of Jesus in prophetic categories remained limited to Jewish Christianity. It is surprising that Luke here characterizes Jesus as (literally) 'man prophet', since nowhere else in Luke-Acts can one find the title 'prophet' explicitly attributed to Jesus. Is Lk 24:19 then an exception? It should be pointed out that Luke has several passages in which a prophet-Christology can be discerned. We think, e.g., of the Nazareth pericope (Lk 4:16–30; see especially Lk 4:24, 'no prophet is acceptable in his own country'), the raising of the young man at Naim (Lk 7:11–17, especially Lk 7:16, 'a great prophet has risen among us'), and the discussion about Herod (Lk 13:31–33, especially Lk 13:33, 'for it cannot be that a prophet should perish away from Jerusalem').

> [Luke's] characterization of Jesus as wonder-working prophet . . .
> is not the survival of some primitive and flawed christological
> viewpoint, it is specifically and recognizably Lucan, depicting the
> first phase of Jesus' mission and the first step in understanding
> him.[12]

Luke was certainly familiar with traditions which endeavoured to express Jesus' personality in prophetic categories. Luke's use of these traditions may have been influenced by the late Jewish Moses-tradition and its typological utilization with the help of Deut 18. In fact, in Acts Luke has taken over traditions which develop Deut 18:15ff. Christologically (Acts 7:22; 3:22f.; 7:37). In particular, Acts 7:22, 'he (Moses) was mighty in his words and deeds', is very similar to Lk 24:19.

It has been established by several scholars that the answer of the disciples derives, on the one hand, from the missionary sermons of Acts and, on the other hand, from the vocabulary of the passion prophecies. 'Jesus of Nazareth' is found in Acts 2:22; 4:10, etc.; 'who was a prophet' (cf. Deut 18:15 – quoted in Acts 3:22 and 7:37);

'mighty in deed and word' corresponds to the content of Acts 2:22; in Acts 7:22 it is applied to Moses in a Jesus–Moses parallel.

'All the people' are contrasted in a typically Lucan way with the 'chief priests and rulers', the Jewish leadership, in the following verse.

> **Verse 20:** 'and how our chief priests and rulers delivered him up to be condemned to death and crucified him.'

It is well known that Luke emphasizes the Jewish responsibility for Jesus' death. Here we find the first part of a polemic antithesis which occurs repeatedly in the kerygmatic formulae of the first part of Acts: You, the Jews, have killed Jesus (but God raised him from the dead; see Acts 2:23–24, etc.). Of course, here in Lk 24:20 the disciples do not yet mention the second part of the antithesis since their eyes have not yet been opened to the reality of the resurrection.

The disciples express the killing of Jesus in the following way: 'they delivered him up' and 'crucified him'. The same verbs are found respectively in Acts 3:13 and Acts 2:36; 4:10. Unlike the passive delivery-statements of the Marcan passion summaries (cf. Mk 9:31; 10:33), in Lk 24:20, 'to deliver' has a juridical sense, in agreement with its use in the passion narrative, which is characterized by the active voice. In analogy with the 'delivery' of Jesus, Luke speaks also of the 'delivery' of Christians (Acts 8:3; RSV: 'committed'; 12:4; 21:11; 22:4; 28:17).

The phrase 'to be condemned to death' (*eis krima thanatou*) is most probably derived from Mk 10:33, 'they will condemn him to death' (*katakrinousin auton thanatōi*), the only Marcan prophecy in which Jesus' condemnation is mentioned.

In its present situation Lk 24:20 prepares for the expression of the disciples' disappointment in Lk 24:21. This disappointment derives not from the fact that the adverse action of the Jewish leaders made Jesus' work fail, but rather from the fact that his death has proved that they were mistaken about Jesus' person. Lk 24:25–27 will then show that in the 'suffering' (i.e. death) of Jesus lies the starting-point for the correction of the disciples' statement. The 'must' of the suffering (i.e., death) of the Messiah was foretold in the scriptures. It corresponds to God's plan. Lk 24:20 thus prepares for Lk 24:25–27.

> **Verse 21a:** 'But we had hoped that he was the one to redeem Israel.'

The disciples' statement ends with an exclamation of disappointment: the hope that Jesus would deliver Israel has not been fulfilled, because he is dead. The disciples' hopelessness is caused by Jesus' 'absence'.

The men do not altogether deny the validity of their preceding description, but complain that a further expectation is apparently not going to be carried out, namely, 'that he was the one to redeem Israel'. The word 'redeem' is full of Old Testament associations, recalling the deliverance from Egypt and the entry into the promised land, as also the return from the Babylonian exile. Here this hope is expressed in terms very similar to Lk 1:68, 'he has redeemed his people'. See also Acts 7:35, 'God sent as both ruler and deliverer'. The poignant saying, 'we had hoped that he was the one to redeem Israel', appears to recapture the actual mood of the disciples between Jesus' death and the Easter revelation. Just like Moses, this Messiah should have liberated Israel from its enemies. We find the same hope expressed in Acts 1:6, 'Lord, will you at this time restore the kingdom to Israel?'

Second part of the conversation (Lk 24:21b–24)

> **Verse 21b:** 'Yes, and besides all this, it is now the third day since this happened.'

The second half of verse 22 expresses a strong contrast (*alla ge*) with the preceding statement: 'not only this. . ., but besides'. The preceding clause expressed the (past) hope of the disciples, the present clause states that three days have passed and that therefore all hope is gone.

The mention of 'the third day' corresponds to 'the third day' in Lk 24:7 which is a prediction inserted by Luke himself. On 'the third day' the disciples will experience the fulfilment of the passion prediction recalled in Lk 24:7.

> **Verses 22–24:** 'Moreover, some women of our company amazed us. They were at the tomb early in the morning (23) and did not find his body; and they came back saying that they had even seen a vision of angels, who said that he was alive. (24) Some of those who were with us went to the tomb, and found it just as the women had said; but him they did not see.'

These verses are nothing but a summary of the content of Lk 24:1–12 (the finding of the empty tomb) in words which are entirely Lucan. Luke enumerates everything that is contained in the Christian kerygma (even the experience of the women), and there is very little difference between the kerygmatic formulae and what the disciples say in these verses. But there is this enormous difference: all these words are pointless so long as the inner enlightenment of faith is not given. In this sense verses 22–24 are a continuation of verses 19–21. What should lead to the triumph of paschal faith leads only to despair and unbelief without this inner enlightenment. For them, Jesus is dead, and with him their faith in him.

'Moreover' (*alla kai*) corresponds to the first *alla* in Lk 22:21b. Even the message of the women, which intrudes into the hopelessness of the disciples as a foreshadowing of the Easter event, cannot remove their disconsolateness and disappointment.

The clauses 'they did not find his body' and 'they did not find the body of the Lord Jesus' (Lk 24:3) correspond almost verbally. Here as there, there is a contrast between what they did find (an empty tomb) and what they did not find (his body, him).

The plural 'angels' refers to the 'two men' of Lk 24:4. The disciples' words about the women suggest how 'two men' can easily become transformed into 'angels' in the course of the tradition. Strictly speaking, they do not say that the women saw two angels, but 'that they had seen a vision of angels'. And these angels asserted that Jesus was alive.

The clause 'he was alive' (*auton zēn*) reminds us of 'why do you seek the living (*ton zōnta*) among the dead?' (Lk 24:5). The present verse emphasizes that the women informed not only the Eleven but also the wider circle of disciples. The two travellers, who do not belong to the Eleven, know about the empty tomb. This is prepared for in Lk 24:9 where the women 'told all this to the eleven and to all the rest'. That the two disciples are nevertheless hopeless may be connected with Lk 24:11, 'but these words seemed to them an idle tale, and they did not believe them'. The insensible talk of the two disciples illustrates the matter-of-fact statement of unbelief in Lk 24:11.

Lk 24:24 seems to fall back on Lk 24:12, although it is possible that the latter, which has Peter alone go to the tomb, and the former, which says that 'some of those who were with us went to the tomb', derive from different layers of Lucan tradition or redaction. Some men of the circle of the disciples also went to the tomb (see Lk 24:12) and confirmed the report of the women, but – and this is the primary complaint – 'him they did not see'. This clause seems to form an inclusion with what had been said of these two disciples in Lk 24:14, 'their eyes were kept from recognizing him'. The disciples are pronouncing these words while they themselves do not recognize the risen One who walks with them! They have all the keys but do not cross the threshold, because the door of faith by which they should enter is still beyond them. They have to be raised to that level by the grace of faith; without that all the keys are useless. Therefore, they still need the light of faith by which they will see not only the facts but also and especially the meaning of the facts.

This interpretation shows that Luke understood this story as an exemplary case. The situation of the two disciples is the situation of all those who have not yet received the grace of the Easter faith, those who are instructed about the facts, but cannot yet see the true meaning of these facts. Whatever is said of the two disciples on the road to Emmaus is true of the 'road' every Christian has to go, perhaps more than once in his or her life, for every step of growth contains the possibility of closing oneself to the meaning of the facts, which is then called loss of faith.

(3) *Third part of the conversation (Lk 24:25–27)*

> **Verses 25–27:** And he said to them, 'O foolish men, and slow of heart to believe all that the prophets have spoken! (26) Was it not necessary that the Christ should suffer these things and enter into his glory?' (27) And beginning with Moses and all the prophets, he interpreted to them in all the scriptures the things concerning himself.

In verses 25–27 the conversation along the road reaches its culmination. Through the instruction which the risen Christ gives to the disciples, the unsatisfactory Christological statement (Lk 24:19f.) is corrected. Lk 24:20f. showed that it was especially Jesus' death which made the disciples doubt Jesus' Messiahship. The solution of the 'riddle of the passion' is brought about in a way determined by the theological thought of the evangelist. The messianic suffering as well as the attainment of his glory stand under the divine 'must'. More precisely, verses 25–27 are dominated by two motifs: first, the suffering which is not understood by the disciples as a constitutive element of Jesus' messianic existence, and second, the divine 'must' which surrounds the passion and glorification and is revealed in these events by means of the testimony of the scriptures.

The expression 'all that the prophets have spoken' is also found in Acts 24:14 (cf. 26:22, 27; 28:23). The word 'all' may be important. It may suggest that the disciples concentrated on the parts of scripture which promised redemption for Israel (cf. Lk 24:21), but overlooked the texts which spoke of the suffering experienced by God's chosen messengers.

Verse 26 is undoubtedly the core-statement of the conversation along the road. Luke emphasizes the paradoxical fact that the Lord who is destined for heavenly glory is at the same time a man humiliated in suffering and death. The necessity for the Messiah to suffer and thus enter his glory which is here explained from the scriptures had not been envisaged in any previous form of messianic expectation. However, this was the early Christian understanding of the Messiah on which Luke built. For the early Christians this understanding opened up the scriptures in a new way. For Luke this understanding was to be accepted as a gift of the risen Christ. It is only the way through the cross to glory that actualizes the Messiahship proclaimed from the outset. Thus Luke's picture of the Messiah is shaped by the crucifixion and resurrection of Jesus.

It has been noted that in the Lucan redaction of Mark's prophecies of the passion (Lk 9:22, 43b–45; 18:31–34), the messianic secret and the emphasis on the disciples' lack of understanding are interpreted respectively as the secret of the passion and as lack of understanding concerning the passion. This is confirmed by further references to the passion, e.g., Lk 9:31–32, which is an important parallel to Lk 24:25–27; Lk 22:15, in which Jesus' farewell meal is situated in time: 'before I suffer'; and Lk 22:23, where Luke introduces the idea of 'questioning' and thus emphasizes that the passion of the Lord remains incomprehensible to the disciples until the very end.

Whereas in the Marcan passion prophecies the phrase 'must' (*dei*) appears only once, it is found six times in Luke in the context of references to the passion. This does not mean that this 'divine must' of the passion did not appear in the pre-Lucan tradition. But the exclusiveness with which the phrase *dei* ('must', 'should') is understood in the sense of a salvation-historical interpretation of Jesus' fate is peculiar to the Lucan redaction (cf. Lk 17:25; 18:31; 22:37). Especially noteworthy in Lk 24 is the threefold reference to the suffering of the Messiah and its being 'according to the scriptures' (cf. Lk 24:7, 26, 46). It has been noted that with the help of these references Luke binds together what were originally divergent traditions, and also that the proof-from-prophecy theology is the heart of Luke's concern in chapter 24.

Lk 24:26 connects the passion statement with the title 'Christ'. What meaning does this title have? Our present verse is related to Lk 24:20, which deals with the 'delivery' and death of Jesus of Nazareth (Lk 24:19). The Christ-title in Lk 24:26 is determined by the passion statement of Lk 24:20: its meaning is found in the passion and resurrection as proclaimed by the first Christians, and not vice versa. That is most probably why Luke uses here the imperfect *edei* ('should'), not *dei:* the actual suffering of Jesus was a messianic suffering (cf. Acts 17:3). Since Jesus is the Christ, he 'must' suffer. It is clear, therefore, that we do not have here a proof that 'the' Christ must suffer, but rather, that *Jesus* as Christ must suffer. Acts 3:18 shows that Luke places the Christ-title in a context of salvation history: 'But what God foretold by the mouth of all the prophets, that his Christ should suffer, he thus fulfilled'. Jesus is not called 'Christ' in virtue of his relationship to God, but because he fulfils God's promise.

We should also draw attention to the specifically dialectical combination of passion and glory in the background to the divine 'must'. Similarly, the basic law of Christian existence is described by Luke as 'through many tribulations we must (*dei*) enter the kingdom of God' (Acts 14:22), i.e., 'through suffering to glory'.

Appealing to 'Moses and all the prophets', the risen Lord declares that the fate of Christ is in accordance with the scriptures. The preceding considerations regarding the 'must' of Jesus' suffering and the meaning of the Christ-title should be placed in the wider context of the Lucan 'faith in Providence', since in it they have their ultimate root. That is why in Luke the reference to the testimony of the scriptures 'limps after' so strangely: it confirms afterwards (Lk 24:27) what has already been established (Lk 24:26). In this context reference has rightly been made to Luke's characteristic relativization of proof from scripture. On the one hand, this is due to the changed kerygmatic situation: missionary preaching to Gentile Christians could not simply resort to scriptural proof of Jesus' Messiahship, since the listeners did not have the necessary background. On the other hand, the strong dependence on proof from scripture in the context of Jesus' passion is to be understood through the Lucan theologoumenon of the divine plan of salvation. Salvation is here because God's plan and providence will it this way. Scripture is not the revealed blueprint of God's plan, but it does derive from his very nature. Even for Luke scripture and revelation are not the last instance; the plan of God takes precedence over them. Lk 22:22 clearly indicates how Luke wants the so-called proof-from-scripture to be understood: the law, the prophets and the Psalms are the mouthpiece of Providence, the 'prognosis of God'.

> The veil of mystery is now to be lifted, according to divine determination, in the only way it could be lifted: by the personal presence and instruction of the risen Lord, who 'opens' the scriptures by showing their realization in himself. . . . The 'things concerning Jesus of Nazareth' that the travelers could not grasp (v. 19) are now the focal point of the Easter exposition of all Scripture. No more than the events themselves could the Scripture by itself beget faith in the messiah's triumph; *only he can bestow that as his personal gift*. . . . Scripture is illumined by the risen Lord in terms of its 'alpha' and 'omega,' Moses and the Messiah: both 'mighty' prophets (Lk 24, 19/Acts 7, 22), both 'saviours' and 'leaders' of a wayfaring people (Lk 24, 21/Acts 7, 35; 5, 31; 3, 15), and both, according to the central mystery of the divine plan, subjected to the people's rejection and 'denial' (Acts 7,35; 3,13f.; Lk 24, 20). Bounded so harmoniously by the prophetic leaders who begin and end it, all of Scripture can be understood in its christological unity. So too can the Emmaus dialogue be understood as a unity determined by the *Mosaic prophecy* invoked at its beginning (v. 19) and end (v. 27).[13]

Recognition of the risen One in the meal (Lk 24:28–32)

Unlike the other Easter traditions, where the word of the risen Lord leads to faithful recognition, in Lk 24:28–32 the recognition is closely related to the meal, although it is not said in so many words that the giving of the bread opened the disciples' eyes. The meal proper is introduced by verses 28–29. The aim of the disciples is to make Jesus stay with them for the meal, as the evangelist emphasizes: 'stay with us . . . to stay with them. When he was at table with them. . .' (Lk 24:28–30).

Verses 28–29: So they drew near to the village to which they were going. He appeared to be going further, (29) but they constrained him, saying, 'Stay with us, for it is toward evening and the day is now far spent.' So he went in to stay with them.

με ι′νον   μεθ′ ημων̄

The expression 'he appeared to be going further' is not a very accurate translation. A preferable translation would be: 'he pretended to be going further'. The clause has been compared with Mk 6:48, 'he meant to pass by them'. See also Job 9:11, 'Lo, he passes by me, and I see him not; he moves on, but I do not perceive him'. Jesus' pretending to be going further constitutes an effective contrast with the prayer-like invitation 'stay with us'.

The disciples urged (*parebiasanto*) Jesus to stay (*meinon*) with them. The same term is found once more in the New Testament, namely in Acts 16:15 (RSV translates 'prevailed'), in the same context of an urgent invitation to a meal. In fact, the similarities between Lk 24:28ff. and Acts 16:15 are so striking that Luke may very well see a connection between Jesus' 'staying' and the missionaries' staying in the house of Lydia (Acts 16:15). Among the Synoptics, Luke uses 'to stay', 'to remain', most often (twenty times in Luke-Acts, against two times in Mark and three times in Matthew). For the use of 'to stay' (*menein*) in the context of a theological statement, see also Lk 22:28, 'You are those who have continued (*diamemenēkotes*) with me in my trials', and Acts 11:23; 13:43; 14:21f., in the sense of remaining faithful to the Christian life.

What is the meaning of the time indication, 'for it is toward evening and the day is now far spent'? It is striking that the feeding of the five thousand (Lk 9:10b–17) and the meal at Emmaus have the same time setting (compare 9:12, 'now the day began to wear away [*ērxato klinein*]', and Lk 24:29, 'the day is now far spent [*kekliken*]'). Luke may very well intend to refer to the feeding of the five thousand, a suggestion which is further supported by two other common features: the use of the imperfect (*ep-*)*edidou* ('gave', Lk 9:16 and 24:30) and *kataklinein* ('sit down', Lk 9:15 and 24:30). Many scholars believe that the meal sequence (Lk 24:28–31) has been modelled on Luke's version of the feeding of the multitude (Lk 9:11–17), and, to a lesser extent, the institution of the Eucharist (Lk 22:15–20). In other texts too it can be shown that Luke emphasizes the eucharistic reminiscences already present. This also explains the imperfect (*ep-*)*edidou:* Jesus' unique giving is continued in the 'giving' of the eucharistic gifts. In all this we should not overlook the use of the phrase 'the breaking of the bread' in Lk 24:35 and its connection with the community meal (Acts 2:42, 46; 20:7, 11). The common meal of the post-Easter community is the background against which Luke understands the Emmaus account. The community meal and the experience of Jesus' 'staying' in the midst of his disciples are closely related. The present indication of time, 'for it is toward evening and the day is now far spent', reminds us of the time of the community meal.

So Jesus 'went in' (*eisēlthen*); the same expression is found in Lk 7:36; 10:38; 11:37; 14:1. He went in to 'stay' with them (cf. Lk 19:5, 'I must stay at your house today').

> **Verse 30:** When he was at table with them, he took the bread
> and blessed, and broke it, and gave it to them.

They have their meal together. This is a favourite theme of Luke's and is here understood as a continuation of the table-fellowship between Jesus and his disciples during his ministry. The Emmaus account reaches a second culminating point with the description or, better, the indication of the meal. The verbal forms which describe the meal action proper, 'took . . . blessed . . . broke . . . gave', are solidly rooted in the tradition of the institution of the Eucharist. Scripture bears witness to the risen Christ, but the Eucharist makes the risen Christ himself present in living form. The Eucharist is the great sign of the resurrection, the sign by which we can know that Christ is alive and present.

Was the meal at Emmaus a eucharistic celebration or an ordinary meal? Apart from the fact that in Lk 24:30 the meal is referred to rather than described (nothing is said about the disciples' actually eating), this question can be taken up only with regard to the form- and redaction-critical data. Present-day research generally recognizes the eucharistic character of the account, at least in the Lucan redaction. However, the tradition of meals of the earthly Jesus with his disciples may also have exerted some influence on the Emmaus account.

The question should not be: was the meal at Emmaus a eucharistic celebration?, but: what did the meal at Emmaus mean for the Hellenistic readers of the gospel? Any attempt to describe 'what really happened at Emmaus' disregards the real aim of the account. It is a *Christian* account. If the action culminates in the recognition at the breaking of the bread, the Hellenistic readers could not fail to understand it as a eucharistic celebration.

> **Verse 31:** And their eyes were opened and they recognized
> him; and he vanished out of their sight.

'Their eyes were opened' (cf. Lk 24:16, 'their eyes were kept from recognizing him'), 'and they recognized' their guest, who had now become their host. The story suggests that the disciples' journey coincided with the duration of their blindness (Lk 24:16), since their eyes were opened only when the 'going with them' had terminated in the eucharistic 'being at table with them'. This is Luke's way of affirming that the resurrection of Jesus is to be interpreted in terms of the fellowship of the risen Christ with his community, a fellowship which is in continuity with all his previous associations with tax collectors and sinners, climaxing at the cross where he died together with two criminals, to one of whom he said 'today you will be with me in Paradise' (Lk 23:43).

The internal faculty of seeing has been prepared by the interpretation of the scriptures ('the service of the word'), which has created a desire to see (cf. Lk 24:32). The seeing of faith comes into being in the Eucharist: they see the risen Christ presiding, blessing, breaking the bread, and distributing it to them. So, in faith, they discover the risen One among those who belong to him. It is not a sign that forces one to believe. Personal decision is involved, but even this decision is a gift. In Luke's view, the opening of the scriptures by the risen Lord and the opening of the eyes by that same Lord in the Eucharist belong together.

Recognition is clearly a key concept of the Emmaus story (Lk 24:16, 31, 35). It is situated at the moment of the breaking of the bread, because both in Jesus' ministry and in the ministry of the early Church, the breaking of the bread is associated with the instruction concerning Jesus' person and mission.

> In Lk's mind, *the Master breaking bread with his followers is the Master sharing his mission and destiny with them!* . . . the combination of *messianic destiny and Master-disciple solidarity* . . . , for Lk, forms the heart of the christological revelation formerly veiled in cryptic *gesture-and-word* of the earthly Jesus, but fully accessible in the Easter Christ's lucid word-and-gesture.[14]

'He vanished out of their sight', but remains visible to those whose eyes are open. The moment of visibly showing himself comes to an end, but the faithful disciple knows that he is now as much as ever present among his community as the risen One, even if not visible in the same way. He has indeed entered into his glory (Lk 24:26). Therefore, the disciple should not be surprised at not seeing the risen Christ.

> **Verse 32:** They said to each other, 'Did not our hearts burn within us while he talked to us on the road, while he opened to us the scriptures?'

Looking back on the preceding scene, Lk 24:32 connects the conversation along the road and the meal scene. By means of a wondering question Luke lets the disciples reflect on the previous happenings. Similar features are found in Acts 9:27; 11:13, 16; 12:17.

The disciples now realize why it was that the 'stranger's' exposition of the scriptures had set their hearts aflame. They express once more their experience of how their faith came into being, once more calling attention to the Christological interpretation of the scriptures by the risen Christ, the beginning of real faith which reached completeness in the Eucharist. The faithful become aware of the risen Christ's presence when the scriptures are interpreted in the light of the Easter event and the eucharistic meal is celebrated; their hearts are set on fire and they recognize him.

Conclusion of the account (Lk 24:33–35)

Verses 33–35 form an appendix to the account, serving as a connecting link between the Emmaus pericope and the Jerusalem appearance which is to follow.

> **Verse 33:** And they rose that same hour and returned to Jerusalem; and they found the eleven gathered together and those who were with them,

The phrase 'that same hour' is parallel with the indication of time in Lk 24:13, 'that very day'. Luke brings all the Easter events together in one day. How the two disciples could possibly return to Jerusalem on the same day is none of Luke's concern. His intention is theological.

> The travelers left Jerusalem in confusion and disappointment; they now return there aglow with the revelation of the risen Lord. There is thus the closest relationship between the 'journey' motif, with its contrasting moments of *concealment* and *revelation*, and the return to Jerusalem, presented almost as a home-coming.[15]

home coming

The favourite Lucan use of 'to return' (*hupostrephein*) should be explained by the frequency of the return motif in the Lucan narrative technique. Luke likes to mention the return of his characters, especially at the end of an account (Lk 1:23, 56; 2:20, 39; 4:14; 5:25; 7:10; 23:48; 24:52). But here the return has also a theological meaning: through the return of the travellers the Emmaus account is closely connected with Jerusalem. However, Jerusalem is more than a geographical entity. As the place of Jesus' suffering, death and resurrection, it is for Luke the city of all fulfilment of salvation history. The movement away from Jerusalem and the future community is reversed into a movement towards the city by the appearance and the recognition of the risen Lord.

The designation 'the eleven' occurs only in the concluding chapters of the gospels and the first two chapters of Acts. Luke uses it four times (Lk 24:9, 33; Acts 1:26; 2:14). In the first two instances he mentions their associates as well: 'all the rest' (Lk 24:9) and 'those with them' (Lk 24:33), but this is no longer the case after the election of Matthias. Luke states that the associates too receive from the women the news of the empty tomb and the divine revelation, and that the Eleven and 'those with them' believed in the resurrection because of the appearance of the risen One to Peter. They are also present at the risen Christ's appearance to the apostles and at his ascension (Lk 24:36–52). They all become 'witnesses of these things' (Lk 24:48). Presumably Matthias was among them and was thus qualified to be elected an apostle (Acts 1:21–22).

Verse 34: who said, 'The Lord has risen indeed, and has appeared to Simon!'

The theological interpretation of the return-motif also explains the insertion of the Easter confession of the disciples at Jerusalem. In Jerusalem there comes the first confession of the Easter faith. The disciples at Jerusalem address their confession to the travellers, and not the other way as we would have expected. Indeed, we would expect the two travellers to relate their experience to the Eleven. But before they can do so, Luke puts into the mouth of the Eleven a piece of early Christian kerygma: 'The Lord has risen indeed, and has appeared to Simon'.

This kerygmatic formula is very similar to I Cor 15:3–5, 'he was raised . . . and that he appeared to Cephas'. The only significant difference in Luke's text is the addition of *ontōs* (RSV translates 'indeed'; we would prefer 'really'). The introductory *ontōs* is undoubtedly a response to the incredulity of the disciples at the news of the empty tomb (Lk 24:11). What the empty tomb could not bring about is now achieved, for the risen Lord himself has appeared to Simon. Thus Luke presents the 'dialectic of human experience versus Easter revelation' (R. J. Dillon) which dominates the whole of Lk 24. In both 24:34 and 23:47, the only two occurrences of the word in Luke, *ontōs* may be taken to indicate an unexpected state of affairs realized by God against all human calculation and capability. This 'really' is exactly what Luke is going to dwell on in the next pericope, Lk 24:36–53. Some scholars have considered Lk 24:34 the oldest form of the kerygma; because of its 'catechism-like' brevity and simplicity they consider it older than I Cor 15:3–5. But it would seem that Lk 24:34 should be understood as an extract (in German, *Auszug*) from a formula like I Cor 15:3–5 (or an older form of the latter) rather than as its starting-point. This does not necessarily mean that Lk 24:34 is directly dependent on I Cor 15:3–5.

It should not be overlooked that Lk 24:34 and I Cor 15:3–5 show different interests. In I Cor 15 Paul is dealing with the resurrection of the faithful. In order to show that this aspect of his 'gospel' is not an invention of his, Paul appeals to what he himself has received. His appeal to the Christ-formula is intended to give a solid foundation to the whole chapter. Therefore, he accurately quotes the tradition. In

Lk 24:13–35, however, the author is not obliged to defend the legiti-
mate character of his message. It is not surprising then that Luke does
not quote the kerygmatic formula accurately and completely. We are
given here, rather, an enthusiastic proclamation of the Easter faith.

The importance of the statement is emphasized by its place at the
end of the account, but also by the fact that it is pronounced by
the circle of disciples gathered around the Eleven. We have here the
faith-proclamation of the Church.

But we should go a step further and look at the Emmaus account
in the context of the whole of Lk 24. Luke is concerned with the
question how the Easter faith came into being. The unbelief mentioned in Lk 24:11 is taken up again in Lk 24:34. Neither the finding of
the empty tomb nor the experience of the two disciples on the road to
Emmaus, but the appearance of the risen Christ to Peter is the foundation of the Easter faith.

Literally, the text does not say 'he appeared' but 'he was seen'.
'Seeing' here is a kind of confession metaphor expressing the Christological affirmation that this One is the Lord. It means that something of
what was to constitute the 'seeing' at the parousia (see Mk 14:62) is
transferred to the resurrection appearances.

Luke does not say where and when this appearance to Peter
occurred. In the present arrangement of the gospel sequence it must
have occurred in the Jerusalem area between Peter's morning visit to
the tomb when he did not see Jesus (Lk 24:12, 24) and the evening
return of the two disciples to Jerusalem. But if Luke received the
'formula' found in Lk 24:34 from early tradition, he may have known
little about the where and when of the appearance, and the present
setting given to it may not tell us anything about the original circumstances of the appearance. Luke was apparently interested in emphasizing the priority of the appearance to Peter: first the Lord appeared
to Peter, then to the two disciples on the road to Emmaus, and finally to
the Eleven and those who were with them. Through the reference to
the appearance of the risen Lord to Peter the experience of the two
disciples is turned into a 'Church' experience. The Easter experience of
Peter legitimates any other Easter experience.

Verse 35: Then they told what had happened on the road,
and how he was known to them in the breaking of the bread.

By way of conclusion, 'what had happened on the road' and 'how he
was known to them in the breaking of the bread' recapitulate the whole
pericope in its two aspects, the travellers' dialogue and the meal scene.

Only after they have heard the Easter kerygma do the two
disciples relate their experience. Their report falls into two parts: first,
the events on the road and, second, the recognition at the breaking of
the bread. The whole pericope, centred on the 'liturgy of the word'

(Lk 24:19–27) and the 'eucharistic meal' (Lk 24:30–31), has a liturgical colouring. It is an early catechesis, in a liturgical setting, highlighting the encounter with the risen Christ in the Eucharist. Luke apparently also wants to say that nobody can encounter the risen Christ without becoming his messenger.

The literary form and original background of the Emmaus account

The account obviously expresses the early Christian conviction that an inspired or Spirit-filled reading of the scriptures and the Christological interpretation resulting from it are to be ascribed to the risen Christ himself. At the same time it contains a theology of the Eucharist which is understood as a communion at table with the risen Christ and a sign of his continued presence among those who belong to him. How would such a two-stage account, i.e., the experience of the two disciples and the early Christian experience expressed in it, best be described? Some speak of an 'edifying story'. Others have proposed using the French term *geste*. A term closer to the biblical and Semitic spirit may be 'event-parable'. The event, the story of the two disciples on the road to Emmaus, serves as a revelation of another deeper reality, the early Christian experience of the presence of the risen Christ.

In what situation in life (the German term *Sitz im Leben* is often used in this context) did this Emmaus account take shape? In other words, which theological concerns of the early Christian community determined the selection of this pericope and the manner in which it was narrated (its literary form)? The account is rooted in a double situation: on the one hand, the proclamation of the Christological fulfilment of the scriptures and, on the other hand, the celebration of the Eucharist. It is here that the Emmaus account received its real depth and meaning.

But it may be possible to determine further the actual situation in the life of the early Christian community. Some scholars have pointed to the close parallelism between the Emmaus account and Acts 8:26–39, the story of Philip and the Ethopian. We have the following parallels:

Lk 24:13–35	*Acts 8:26–39*
— two disciples on the way from Jerusalem (verse 13)	— the Ethiopian on the way from Jerusalem (verses 26–27)
— the two disciples talk on the way about the recent events in Jerusalem, namely the condemnation and death of Jesus (verse 14).	— the Ethiopian reads on the way Isa 53:7f. about the death of the Suffering Servant (verse 28; cf. 32–33).

Lk 24:13–35	*Acts 8:26–39*
— Jesus joins the disciples and asks them what they are talking about (verses 17–18).	— Philip asks the Ethiopian whether he understands what he is reading (verse 30).
— the disciples tell Jesus about the events which they do not understand (verses 18–24).	— the Ethiopian says that he does not understand what he is reading (verse 31).
— Jesus explains the scriptures to them starting from Moses and all the prophets: they are talking about him as dying and rising Messiah (verse 27).	— Philip announces the good news to the Ethiopian, starting from the text of Isaiah (verse 35).
— the disciples invite Jesus to stay with them (verse 29).	— the Ethiopian invites Philip to get into his chariot and sit beside him (verse 31).
— Jesus breaks the bread (verse 30).	— the Ethiopian is baptized by Philip (verse 38).
— Jesus suddenly disappears (verse 31).	— Philip suddenly disappears (verse 39).
— The disciples return to Jerusalem (verse 33).	— the Ethiopian continues his journey (verse 39).

The parallels are certainly striking. But there are also differences which should not be overlooked and which could inform us about the precise situation in life of the two parallel accounts in early Christianity. In Acts 8 the deacon Philip acts directly, although he does not act of his own accord but under the impulse of the angel of the Lord (Acts 8:26), and driven by the Holy Spirit who is none other than the Spirit of the ascended Lord (Acts 8:29, 39). In Lk 24 it is Christ himself who acts directly, explaining the scriptures in a Christological sense and presiding at the meal (though the author may very well be thinking of the Christological interpretation of the scriptures and the presiding at the Eucharist by Christian ministers).

How can we further describe the situation in life, taking into account the close parallels as well as the differences? Ultimately the two accounts refer to the same experience of the Church: the apostolic mission with its double aspect of the proclamation of the word and the sacramental ministry. The account of Acts 8 describes this ministry in its material reality in a way which could be described as epic. The account of Lk 24 evokes this apostolic ministry in its deeper reality, visible only to faith, as an epiphany of the risen Christ. We could put it this way: in the account of Acts 8 the apostolic ministry (the proclamation of the word and the administration of the sacraments) is to the fore, the deeper reality being the work of the risen Christ through his Spirit. In Lk 24 the activity of the risen Christ is to the fore, while his hidden activity through the Church is the deeper reality hinted at. In Acts, the activity of the ministry evokes the risen Christ manifesting himself through the minister to the eyes of faith. In Lk 24, the words and gestures of Jesus evoke the double ministry of the Christian ministers (the word and the Eucharist). To one who understands the account correctly, the event at Emmaus appears to be a *parable* which reveals the hidden meaning of the missionary activity, and manifests that ministry of which it is the 'sacrament'. Conversely, the apostolic activity of Philip, the travelling missionary, helps us to situate more precisely the ecclesial experience which marks the literary elaboration of the Emmaus account.

The actual experience is the reception of the strange travelling missionary. The group which welcomes him, no doubt Jewish or at least influenced by Judaism, hears from his mouth the message of the fulfilment of the scriptures in the death and resurrection of the Lord. They offer him hospitality. Together they enter into communion with the risen Christ in the breaking of the bread. So, Jesus who joins the two travelling disciples is the One who, concretely and visibly, adopts the face of Philip, Peter and others down to the present time in the performance of their ministry.

> . . . the hypothesis is quite plausible that Lk's Emmaus *tradition* was the account of the risen Christ encountered as a *wayfaring stranger entertained as a houseguest* (in the house of Cleopas?) and, while reclining at table with his host, *reenacting the miraculous feeding of bread and fish*, whereupon his astonished hosts-turned guests recognized his identity. . . . The Stranger hosted at a meal, who turns out to be the Lord in the breaking of the bread, contains a hint of the *self-image of itinerant Christian missionaries of the early years*. . . . the situation of the earthly Jesus as *houseguest* is a strong and recurrent feature of the *traditions proper to the gospel of Lk*, just as Lk's version of the Q sayings forming the *instruction to the missionaries* gives prominent play to the directive governing the travellers' acceptance of *hospitality and table-fellowship* in the households along their route (Lk 10:5–7 *diff*. Mt).[16]

The purpose of the account is therefore theological. It aims to make us think of the Christian experience and reveal its meaning. It intends to show us how, in the hearing of the Christian message and in the participation in the Eucharist, the reality of the encounter with the risen Christ takes place – a reality which is in no way less real than the encounter of the two disciples with the risen Christ.

NB

The historical value of the Emmaus account

The gospels are interpretative testimonies of events which took place in Palestine about 2,000 years ago. The evangelists are not interested in the merely material facts but in the meaning of these facts for faith in a certain historical situation of the Christian communities. Therefore it is obvious that in a text like that of the Emmaus account we do not find an objective, photographic picture of the facts.

Going a step further, we could say that at the basis of this theological reflection there is a certain event which actually occurred to the two disciples. But we are no longer in a position to find out exactly what this event was, because we cannot simply separate the interpretative element from the account.

That there was such an event at the origin of the account could be concluded from, first, the certainty we have that Luke did not invent the whole story himself but rather used some extant tradition and, second, the occurrence of certain names like Emmaus and Cleopas, which seem to have no other point than historical recollection.

We should, however, remain open to the objection that this evidence is not entirely conclusive. For quite some time elapsed between the first days after Jesus' crucifixion and the composition of the gospel of Luke, and during this time the early Christian tradition was very active as regards the interpretation of the data. The names occurring in the account could possibly just prove that some early Christian knew how to tell a good story.

Such explanation would not destroy Christianity as an historical reality. The whole question is whether we can accept the possibility that in some particular instance the *meaning* of the resurrection of Christ was expressed in a narrative form which was merely literary, i.e., without strict historical basis. This possibility cannot be denied in principle. Questioning the historicity of this particular account would not mean questioning the resurrection as the foundation of Christianity as such. The Emmaus account itself makes clear that it is not meant to lay such a foundation. At the end it explicitly and purposely points to the foundational character of the appearance of the risen Christ to the *official* apostolic witnesses who are sent to witness to this fact (cf. Lk 24:34). The appearance to the disciples of Emmaus does not belong to this category.

A more nuanced judgment of the 'historicity' of the Emmaus account is not an impoverishment. On the contrary, as soon as we pay less attention to the story as a kind of historical anecdote, we discover more clearly the *meaning* of the Christian existence of which it is the expression. Then we see that the account speaks of the missionary announcement of the gospel and of a truly significant celebration of the Eucharist, the decisive experience of the risen One without which the preceding apostolic witness to the *fact* of the resurrection remains empty.

7 Appearance in Jerusalem and the Ascension *(Lk 24:36–53)*

Just as the whole of Luke's resurrection chapter consists of three clearly distinguished sections (Lk 24:1–12, 13–35, 36–53), so the third of these sections too falls into three paragraphs which we can formally distinguish as:

(1)   narrative (Lk 24:36–43);
(2)   Jesus' discourse (Lk 24:44–49);
(3)   narrative (Lk 24:50–53).

This formal distinction corresponds to a distinction in contents. The first part (Lk 24:36–43) is clearly a recognition scene in which Jesus reveals the reality of the resurrection. But the result of the invitation to physical verification is that the disciples 'still disbelieve' (for joy!) (verse 41). This lack of faith is not merely a heightened threshold for the risen Christ's eating before them which would be the conclusive proof of his identity. One should not overlook the absence of any affirmation that the disbelieving disciples were finally convinced by Jesus' eating. Therefore, it cannot be taken for granted after Lk 24:43 that the disciples have reached the Easter faith. Any such 'conclusion' of the 'demonstration' is missing. In fact, the first explicit, positive response from the disciples is recorded in Lk 24:52, 'and they worshipped him'. Lk 24:36–43 is understood only in close relation to Lk 24:44–49, which contains the testimony that sheds light upon the meaning of the experiences related in the preceding narrative. The emphasis is clearly on the words of the risen Christ, which are at no time interrupted by any reaction of the disciples. The third and final part is a solemn farewell scene (Lk 24:50–53) in which no further word of the risen Christ is recorded. It is distinguished from the two previous parts by a change of location (Lk 24:50a, 'then he led them out as far as Bethany . . .'). Thus the formal tripartite structure corresponds to the contents:

(1)   recognition scene (Lk 24:36–43);
(2)   instruction of the disciples (Lk 24:44–49);
(3)   farewell (Lk 24:50–53).

Exegesis of the text

(i) *Recognition scene (Lk 24:36–43)*

> **Verse 36:** As they were saying this, Jesus himself stood among them, and said to them, 'Peace to you!'

Luke apparently composed the first part of this verse to connect the present pericope with the Emmaus account. The clause 'and said to them, "Peace to you!"', omitted by the so-called Western text and many translations, has often been taken to be an interpolation patterned after Jn 20:19. But more and more scholars agree on its authenticity.

Who are those who 'were saying this'? According to Lk 24:33, 'the eleven gathered together and those who were with them'. But in Lk 24:34 they were referred to as people who believed in the resurrection since they proclaim, 'The Lord has risen indeed'. How then can the present pericope present the same people as doubting and misinterpreting Jesus' appearance? This apparent contradiction clearly indicates that the present pericope and the Emmaus account did not form an original unity. It is also possible that in the different sections of Lk 24 the evangelist wants to describe different ways in which people came from initial unbelief to belief and recognition, and therefore cannot take into account the earlier recognition scenes. He starts afresh each time from unbelief and lack of recognition.

In Luke's redaction Jesus' appearance is made to ratify the words of the two disciples referred to at the end of the Emmaus account. It was 'as they were saying this' that 'Jesus stood among them'. The latter clause expresses the essence of the resurrection. During the last supper Jesus had said, 'I am among you as one who serves' (Lk 22:27). Now, after his death and resurrection, he stands 'among them'. He is the same person as the One they have known before.

Since the present pericope and the Emmaus account did not belong together originally, we should not conclude from Jesus' sudden appearance that he followed the two disciples from Emmaus so that he arrived only a little later. Neither does this mean that the risen Christ walked through closed doors or through walls, as is sometimes implied, especially in the interpretation of the similar incident in Jn 20:19. It rather means that *he is always there*. As the risen Christ he is present in the fullest sense (compare Mt 28:20, 'I am with you always'). In his glorified existence Christ is no longer subject to the conditions of time and space which are characteristic of earthly bodily existence. The Emmaus account said that the Christ entered into his glory (Lk 24:26). So at any time and in any place, he can make himself visible, because he is present everywhere and at any time. However, men can see Christ only when he is *revealed* to them. It is these 'revelations' which we refer to as 'appearances' of the risen Christ.

But it is precisely this kind of appearance that caused a problem to Luke's Greek readers. They could never ascribe such appearances to a body: for them, the body was considered the prison of the soul and tied it down to a particular place. Only a soul freed from its bodily prison could appear at any time and in any place. If such a soul appeared, the form in which it became visible was not real. It was a 'ghost', a 'spirit' (cf. Lk 24:37), which adopted a visible form which only seemed to be a body. That is why Luke had previously asserted the true bodiliness of the risen Christ (Lk 24:3–5; cf. 23:55), and why he inserted a very Greek expression into the kerygmatic formula of Lk 24:34, 'The Lord is *truly* (*ontōs*; RSV: 'indeed') risen'. He thus prepared the way for the present pericope, in which he deals explicitly with this problem.

In greetings and similar expressions, 'peace' meant the sense of well-being or salvation. We thus have 'go in peace' (e.g., Lk 7:50) as a farewell, and 'peace' with a dative as a greeting on arrival (Lk 10:5). The words 'peace to you' represent the normal greeting of the day. The nucleus of the Q version of the instructions to missionaries found in Lk 10:5–7, which combines the gestures of peace-greeting and table-sharing, presents a remarkable analogy to Lk 24:36–43, where the risen Christ seems to follow precisely the procedure prescribed for his itinerant representatives.

Verse 37: But they were startled and frightened, and supposed that they saw a spirit.

The language of this verse contains apocalyptic overtones (cf. Lk 24:5). The Greek term for 'startled' is found in Luke only (Lk 21:9 and here) and that for 'frightened' in Luke-Acts only (Lk 24:5 and here; Acts 10:4; 24:25), except for Rev 11:13. The disciples are startled and frightened by the sudden appearance of what they take to be a 'spirit', i.e., a ghost. Luke's intention to confront possible interpretations of the appearances as being those of a 'spirit' with only an apparent body, is very clear. Only here and in Lk 24:39 does one find *pneuma*, 'spirit', used as a synonym for *phantasma*, 'ghost'. As a term for 'seeing' in the appearance stories of the gospels, *theōrein* occurs only in Lk 24:37 and 39, and in Jn 20:14. Mt 28:1 refers to the desire of the women 'to see' (*theōrēsai*) the tomb, but the verb does not recur in the report of the appearances themselves. The verse is certainly formulated by the evangelist himself.

Verse 38: And he said to them. 'Why are you troubled, and why do questionings rise in your hearts?'

The cause of the disciples' misunderstanding and confusion is indicated in the question 'Why are you troubled, and why do questionings arise . . . ?' The phrase 'troubled' was used only once before in this gospel, namely of Zechariah at the appearance of the angel (Lk 1:12). Thus Luke suggests the glorious condition of Jesus. His presence should be a source of joy, not of fear (cf. Lk 2:10). So Jesus asks the reason for the disciples' being 'troubled' and for their 'questionings'. The latter term (in Greek, *dialogismoi*) is found six times in Luke, against only once in Mark and Matthew. Jesus has come 'that thoughts (questionings) out of many hearts may be revealed' (Lk 2:35). He reveals the secret questionings of the scribes and Pharisees concerning the Son of man's authority to forgive sins (Lk 5:22). Again 'he knew their thoughts (questionings)' about healing on a sabbath (Lk 6:8). Jesus also realized that the disciples did not understand his prophecy of the passion (Lk 9:44–45) because they were discussing among themselves and entertained thoughts as to which of them was the greatest (Lk 9:46, 47; twice *dialogismoi*). So, as long as Jesus' disciples entertain such thoughts, then and now, they belong in reality to the opposition (cf. Lk 5:22; 6:8).

Paul uses the same term *dialogismos* where he depreciates the sophistries of Greek philosophy (e.g., Rom 1:21; I Cor 3:20). We have already mentioned that the idea of the risen Christ being a 'ghost', or a soul with only an apparent body, was the result of Greek thinking, which sharply distinguished between soul and body. The doubts and mistaken interpretations ascribed to the disciples reflect the doubts and false explanations of those who opposed the early Church's preaching of the resurrection.

> **Verse 39:** 'See my hands and my feet, that it is I myself; handle me and see; for a spirit has not flesh and bones as you see that I have.'

The first step in the demonstration is that the appearance is a real bodily self. The disciples are invited to take a good look at Jesus' hands and feet in order to verify that there is bodily continuity between the Jesus who suffered and died and the risen Christ who appears here to them. On the one hand, Luke states that Jesus appeared in a bodily form not subject to ordinary, physical restrictions (cf. Lk 24:36), but, on the other hand, he also emphasizes its solidly corporeal nature.

But mere recognition of bodily presence does not necessarily mean faith, and therefore Jesus continues: 'it is I myself'. Just as in Mk 6:50 ('it is I'), these words are a device by which full recognition will be achieved. The Greek phrase contains the words 'I am' (*egō eimi*). Many may come and say 'I am he' (Lk 21:8), but only Jesus, who before the Sanhedrin affirmed 'I am' (Lk 22:70), can legitimately make this claim.

Egō eimi autos is the central affirmation of the whole passage, stated in the showing of the wounds and the invitation to touch them, as well as in the greeting, the eating and the instruction concerning things past. It proclaims the *identity of the risen Christ with the earthly Jesus* and hence the unbroken journey started at Lk 9:51 (his *analēmpsis*, his 'being received up') in the three phases of the pericope: the narrative, the discourse, and the final narrative. His journey has not been broken by his death.

The Christological affirmation is accompanied by the invitation to 'handle' (*psēlaphan*) Jesus. This verb is found only four times in the New Testament (Lk 24:39; Acts 17:27; Heb 12:18; I Jn 1:1). I Jn 1:1 is especially worth quoting: 'That which was from the beginning, which we have heard, which we have seen with our eyes, which we have looked upon and *touched with our hands*, concerning the word of life'. The disciples are invited to touch Jesus to make sure that he really has flesh and bones. The phrase 'for a spirit has not flesh and bones' has reminded some scholars of a very similar passage in Homer's *Odyssey* XI, 219, 'because they have no more flesh nor bones on their muscles' (*ou gar eti sarkas te kai ostea ines echousin*).

Verse 40: And when he had said this, he showed them his hands and his feet.

This is yet another verse omitted by RSV and many others on the grounds that it is missing from the so-called Western text and certain Syriac manuscripts. The verse is then believed to be an interpolation patterned after Jn 20:20, 'When he had said this, he showed them his hands and his side'. But, as we have already said, there is a growing consensus to consider this and other verses of Lk 24 missing from the Western text as authentic. Luke may have known the same tradition as the one on which Jn 20:20 drew, but since he did not mention the pierced side of Jesus (cf. Jn 19:34), he changed 'hands and side' into 'hands and feet'. The verse indicates that Jesus did what his words implied and showed his disciples the places where the nailprints were.

Verses 41–43: And while they still disbelieved for joy, and wondered, he said to them, 'Have you anything here to eat?' (42) They gave him a piece of broiled fish, (43) and he took it and ate before them.

These verses constitute the second step in the demonstration of the reality of the resurrection. The disciples were not yet entirely convinced. They found it hard to believe that Jesus had really risen from the dead. 'They still disbelieved' (cf. Lk 24:11; Acts 28:24), though, in his own typical way, Luke excuses them somewhat by saying that it was 'for joy': this was too good to be true! They also 'wondered' (cf. Lk 24:12). Doubt and fear were combined in this wondering, as in the disciples' reaction to the second prediction of the passion (Lk 9:43–45).

The disciples' unbelief helps motivate the second step of the demonstration. Jesus now asks: 'Have you anything here to eat?' A ghost would definitely not eat anything. The same argument is used in Acts 10:40–41, 'but God raised him on the third day and made him manifest; not to all the people but to us who were chosen by God as witnesses, who ate and drank with him after he rose from the dead'. And in Luke's version of the raising of Jairus' daughter, Jesus immediately 'directed that something should be given to her to eat' (Lk 8:55), unlike Mark where this command only follows a little later (Mk 5:43). Thus Luke emphasized the reality of the girl's raising. It is usually maintained that the eating is intended as a demonstration of the risen One's physical reality. While this may indeed be Luke's intention, it should not be overlooked that no recognition is recorded after the eating. 'He ate before them' which is usually understood as 'before their eyes', should preferably be rendered 'he ate at their table, . . . in their company, . . . as their guest'. This rendering does not deprive the statement of its demonstrative power, but does especially highlight the renewal of table-fellowship between Jesus and his disciples, and emphasizes *continuity*, *reunion* (compare Lk 13:26 and Acts 27:35).

Both in Acts 10:40–41 and in our present text, Luke emphasizes the two aspects of *continuity* and *discontinuity*. The disciples ate and drank with the risen Christ as they ate with Jesus before his death, but at the same time Luke also says that, even while he was eating with them, he was visible only to the witnesses preordained by God; and this is, of course, different from the situation before Jesus' death when he was visible to anybody. Indeed, in Lk 24:41–42 as in Acts 10:40–41, Luke certainly means that Jesus was visible only to those 'who were chosen (more literally, 'preordained', 'previously appointed') as witnesses'. How then should we think of the risen Christ as eating a piece of fish which was, no doubt, visible to all? Or how should we imagine the risen Christ walking the three miles to Bethany (Lk 24:50) and talking with his disciples (cf. Acts 1:3ff.), while not being seen by other people? It is indeed difficult to look upon such accounts as simple reports. We should, therefore, make a clear distinction between *what* Luke wants to say, i.e., the reality of the person of the risen Christ and his continuity/discontinuity with the earthly Jesus, and *how* he says it, namely in a very realistic, material way. Faith in the *reality* of the resurrection is expressed in very *realistic* language. These considerations will prevent us from having too material an understanding of the resurrection which Luke himself certainly did not have. If, on the contrary, we take Luke's words as the literal historical truth, they would obscure the true meaning of the resurrection and lead to a crude, materialistic resurrection belief.

Jesus' instruction to the disciples (Lk 24:44–49)

Verse 44: Then he said to them, 'These are my words which I spoke to you, while I was still with you, that everything written about me in the law of Moses and the prophets and the psalms must be fulfilled.'

The theology as well as the vocabulary and style of this verse are perfectly Lucan. It introduces a paragraph which contains a major statement of Lucan theology. It expressly restates a theme prominent in the Emmaus account, the need to interpret the Christ event in the light of the scriptures. In the Emmaus account the two disciples themselves remembered how they had seen in Jesus the fulfilment of Israel's hope as expressed in the Old Testament (Lk 24:21). But they misinterpreted these prophecies, so that Jesus had to interpret these texts to them (Lk 24:27). Here Jesus himself reminds the disciples of his own words about the fulfilment of the whole scripture.

'These are my words which I spoke to you' means 'the events (of my death and resurrection) explain the words which I spoke to you'. We should note the tension between the phrase 'while I was still with you', meaning that he is now in his glory (cf. Lk 24:26), and the fact that Luke has just said that Jesus ate before his disciples (Lk 24:43), and will say next that Jesus 'led them out as far as Bethany' (Lk 24:50). This means that, even when Luke speaks of eating and walking, Jesus' relations with the disciples are not what they were before his glorification.

Luke inserts here the 'must' (*dei*) of Mk 13:10 which he had previously omitted (compare Mk 13:10 and Lk 21:13). But he gives it a very different meaning, because he has taken it out of its apocalyptic context to fit it into a pattern of prophecy and fulfilment.

The Christ event fulfilled 'everything written about me in the law of Moses and the prophets and the psalms', i.e., in the three divisions of the Hebrew Bible. This is the only place in the New Testament where this threefold division is explicitly mentioned and where, therefore, the Psalms are mentioned alongside the law and the prophets. This may be because the Psalms provided the greater part of the messianic texts.

Verses 45–46: Then he opened their minds to understand the scriptures, (46) and said to them, 'Thus it is written, that the Christ should suffer and on the third day rise from the dead,

In the present composition of Lk 24, it appears that neither the scriptures nor the message of the women had been of any avail. But now Jesus 'opened their minds', i.e., he enlightened them from within 'to understand the scriptures'. The Christological reading of the scriptures has a definitely Lucan character (Lk 24:26; Acts 3:18; 17:3).

Moreover, the idea of opening the mind to understand the scriptures is specifically Lucan (seven times in Luke-Acts, against once in Mark and nowhere else).

The risen Christ opened their minds to the scriptures, just as he had done for the disciples at Emmaus (Lk 24:25–26, 32). In fact, the formulation of verse 46 is very similar to Lk 24:26, 'Was it not necessary that the Christ should suffer these things and enter into his glory?' 'It is necessary' corresponds to 'it is written'. In both texts Jesus is referred to as 'the Christ', and the same verb *pathein* is used for 'to suffer'. The use of 'to suffer', meaning the whole of the passion including Jesus' death, is typically Lucan (Lk 22:15; 24:26; Acts 1:3; 3:18; 17:3).

The phrase 'the third day' reminds us that the two men on the road to Emmaus confirmed that this was the third day since the suffering had taken place (Lk 24:21). On that same 'third day' Jesus' credentials are validated.

> **Verses 47–48:** 'and that repentance and forgiveness of sins should be preached in his name to all nations, beginning from Jerusalem. (48) You are witnesses of these things.'

Verse 47 is Luke's equivalent of Mk 13:10, 'And the gospel must first be preached to all nations'. Luke has already used the phrase 'must' in Lk 24:44. He drops the word 'gospel' which he often avoids, but takes over 'should be preached . . . to all nations'. The clause 'repentance and forgiveness of sins . . . in his name' is new. The idea of repentance is more emphasized in Luke than in Mark and Matthew. In fact, repentance is presented as a central element in Jesus' preaching (Lk 5:32; cf. 15:7, 10). Joined to 'forgiveness of sins' (Lk 3:3; 24:47; Acts 2:38; 5:31; 26:18, 20) or to faith and new life (Acts 11:17, 18, etc.) it becomes Luke's favourite term for conversion.

'That repentance and forgiveness of sins should be preached in his name to all nations' is also derived from a Christological reading of the scriptures, since this clause is also dependent on 'thus it is written'. This means that for Luke the mission is founded not only on Jesus' command, but also on Old Testament prophecy. The statement expresses a typically Lucan understanding of the Christian mission. 'And Peter said to them, "Repent, and be baptized every one of you in the name of Jesus Christ for the forgiveness of your sins; and you shall receive the gift of the Holy Spirit" ' (Acts 2:38; see also Acts 3:19; 5:31; 10:43; 13:38–41). It has been convincingly shown that conversion or metanoia towards the forgiveness of sins is a characteristically Lucan theme. The idea is not so much that of an individual conversion, but rather of the conversion of the *laos* (the Jewish people; see, e.g., Lk 2:32; Acts 4:10–12) and the *ethnē* (the Gentile nations). But whereas *ethnē* standing alone in the plural refers to the Gentiles, the phrase *panta ta ethnē* ('all the nations') may include the Jews. The universalist perspective of 'to all the nations' fits very well in Luke's theology (cf. Acts 2:38f.; 3:19f.; 4:12), but the expression is also found in Mk 13:10; Mt 28:19 (see Chapter Five above).

The 'forgiveness of sins', enacted in baptism (cf. Lk 3:3; Acts 2:38), leads to the formation of a new people. This last consideration brings out the ecclesial character of the commission to the apostles, somewhat closing the apparent gap between this text and Mt 28:19. But there remains a considerable difference in perspective. Matthew is more ecclesial in the sense that he emphasizes the Church's internal 'teaching' which leads people to accept a Christian way of life. Speaking of preaching and conversion, Luke thinks rather of the missionary aspect as such, as it is described in Peter's and Paul's missionary activity in Acts.

The phrase 'in his (i.e., Jesus') name' expresses in a special way the presence of Christ and fits very well into verse 47. The scriptures promise that repentance will be preached to the nations on the basis of the name of Jesus. 'The name of Jesus' is Luke's way of expressing the reality and the efficacy of the ascended Christ at work during the age of the Church.

The clauses 'beginning from Jerusalem' and 'you are witnesses' take up the theme of the beginning of Acts, more specifically Acts 1:8, 'But you shall receive power when the Holy Spirit has come upon you (cf. Lk 24:49); and you shall be my witnesses in Jerusalem and in all Judea and Samaria and to the end of the earth'. This 'beginning from Jerusalem' corresponds to 'beginning from the baptism of John' (Acts 1:22), and 'beginning from Galilee' (Acts 10:37). The idea of witness as well as that of the centrality of Jerusalem are very Lucan. Here we are in the centre of Jesus' way from Nazareth over Galilee to Jerusalem, and then from Jerusalem, and Judea, to the end of the world. Jerusalem is the centre of salvation history, from which the centrifugal mission, i.e., Christ journeying in the person of his apostles to the end of the world, will start. Writing this, Luke obviously has the whole book of Acts in mind.

> **Verse 49:** 'And behold, I send the promise of my Father upon you; but stay in the city, until you are clothed with power from on high.'

A solemn 'and behold' introduces Jesus' final words. 'The promise of the Father' is a somewhat unusual designation of the Holy Spirit, emphasizing the role of the divine promise in his coming. We find the same idea expressed in Acts 2:33, 'Being therefore exalted at the right hand of God, and having received from the Father the promise of the Holy Spirit, he has poured out this which you see and hear' (see also Acts 1:4).

All this is the fulfilment of the promise of the Spirit for the whole messianic community: 'And it shall come to pass afterward, that I will pour out my spirit on all flesh. . .' (Joel 2:28), to which Peter will refer on Pentecost (Acts 2:16–21). The fact that Luke no longer speaks of the promise of 'God', as in the Old Testament, but of 'the promise of my Father' is certainly due to advanced Christian reflection. Jesus is implicitly called the Son, and the Spirit is his Spirit too. The risen Christ has the power to 'send' the Spirit.

The disciples are told to 'stay in the city', i.e., Jerusalem, the centre of salvation history. There they will receive the Spirit. The same idea is found in Acts 1:4, 'And while staying with them he charged them not to depart from Jerusalem, but to wait for the promise of the Father. . .'. In Acts 1:4–8 the two themes of the gift of the Spirit and the Gentile mission are inseparably linked.

The disciples are not to attempt the task of evangelization with their own resources. They are commanded to go on a universal mission, but not before they have received the 'power from on high'. Their mission is God's own operation. Their ministry will extend the ministry of Jesus who said, 'The Spirit of the Lord is upon me, because he has anointed me to preach good news to the poor. . .' (Lk 4:18–19). The association of 'power' and the 'Spirit' is typical of Luke (cf. Lk 4:14; Acts 1:8). Especially enlightening is Lk 1:35, 'The Holy Spirit will come upon you, and the power of the Most High will overshadow you'. Luke seems to have regarded 'power' as the energy of the Holy Spirit. It is linked with the historical ministry of Jesus as well as with the present life of the Church.

The evangelist may be thinking specifically of the powerful witness of the apostles supported by the working of miracles (Acts 3:1–10, etc.). It is also possible that we have here an allusion to II Kgs 2:9–13, where Elisha asked for a double share of the spirit of Elijah, who was then taken up into heaven. This would fit well into Luke's Elijah typology, which has certainly played a role in his redaction of the ascension texts.

Summing up, we may say that not only the different stylistic and theological elements but also the whole movement of thought of Lk 24:44–49 are very Lucan. The evangelist summarizes here his understanding of Jesus' life as the centre of salvation history. He mentions the whole Old Testament (law, prophets and Psalms). Then he refers to the central place of Jesus among his disciples quoting the scriptures to them, which, however, they fail to understand. Finally, he envisages the future period of the Church in which the risen Christ will open his disciples' minds to a Christological understanding of the scriptures, and which Luke is going to describe in Acts.

This pericope says practically the same as Mt 28:16–20, but in a Lucan way. Without mentioning the Spirit, Matthew said that the risen Christ would be with his disciples 'to the close of the age' (Mt 28:20).

For Luke, however, the Spirit is precisely the power by which the risen Christ is present. Therefore, it is said that those who will witness to the risen Christ 'to the end of the earth' (Acts 1:8) will receive the Spirit. The Acts of the Apostles is the book of the Spirit, of ever-repeated Pentecosts (Acts 2:1–4; 10:44–45; 19:1–7).

Farewell blessing and ascension (Lk 24:50–53)

The ascension account is the continuation of the preceding pericopes. It constitutes the conclusion of the gospel and is closely related to the appearance accounts: Jesus disappears in his glory as heavenly Lord (Lk 24:50–51); the disciples worship him; their faith fills them with great joy, and they give thanks in the Temple (Lk 24:52–53).

A major textual-critical problem in this pericope is whether or not it originally included a reference to the ascension. The so-called Western text and a few other manuscripts read: 'While he blessed them, he parted from them', whereas the other manuscripts continue 'and was carried up into heaven'. An increasing number of textual critics and exegetes opt for the longer reading. The manuscript evidence for the longer reading is strong and its omission by the Western text can easily be explained. Evidently it wanted to get rid of the apparent contradiction between Lk 24, where Jesus appears to ascend within twenty-four hours after his resurrection, and Acts 1, where he is taken up into heaven after forty days. But it should be noted that even with the shorter text there is still a reference to the ascension in Lk 24, since Acts 1:2, in particular the phrase 'he was taken up', refers back to and interprets 'he parted from them' in Lk 24:51.

The different descriptions of the ascension at the end of the gospel and at the beginning of the Acts of the Apostles correspond to the different perspectives and stages of Luke-Acts at these two points. While the gospel scene brings the story of Jesus to a triumphal conclusion, the scene in Acts presents the end of Jesus' life on earth as the beginning of the 'time of the Church'. So the differing accounts have much to do with the conjunction of the two Lucan books.

Both the recognition scene (Lk 24:36–43) and the witnesses' commission (Lk 24:44–49) are accounted for by the traditional schema of the appearance to the Eleven; but the heavenly translation at the conclusion of such an appearance has no counterpart elsewhere in the tradition of the Easter narratives.[17]

Once we have decided in favour of the longer reading in verse 51, we naturally also maintain the longer beginning of verse 52, 'And they *worshipped him and* returned to Jerusalem with great joy'. The external evidence is the same as for the previous verse, and the idea of worship, mentioned immediately after the ascension, fits very well.

Verse 50: Then he led them out as far as Bethany, and lifting up his hands he blessed them.

In what has been called Luke's 'theological geography' of Jerusalem, the evangelist emphasizes Christ's presence in the Temple. After the death and resurrection of Christ, he emphasizes that 'he led them out'. The risen Christ goes out of Jerusalem into the world, 'beginning from Jerusalem' (Lk 24:47).

The risen Christ led his disciples out 'as far as', i.e., 'in the neighbourhood of' Bethany, where the events of the passion had begun (Lk 19:29). According to Acts 1:12 the place of ascension was 'the mount called Olivet'. It is pointless to attempt to harmonize the two locations. Luke, who does not seem to care about chronology ('the third day' or 'after forty days'?), does not care about mere geography either.

The clause 'and lifting up his hands he blessed them' seems to present Jesus as the messianic high priest in his relationship to his believers. See similar expressions in Lev 9:22, 'Then Aaron lifted up his hands toward the people and blessed them'. An even more interesting text is Sir 50, where we find the image of a blessing priest and a responding community: 'Then Simon came down, and lifted up his hands over the whole congregation of . . . Israel, to pronounce the blessing of the Lord . . . and they bowed down in worship . . .' (Sir 50:20–21). The community then answers with what is apparently an elaboration of the priestly blessing in Num 6:22–27, and in which, for our present context, the 'gladness of heart' (Sir 50:23) is significant (cf. Lk 24:52). Luke's intention of concluding with a priestly blessing can also be gathered from his repeated use of 'to bless/blessing' at the beginning (Lk 1:42, 64; 2:28, 34) and at the end of his gospel (Lk 24:30, 50, 51, 53). The important difference is that, whereas in the first texts we are in a Temple context, at the end the blessing takes place outside the Temple, possibly symbolizing the beginning of the new age of the Church.

Luke concludes his gospel with the great high priest blessing his community. The blessing means assurance of God's favour and support. Jesus' blessing in fact means the same as his assurance that he will be with his disciples always (Mt 28:20).

Verse 51: While he blessed them, he parted from them, and was carried up into heaven.

'While he blessed them', Christ departed from his disciples. He, as it were, departed from them and was taken up into heaven in this attitude of blessing them. It was a lasting blessing, a lasting guarantee. The Greek expression which is translated 'he parted from them' certainly refers back to Lk 24:36, where it was said that 'he stood among them'. This time it is no longer a temporary disappearance, as, e.g., in Lk 24:31, but a final departure. No wonder, therefore, that Luke also adds: 'he was carried up into heaven'. Acts 1:9–11 certainly contains

expressions borrowed from the assumption of Elijah (II Kgs 2), but
Lk 24:49–51 also reveals traces of such influence, particularly the
promise of the disciples' investiture with the power of the Spirit, which
recalls Elijah's bequest of his 'spirit' to Elisha (II Kgs 2:9–10, 15;
Sir 48:12).

Luke uses here a strange verb for the ascension: *anephereto*. It
may be related to the priestly blessing just mentioned, for the verb is at
home in sacrificial terminology (cf. Heb 7:27; 9:28; 13:15). Although
some exegetes explicitly reject the possibility, this might suggest that
Luke understands the ascension as the final oblation of the high priest
to the Father in heaven.

It is important to understand why Luke has an ascension distinct
from the resurrection, a feature not found in Mark and Matthew. In
Luke, it is connected with his presentation of salvation history as a
journey with clear demarcation lines. Christ's ascension is the clear
demarcation line between the period of the earthly Jesus and the
period of the Church. This presentation, therefore, is completely tied
up with Luke's own theological perspective.

Verses 52–53: And they worshipped him, and returned to
Jerusalem with great joy, (53) and were continually in the
temple blessing God.

Like the community in Sir 50:21, the disciples 'worshipped' the
ascending Lord (cf. Mt 28:17, 'And when they saw him they worshipped him'). Now that he is the fully glorified Lord, he can be
worshipped without reservation. This is the first and only time the
disciples *worship* Jesus in this gospel and it has been argued that this 'is
actually the point to which the expected moment of recognition was
deferred by our evangelist'.[18]

The phrase 'they returned to Jerusalem' is paralleled in Acts 1:12.
Both texts express the centrality of Jerusalem in Luke's understanding
of salvation history. But whereas Lk 24:52–53 tells of the disciples'
great joy and continual praising of God in the Temple, Acts 1.12–13
makes no mention of their joy and says that they returned to the upper
room.

The disciples returned 'with great joy' (cf. Lk 24:41; Acts 12:14).
Their anxieties and doubts (Lk 24:17, 37) are gone. Their joy reflects
the worship of the early Christian community 'in gladness and simplicity of heart' (Acts 2:46; RSV: 'with glad and generous hearts'), which
was repeatedly anticipated in the gospel. The disciples' joy is caused by
the knowledge that now that Christ is fully glorified, the kingdom of
God is present in the presence of the Lord which, in turn, is enacted in
the presence of the Spirit.

Finally, Luke says that the disciples 'were continually in the temple
blessing God'. Luke began his gospel with the scene of Zechariah

receiving the promise of the birth of John the Baptist in the Temple. Now at the end of the gospel the group of disciples gather in the same Temple. In fact, the phrases 'with great joy' and 'blessing God' express the disciples' reaction in terms which are characteristic of the eschatological atmosphere in the infancy narrative (Lk 1:14, 64; 2:10, 28). The disciples 'bless' or 'praise' God, as the people previously 'glorified' God, especially after manifestations of Jesus' powerful deeds (Lk 5:26; 7:16; 13:13; 17:15; 18:43). They praise 'the mighty works of God' (Acts 2:11). In fact, they praise God for the greatest thing he has done, the resurrection.

They do so in the Temple, and thus Luke ends the gospel where he started it. The importance of the Temple for the first Christian community is also expressed in Acts 2:46; 3:1; 5:42. Yet between the first mention of the Temple in Lk 1:9 and the present reference, Luke has shown the 'time of Israel' yielding to the 'time of Christ and his Church'.

The literary form of Lk 24:36–53

As we pointed out at the beginning of this chapter, this section is composed of three pericopes: a recognition scene (Lk 24:36–43), an instruction on the meaning of the Easter message (Lk 24:44–49), and finally the farewell scene (Lk 24:50–53). It has been shown that the combination of a recognition scene and instruction is found elsewhere (cf. Jn 20:19–23: recognition scene in verses 19–20 and instruction in verses 21–23; cf. Acts 10:34–43) and may therefore be traditional. But nowhere else in the New Testament is this combination followed by a farewell as is the case in Lk 24:50–53. All other appearances of the risen Christ (Mt 28:9–10, 16–20; Jn 20:14–18, 19–23, 26–29; 21:1–23) end with the words of the risen Christ. Only Luke ends the appearance account with a farewell scene or leave-taking (Lk 24:50–53). This seems to be typically Lucan (cf. Lk 1:38; 2:15; 9:33; 24:31; Acts 10:7; 12:10), and it is probable, therefore, that it was Luke who combined Lk 24:36–49 and 24:50–53.

Lk 24:36–49 is an apostolic Christophany, an appearance of the risen Christ to official witnesses, in which the apologetic motif of recognition (Lk 24:36–43) and the motif of the mission entrusted to the witnesses (Lk 24:44–49) are fused.

Lk 24:50–53 has a different literary form. A study of ascension accounts in ancient Greco-Roman and Jewish literature, including the Old Testament, has led to the conclusion that from the historico-religious point of view, it should be said that Luke treated the ascension as a case of being carried up to heaven comparable to that of Elijah. A study of the New Testament leads to the conclusion that the Lucan conception and account of the ascension present a unique case in early Christianity.

The historicity of Lk 24:36–53

General considerations

All through Lk 24:36–53 we have found a language and theological concerns which are very characteristic of Luke. We list here the most important elements:

(1)   The emphasis on the bodily reality of the risen Christ, to be understood in the light of the Hellenistic mentality with which Luke was faced.
(2)   The salvation-historical perspective of a *journey*, according to which the appearing Christ somehow still belongs to the central period of the earthly Jesus.
(3)   The explanation of the scriptures by the risen Christ who alone can open the disciples' eyes to understand the scriptures and interpret them Christologically (the Christ had to suffer . . .).
(4)   The commission of the disciples to preach conversion for the forgiveness of sins to all nations.
(5)   The centrality of Jerusalem and the centrifugal character of the universal mission.
(6)   The idea of the disciples as witnesses to the fact of the resurrection.
(7)   The promise of the Spirit; the period of the Church as the period of the Spirit of (the somewhat absent) Christ.
(8)   The ascension of Christ as the *terminus ad quem* of the central period of the earthly Jesus.
(9)   The disciples' joy and their praising God in the Temple.

All these features are very Lucan, and it is clear that Luke is developing his own theological viewpoint in these Easter texts. Can we still separate these redactional Lucan interests from extant traditions which Luke may have used? Some years ago an attempt was made to determine the frequency of Lucan characteristics throughout Lk 24:36–53. This showed that the Lucan features are scattered in the recognition appearance (Lk 24:36–43), very abundant in Lk 24:44–45, less numerous in Lk 24:46–49, where we find the classical themes of the kerygma presented in a mission instruction, and again very abundant in Lk 24:50–53.
These considerations then led to the following hypotheses:

(1)   Luke seems to have followed fairly faithfully a tradition on the recognition appearance in verses 36–43 which seem to go back to the same tradition as Jn 20:19–20.
(2)   He seems to have had a much greater share in the composition of verses 44–45, apparently in an effort to connect the recognition appearance with the instruction pericope.
(3)   It is said that verses 46–49 contain relatively few Lucan

characteristics. But these verses are very similar to the kerygma formulas of Acts. Unlike A. George, we think with others that these kerygma formulas are very Lucan and this inclines us to think that verses 46–49 are also rather Lucan.

(4)   Verses 50–53 contain many Lucan characteristics and seem to be an entirely Lucan composition, as is in fact affirmed by many scholars.

The historicity of the ascension

Form- and redaction-critical study of Lk 24:50–53 and Acts 1:1–12 has isolated Lk 24:50b–52a and Acts 1:9–11 as minimal units. For our study this means that the following text remains: '. . . (as far as Bethany). Lifting up his hands he blessed them. While he blessed them, he parted from them, and was carried up into heaven. And they worshipped him.' From a comparative study of this text and Acts 1:9–11, it has then been deduced that the double account of the ascension is due solely to Luke's redactional work. Analysis of the motifs found in the two accounts has led to a similar result.

The whole account is ultimately reduced to the motif of being 'carried up to heaven'. How did Luke arrive at this central motif of his account? In order to answer this question the other Lucan texts which deal with the ascension or the exaltation have been studied (Lk 9:51–52a; 24:26; Acts 1:1–2, 21–22; 2:32–35; 3:19–21; 5:30–32; 13:32–33). This study resulted in the conclusion that Luke himself reinterpreted the early kerygma of the exaltation. He actualized it in a visible fact and expressed it literarily as a carrying up to heaven.

This Lucan interpretation is undoubtedly in accordance with his theological preoccupation. It is connected with his understanding of the whole of salvation history as a *journey* along which he places clear demarcation lines to separate the successive periods. The ascension is the demarcation line between the period of the earthly Jesus described in the gospel and the period of the Church described in the Acts of the Apostles. This means that the ascension is entirely bound up with Luke's own theology.

This last remark should give us an idea how the historical question should be approached. No matter how much it was inspired by the Holy Spirit, Luke's theology took shape in his mind in connection with the questions and problems he faced in the Greek world to which he addressed his gospel. Then we know the true source of the account of the ascension and should not worry too much about the so-called historical contradictions. They would be contradictions only if the ascension in itself were to be understood as an historical observable fact. Luke is well aware that it is a literary unfolding of the one saving event, the glorification of Christ. Narratives with time and space sequences are then no more than literary-theological unfoldings of the many aspects of that one eschatological event.

8 The Appearances of Mark 16:9–20

The different endings of the gospel of Mark

On the basis of both internal and external evidence, there is now almost general agreement that Mark ended his gospel at Mk 16:8. This ending, however, appeared too abrupt to some readers, and several attempts were therefore made to provide a more appropriate ending.

The shorter ending

After Mk 16:8 some manuscripts add a conclusion which reads as follows: 'But they reported briefly to Peter and those with him all that they had been told. And after this, Jesus himself sent out by means of them, from east to west, the sacred and imperishable proclamation of eternal salvation.'

The language of this passage is totally unlike that of Mark. The intention of the text is obvious. It is composed to round off Mk 16:8a and to indicate that the women obeyed the command given in Mk 16:7. Thus it contradicts Mk 16:8b, 'they said nothing to any one'. Codex Bobiensis, which is the only manuscript which has the shorter ending alone, omits the phrase 'they said nothing to any one'. Since this Codex was transcribed in the fourth or fifth century the latest possible date for the composition of the shorter ending is the fourth century, but it is most probably much older, and many scholars consider a date near the middle of the second century likely.

In practically all manuscripts which contain the shorter and the longer endings the former is placed before the latter. The shorter ending, which emphasizes the inauguration of a world-wide mission, is not canonical, i.e., not part of the canon of holy scripture.

The longer ending, Mk 16:9–20

Whereas the shorter ending was composed to round off the gospel of Mark, the composer of the longer ending does not appear to have had this intention, for, while it relates several appearances of the risen

Christ, it fails to narrate the appearance in Galilee, promised in Mk 16:7. There is also an apparent tension between Mk 16:8 in which the subject ('they') is the women and Mk 16:9 in which the presumed subject ('he') is Jesus.

The longer ending has been commonly held to be an artificial summary of resurrection appearances recorded in Matthew, Luke and John. But this commonly accepted view has recently been questioned by some scholars who list a number of differences between Mk 16:9–20 and the resurrection appearances narrated in the other gospels. They also point out the similarities as well as the dissimilarities to I Cor 15. This leads to the conclusion that the longer ending is not merely an artificial summary of resurrection appearances in the other gospels, but rather a free composition based on tradition and supplemented in part from the resurrection narratives in Matthew, Luke and John. The statement about the ascension, the missionary charge and the command to baptize may be considered independent traditions.

The form, vocabulary and style of Mk 16:9–20 make almost all scholars decide against Marcan authorship. But although the text is not authentic, i.e., not the work of Mark, it is considered canonical by all Catholic and many non-Catholic scholars.

Because the longer ending is undoubtedly dependent on Matthew, Luke and John, it is to be dated after these gospels. But by about A.D. 180 Irenaeus quotes the text as belonging to the gospel of Mark, and there are possible allusions to it in Justin's *Apology* (*c.* A.D. 140) and Tatian's *Diatessaron*. It is therefore usually dated in the earlier part of the second century A.D.

The Freer Logion

In the Freer Museum at Washington there is a fourth- or fifth-century manuscript discovered in Egypt in 1906 in which sixteen lines of text are appended to Mk 16:14 of the longer ending. The addition reads as follows: 'And they excused themselves, saying, "This age of iniquity and unbelief is under Satan, who prevents the truth of God and his power from being apprehended by the unclean spirits, therefore reveal your righteousness now," [they said to Christ]. And Christ answered them, saying, "The term of the years of Satan's authority has been fulfilled, but other terrors are at hand; even for those sinners for whose sake I was delivered to death, that they might return to the truth and sin no more, and they might inherit the spiritual and incorruptible glory of righteousness, which is in heaven" '.

The word of association which attracted the Freer Logion appears to be 'unbelief' in Mk 16:14, '. . . and he upbraided them for their unbelief . . .': 'And they excused themselves saying, "This age of iniquity and unbelief. . ." '

The two dominant themes of the logion are persecution and the longing for the parousia. It has been pointed out that it is strikingly similar to Acts 3:19–21. The Freer Logion is not canonical.

Exegesis of Mk 16:9–20

Verses 9–11: Now when he rose early on the first day of the week, he appeared first to Mary Magdalene, from whom he had cast out seven demons. (10) She went and told those who had been with him, as they mourned and wept. (11) But when they heard that he was alive and had been seen by her, they would not believe it.

The appearance of the risen Christ to Mary Magdalene is generally believed to be a summary in the author's own words of Jn 20:11–18 to which he has added some information about Mary derived from Lk 8:2.

The section begins very abruptly and clearly does not presuppose Mk 16:5–8. It is as if Jesus had been the subject of a preceding verse in which his resurrection was mentioned. This was most probably the case in the writing from which this text was taken. The indication of time 'early on the first day of the week' is peculiar and does not occur as such anywhere else in the resurrection narratives of the gospels. Neither does the Greek verb used for 'he appeared' (*ephanē*). It may derive from the Septuagint (cf. Num 23:4, where it is used for a theophany to Balaam) and may be equivalent to 'he appeared' (*ōphthē*) in I Cor 15:5; 'God ... made him manifest' (*ho theos ... edōken auton emphanē genesthai*), Acts 10:40; and 'Jesus was revealed' (*ephanerōthē*), Jn 21:14.

Next, Mary Magdalene is described as if she had not yet been mentioned. She is introduced as one from whom Jesus 'had cast out seven demons'. This recalls Lk 8:2, 'Mary, called Magdalene, from whom seven demons had gone out', but the verbal form (*ekballein para*) used in Mk 16:9 is very different and, in fact, is not found anywhere else in the New Testament. The reference to the expulsion of 'seven demons' indicates that she had been cured of a severe case of possession. The belief (still current) that Mary had lived an immoral life is based on a mistaken identification with the anonymous woman sinner mentioned in the preceding narrative (Lk 7:36–50). This identification is found for the first time in Tertullian.

Verse 10 seems to confirm that the author is summarizing Jn 20:11–18, especially verse 18: 'Mary Magdalene went and said to the disciples, "I have seen the Lord"; and she told them that he had said these things to her', except for the emphasis upon mourning and crying, which can be compared, however, with Jn 16:20, '. . . you will weep and lament'. It refers to a sadness due to a collapse of faith and fits well in a context which deals with belief and unbelief. The phrase 'those who had been with him' recalls Mk 3:14, 'And he appointed twelve, to be with him. . .'.

'When they heard that he was alive (*zēi*) and had been seen (*etheathē*) by her.' The phrase 'he was alive' is typically Lucan (Lk 24:33; Acts 1:3; 25:19). Mk 16:11 and 14 are the only two instances in which the verb *theasthai*, 'to be seen', is used in the appearance accounts.

The disciples 'would not believe' (*ēpistēsan*). This verb is also found in Lk 24:11, 41 in the same context. The theme of unbelief in the resurrection occurs often in the New Testament (Mt 28:17; Lk 24:11, 41; Jn 20:25). It is increasingly emphasized in accordance with the developing tradition, and seems to be of special importance to the present narrator.

> **Verses 12–13:** After this he appeared in another form to two of them, as they were walking into the country. (13) And they went back and told the rest, but they did not believe them.

These verses constitute a clear allusion to the Emmaus account (Lk 24:13–35). Neither the vocabulary nor the style is Marcan. The phrase 'after this' is found twelve times in John. The Greek verb translated 'he appeared' (*ephanerōthē*) is different from that used in the previous paragraph, but we find it twice in Jn 21:1, 14.

Jesus appeared 'in another form'. Some scholars think that the author means 'in a form different from that in which he appeared to Mary Magdalene' (cf. Mk 16:9). According to Jn 20:15, Jesus looked like a gardener to Mary Magdalene. To the disciples on the road to Emmaus he appeared as a wayfarer (Lk 24:15). However, it seems to us that the author is rather referring to the fact that the risen Christ is not recognized as long as he does not reveal himself and does not give the inner enlightenment of faith by which they can recognize him. We would paraphrase, therefore, 'in another form than the way the earthly Jesus looked'. Thus the phrase seems to be related to Lk 24:16, 'But their eyes were kept from recognizing him'; Jn 20:14, 'Saying this, she turned around and saw Jesus standing, but she did not know that it was Jesus'; Jn 21:4, 'Just as day was breaking. Jesus stood on the beach; yet the disciples did not know that it was Jesus'. Only this time the 'summary' is so brief that we are not told how they came from initial non-recognition to recognition of the risen Christ.

The 'two of them' are apparently two of 'those who had been with him' (Mk 16:10). Further, the text speaks of 'the rest' (Mk 16:13) and of 'the eleven' (Mk 16:14). The phrase, therefore, seems to mean that they belong to the closer circle of disciples. The vagueness of the text seems to imply that the author counted on more detailed knowledge which his readers had from another source. He is apparently satisfied with a brief reference.

On that supposition, we can also understand that the author does not explicitly say that and how they came to recognize the risen Christ and believed in him, although this is clearly presupposed in verse 13, 'they went back and told the rest'. The two disciples took the message to the others, 'but they did not believe them'. They had not believed the message of Mary Magdalene (Mk 16:11); they do not believe the message of the two disciples either. This seems to contradict the ending of the Emmaus account, especially Lk 24:34, where the Eleven and their companions say 'The Lord has risen indeed, and has appeared to Simon!' before the two disciples can relate their experience. This emphasis on unbelief (Mk 16:11, 13, 14) suggests that the author of the longer ending understood the Marcan themes of the messianic secret, lack of understanding, and unbelief. The doubt of the disciples is mentioned at points of transition as the link which gives all three of the accounts (Mk 16:9–11, 12–13, 14) a coherent unity and their basic movement.

> **Verse 14:** Afterward he appeared to the eleven themselves as they sat at table; and he upbraided them for their unbelief and hardness of heart, because they had not believed those who had seen him after he had risen.

Verses 14–16 exhibit parallels with Lk 24:36–49; Mt 28:16–20 and Jn 20:19–21.

The phrase *husteron de* ('afterward', 'finally') is not found in Mark. The author refers here to the appearance of the Eleven mentioned in Matthew, Luke and John. But here it is said that Jesus appeared 'as they sat at table' (cf. Lk 24:30, 41–43; Jn 21:12, 13; Acts 10:41), a reference to the early Christian belief in the presence of the risen Christ at the Lord's supper.

The risen Lord 'upbraided them for their unbelief and hardness of heart'. He reproaches them in the strongest terms, which were previously used for the hostile unbelief of the Jews. The verb 'to upbraid' (*oneidizein*) is used for Chorazin and Bethsaida, the unbelieving cities (Mt 11:20); 'unbelief' (*apistia*) describes the attitude of the people of Jesus' home town (Mk 6:6) and of the father of the epileptic boy (Mk 9:24); and 'hardness of heart' (*sklērokardia*) points to an innate human tendency to resist God (Mk 10:5).

This means basically that the entire college of apostles has been tried for faith and has been found wanting. What is said of Thomas in Jn. is here in essence ascribed to all of them: they were unbelieving and resisting those who had borne witness to them of the Lord's resurrection.[19]

Next the author describes the resurrection faith as believing 'those who had seen him after he had risen'. This is very similar to what were once the final words of Jesus in the Fourth Gospel (Jn 20:30–31 being the final comments of the evangelist and Jn 21 being an appendix): 'Blessed are those who have not seen and yet believe' (Jn 20:29).

Shocked by this severe reproach addressed to the disciples, a copyist added here the so-called Freer Logion (see above) in an attempt to soften the reproach and to explain the disciples' lack of faith.

> **Verses 15–16:** And he said to them, 'Go into all the world and preach the gospel to the whole creation. (16) He who believes and is baptized will be saved; but he who does not believe will be condemned.'

These verses are related to Mt 28:16–20 but are not a copy of it. The risen Christ accepts his disciples into service and thereby enables them to believe.

The wording of the commission is very interesting. It reminds us of Mt 28:19; Lk 24:47; Acts 1:8 and Mk 13:10, but goes beyond the Matthean and Lucan texts in that it speaks of 'all the world . . . the whole creation'. A similar expression is found in Col 1:23, 'not shifting from the hope of the gospel which you heard, which has been preached to every creature under heaven . . .'. All peoples without distinction are to hear the gospel message.

The author takes over the typically Marcan expression 'preach the gospel' without any indication of its contents (cf. Mk 1:14; 13:10; 14:9). If Mt 28:18b–20 is already an expression of the early Church's mission consciousness after the destruction of Jerusalem in A.D. 70, this is even more so for our present text.

The language of verse 16 reminds us of Jn 3:17, 18: 'For God sent the Son into the world. . . . He who believes in him is not condemned; he who does not believe is condemned already. . . .' The phrase 'he who believes' (*ho pisteusas*) points to an act, and probably, as 'and is baptized' (*baptistheis*) suggests, a confession of faith at baptism. Baptism is also referred to in Mt 28:19, but here in Mk 16:16 it is more clearly understood as an expression of faith. We may also be getting close here to the idea of baptism as a seal which guarantees that man 'will be saved', i.e., eschatological salvation. It has also been noted that the second part of the verse declares that unbelief alone is the reason for condemnation, not the failure to be baptized.

> **Verses 17–18:** 'And these signs will accompany those who believe: in my name they will cast out demons; they will speak in new tongues; (18) they will pick up serpents, and if they drink any deadly thing, it will not hurt them; they will lay their hands on the sick, and they will recover.'

This conferral of miraculous powers on the disciples recalls Lk 10:17–19, '. . . Lord, even the demons are subject to us in your name!' . . . 'Behold, I have given you authority to tread upon serpents and scorpions, and over all the power of the enemy; and nothing shall hurt you!' Almost all cases referred to here can be documented from other parts of the New Testament (see below). These signs 'will accompany those who believe'; they are part of the divine authentication of those who are sent.

'In my name they will cast out demons' like the man in Mk 9:38f. In Mk 6:13 the Twelve are said to have cast out many demons. As a result of Jesus' success in casting out demons his own name soon came to be used as a means of driving them out. In Acts 16:18 Paul expels a demon 'in the name of Jesus Christ'.

The second sign is that 'they will speak in new tongues'. In I Cor 14:22 Paul says that 'tongues are a sign not for believers but for unbelievers'. Mk 16:17 is often cited for the evidential character of spirit baptism and for the doctrine of tongues as the Spirit's only initial evidence. However, the doctrine definitely lacks sufficient support. The phenomenon mentioned here should be understood in the light of the colourful depiction in I Cor 14. It was particularly prominent from Pentecost onward (Acts 2:4; 10:46, etc.).

'They will pick up serpents' without being hurt. The thought seems to be related to Lk 10:19, 'Behold, I have given you authority to tread upon serpents and scorpions . . . and nothing shall hurt you'. The text may have Ps 91(90):13 in mind: 'You will tread on the lion and the adder, the young lion and the serpent you will trample under foot'. The psalm promises divine protection in every danger to the man who places his trust in God. In Acts 28:5 Paul shakes off a snake into the fire without suffering any harm.

'If they drink any deadly thing, it will not hurt them.' This sign is not found anywhere in the New Testament. But Eusebius, *History of the Church*, III, 39, quotes Papias (*c.* A.D. 130) as referring to the case of Justus Barsabbas (Acts 1:23) who did not die although he drank poison. There is also a similar legend about John in the apocryphal *Acts of John*.

'They will lay their hands on the sick, and they will recover.' In Acts 9:12, 17 Paul is cured of his blindness by the laying-on of hands and in Acts 28:8 Paul himself cures the father of Publius in the same way. In Acts 5:12 we are told that 'many signs and wonders were done among the people by the hands of the apostles'. Some scholars also refer to Jas 5:14–15 and the anointing of the sick mentioned there.

Verse 19: So then the Lord Jesus, after he had spoken to them, was taken up into heaven, and sat down at the right hand of God.

This verse is a summary statement of the ascension recalling Lk 24:51. The phrase 'after he had spoken to them' seems to refer to what precedes, but the preceding words were spoken at a meal (Mk 16:14), and it would therefore appear that Jesus ascended right there and then from the table! In reality there is no immediate connection in time with verses 15–18. The author is not thinking of the words just spoken by the risen Christ, but of all the words of Jesus known to him from tradition.

The phrase 'he was taken up' (*anelēmphthē*, 'he was lifted up') is the same as the one found in Acts 1:2, 22. The terminology of the verse is borrowed from the Old Testament. The clause seems to be a combination of II Kgs 2:11, '. . . And Elijah went up by a whirlwind into heaven', and Ps 110(109):1, 'The Lord says to my lord: "Sit at my right hand . . ." '. The latter text has a relevance to the Church and the disciples who have just been commissioned: from his heavenly throne the risen Lord continues to guide and help them. The resurrection-ascension is the enthronement of the risen Lord who from now on marches victoriously through the world.

> **Verse 20:** And they went forth and preached everywhere, while the Lord worked with them and confirmed the message by the signs that attended it. Amen.

This concluding verse, which has been called 'a kind of condensed Acts of the Apostles', is actually a look back on a considerable period of missionary work. The Eleven 'went forth and preached everywhere' as they were told in Mk 16:15, 'Go into all the world and preach the gospel to the whole creation'.

The Lord sitting at the right hand of God 'worked with them and confirmed the message'. This statement corresponds to Matthew's 'I am with you always' (Mt 28:20). The risen Lord, fully glorified and freed from all earthly limitations, can work with them 'everywhere'. The Lord's 'working together' consists in confirming the word (*logos*), i.e., the Eleven's message about Christ and their preaching. This preaching is accomplished under the impulse of the risen Christ as he gives force to the word in signs. The divine collaboration is again particularly exemplified in 'the signs that attended' (literally, 'followed', *epakolouthountōn*; cf. Mk 16:17, *parakolouthēsei*) the message. The signs do not prove the validity of the message. They are a way in which the Lord puts the valid word of his apostles more forcefully into effect. Thus the author declares his belief in the Lord's continuing work.

9 Preaching the Resurrection Narratives

General considerations

The Easter tradition in the synoptic gospels – as in the whole New Testament – confronts us with a difficult problem. The Easter witness is without any doubt the foundation as well as the medium of the early Christian preaching. But, as the previous chapters of this book have shown, there are ambiguities and discrepancies between the resurrection narratives. Faced with these difficulties we should not resort to questionable attempts at harmonization in which we try to fit all the elements of the different gospels into an 'historical reconstruction' of our own making. Rather, we should make a clear distinction between the *basic affirmation*, common to all, that God has raised Jesus from the dead, and the *way in which* the basic affirmation is expressed. Indeed, while all the evangelists agree that Christ appeared to the Eleven (Twelve; cf. I Cor 15:5), the details of time and place, circumstances and verbal contents of the mission charge, etc., are different. This shows both the strength of our overall certitude and the limitations of our detailed knowledge. It is an indication that we have to look for the essentials elsewhere than in a chronicle of events. The details vary depending on the standpoint from which each evangelist proclaims the Easter message and on the particular moment in history at which he does so. In other words, in proclaiming the Easter message each evangelist was concerned with the particular questions, problems and difficulties which affected his own community. These, and nothing else, explain the differences between the gospel accounts.

The resurrection narratives, then, must be viewed in their historical context. One must realize to what extent their formulation is related to particular historical and theological situations. Therefore, the present-day preacher cannot just reproduce the Easter message of the gospels, but must proclaim it as 'new'.

Contemporary theology has 'rediscovered' the central place of the Easter event, and the Constitution on the Sacred Liturgy of the Second Vatican Council has brought this awareness to the attention of the Church as a whole. But this renewed insight has until now hardly affected sermon literature and sermons themselves. Most authors and homilists apparently prefer to stick to the familiar categories of traditional preaching.

However,

> The conservative Catholic theological thought of the last centuries has been dominated by a medieval philosophical system and has not been primarily based on the Scriptures.[20]

> But a theological stance that does not do justice to the biblical evidence is of little value, no matter how possible or attractive it may be in itself.[21]

To do justice to the biblical evidence it is not sufficient to season one's exposition with a sprinkling of biblical quotations, because these texts can be fitted into a way of thinking and a presentation which are altogether foreign to the biblical message. The homilist will have to turn to the resurrection narratives with his eyes open, aware that his thinking has for long been determined by values and categories which are only very loosely, if at all, related to the scriptures.

Just as in the early Church the resurrection was not so much narrated as proclaimed, the present-day homilist and catechist will have to be intent on proclaiming the message of the resurrection rather than being concerned with a question like 'What actually happened on that first Easter morning?' This question is alien to the intention of the evangelists, who were not trying to give us historical information.

> What actually happened on that first Easter morning, according to the evangelists, is that it became possible to know Jesus as ultimacy in the historicality of the every-day (Mark), that it became possible to live the life of a Christian within the church (Matthew), and that it became possible to imitate Jesus in a meaningful life in the world (Luke).[22]

To be sure, the possibilities indicated by the evangelists are based on the prior event of the resurrection of Jesus, but rather than attempt to describe the 'mechanics' of the resurrection itself, which is in any case beyond description, the evangelists bring to the fore the effects of the resurrection as experienced by the believing community.

We said that the homilist must proclaim the Easter message as 'new', but this statement too should be further qualified. There is a distinct possibility that a question like 'How can I make the resurrection faith more easily acceptable to contemporary man?' would be misunderstood. The resurrection will always remain acceptable and 'visible' only to faith. Today as in any time what was said by Luke of the Athenians can be said of many: '. . . (they) spent their time in nothing except telling or hearing something new' (Acts 17:21). And many a reaction to the proclamation of the resurrection today may be similar to theirs: 'Now when they heard of the resurrection of the dead, some mocked; but others said, "We will hear you again about this"' (Acts 17:32). The latter talked about giving Paul another opportunity to present the Easter message, but in fact they were brushing him off politely. Recent surveys in some traditionally Christian circles have revealed that about 70% of the people interrogated did not really believe in the resurrection of Christ as an event.

In our time as in Paul's the proclamation of the resurrection faith is certainly a stumbling block. In this connection we should remember that

> The task of the interpreter is not to remove the stumbling block but to ensure that it is rightly located. . . .[23]

> In any true and effective proclamation the 'scandal' of the Resurrection must be located accurately and portrayed fully. To interpret the Resurrection either as a crudely materialistic and publicly verifiable resuscitation of a corpse or as an indefinable happening in some supernatural realm of meta-history completely removed from the time-space world and from all historical enquiry would be to locate the 'scandal' falsely. . . . Only when a man is confronted by the eschatological deed of God, veiled in the ambiguities of history and challenging his very being in its own historicity, is the offence of the Gospel truly and fully known.[24]

On the one hand, the homilist should not try to accommodate himself irresponsibly to the taste of his audience and preach an easily digestible gospel. But, on the other hand, it is also true that in many a homily the stumbling block is wrongly located by dealing with secondary features or placing wrong emphases, as, e.g., dwelling on the presence of angels at the tomb, while this feature in reality expresses the much more important conviction that faith-knowledge of the resurrection is possible only through divine revelation.

Not only do many find it hard to believe in the resurrection, but a great number of those who say that they believe in the resurrection of Jesus have confused this resurrection with the resuscitation of a corpse. They see no difference between the risen Christ and, e.g., Lazarus whom Jesus restored to ordinary life. Many homilists share the same misunderstanding. But a close look at the resurrection narratives shows that to the evangelists Jesus' life was not the same before and after his death and resurrection. While Lazarus was *restored to* ordinary life and had to die again, Jesus' life was *transformed* into a glorious existence which is free from the limitations of space and time and no longer subject to death.

It is a mistake, therefore, to consider and present the appearances of the risen Christ as an 'objective proof' of the resurrection. The appearance vocabulary was derived from the Septuagint (cf. Ex 3:6; 33:20–23; Judg 13:21–23) where it is used for God's appearances to Moses and others. Referring to one such appearance the Jewish theologian Philo of Alexandria wrote: 'God appeared to Abraham. It is not said, therefore, that the wise man saw God but that God appeared to the wise man' (*De Abrahamo* 77:77). A similar insight is expressed by St Thomas Aquinas. In his *Summa Theologica* Pars III, quaestio 55, art. 2, he asks the question *An resurrectio Christi demonstrari potest* (whether the resurrection of Christ can be proved). In the corpus of the following article St Thomas replies: 'Apostoli Christum post resurrectionem viventem occulata fide viderunt quem mortuum sciverant', which means, 'the apostles saw the living Christ after the resurrection *with the eyes of faith*, the one whom they knew to be dead (having seen him with their natural eyes)'. The arguments which convinced them of the reality of the resurrection were not just rational proofs but belonged to the realm of signs manifesting a hidden reality (*Summa Theologica* IIIa, qu. 55, art. 5). The sensory aspect of the appearances was subordinate to an interior gift which was directly related to the knowledge of faith. If we had remembered this statement of St Thomas in the past we would have been more cautious about making the resurrection of Christ just another miracle – though the greatest – proving his divinity! The resurrection is much more than a premiss in an apologetic syllogism. However, in the context of a certain Counter-Reformation theology it proved very difficult to assign to the resurrection the place of the central mystery of salvation. It was instead given a prominent place in apologetics, which belongs to the preliminaries of theology.

In the previous paragraphs we described two attitudes toward the proclamation of the Easter faith: the attitude of a great number of people for whom the resurrection is a stumbling block, and the attitude of those who say they believe in the resurrection but are often mistaken as to the nature of this event. However, the homilist should remember that he cannot draw any clear-cut distinction between those who believe and those who do not, for something of the unbeliever remains even in the heart of the believer. In other words, faith should never be merely presupposed or taken for granted. Therefore, the proclamation of the Easter message should always and in the first place be an invitation to faith.

> ... the Resurrection is not a miraculous happening in the dead past, the historic construct of which might be helpfully presented to the sight of the uncommitted observer in order to elicit faith. Apart from faith in the risen Christ, the Resurrection cannot be known. The method of proclamation must take account of this fact, must express it, must never stray from it.[25]

Both faith and the resurrection-reality-for-us are closely related to baptism, the sacrament of faith, in which 'we are buried' with Christ and 'shall certainly be united with him in a resurrection like his' (Rom 6:4–5). Baptism and the experience of our life as baptized Christians will therefore be the (often unexpressed) starting-point of the homilist. Because of this, he will never present the resurrection either as a wholly past or as a wholly future reality.

A look at the different pericopes

The accounts of the finding of the empty tomb

The accounts of the visit of the women to the tomb in Matthew, Mark and Luke are read during the Easter Vigil of years A, B and C respectively. (The second edition of the lectionary [1981] has omitted Mk 16:8 from the gospel reading for year B at the Easter Vigil.)

In general, we should say that sermon literature for the Easter Vigil does not often take the biblical passages as its starting-point. Most homilies develop dogmatic considerations on the resurrection of Christ as victory over sin and death, proof of his divinity and foundation of our faith. Some deal with the resurrection of Christians, often understood as a mere continuation of life after death, as a source of hope and consolation. On this basis, or sometimes without any previous basis at all, the preacher then often exhorts his audience to an ethical 'resurrection', i.e., he invites them to receive Easter confession and communion, and to renew their moral life.

If it is decided, however, to deal with the gospel texts themselves, there are still a few things we should definitely try to avoid.

Firstly, we should resist the temptation to develop the 'bare facts' for their own sake or to 'complete' the presentation of the evangelists, which is considered too restrained to appeal to the audience. Chapters Two, Three and Four of this book have sufficiently demonstrated that we are not dealing here with 'bare facts' or with an objective eye-witness record of what actually happened on that first Easter morning. Some writers and homilists even volunteer additional information and tell us that the tomb was situated eighteen steps below the place of the crucifixion. We are invited to approach the tomb or to 'hide ourselves in spirit' under a bush to observe the events! Or we get a touching description of that beautiful morning in springtime during which the events took place. But it does not seem to do justice to the unique character of the Easter message when it is presented as something that can be situated without further ado in the cycle of seasons in the northern hemisphere.

In this context an example from the local customs of the Philippines may be relevant. What should be the homilist's attitude toward the *encuentro* or *salubong*, the enactment of the meeting of the risen

Christ and his mother, celebrated in the early morning of Easter? There is indeed no mention of an appearance of the risen Lord to his mother in the New Testament. So what should the homilist do about it? On the one hand, he should certainly avoid describing this meeting with a wealth of details which would give the impression that we are dealing here with a fact which could be *observed* by anybody who happened to be around. On the other hand, it is true that we call Mary the first among the believers, and that she too came to faith in the full sense of the word only after the resurrection. This means that the risen Christ was *revealed* to her, or, in other words, that she met the risen Christ. The homilist, therefore, could start his sermon from the *encuentro* which takes place before the early Easter mass. But rather than dwell on sentimental details, he should develop it as the expression of Mary's Easter faith experience. Next he should relate her faith to ours, and then develop the central meaning of the Easter faith for our life as Christians.

Secondly, though it is obvious that in homilies on the visit of the women to the tomb the empty tomb is dealt with, it should never be allowed to occupy the central position in the preacher's presentation. Mk 16:1–8 and parallels are not 'the gospel of the empty tomb'. The gospel text deals with the *divine revelation* of the resurrection, as is indicated by the presence and the words of the angel(s). The angel turns our attention from the empty tomb to the risen Christ. Moreover, there is no basis in the New Testament for saying that the apostles proclaimed the empty tomb. It is never mentioned in their preaching. They proclaim not the empty tomb but the risen Christ.

Thirdly, our reading of the texts should have convinced us by now that the empty tomb is nowhere presented as a proof of the resurrection. The reasoning of the evangelists is never: 'He is risen, *because* he is not here', or 'He is not here, *therefore* he must have risen'. The discovery of the empty tomb causes only confusion and does not lead anybody to faith, except perhaps in Jn 20:8 where, after Peter's entrance into the tomb which does not cause any faith (Jn 20:7), it is said, 'Then the other disciple, who reached the tomb first, also went in, and he saw and believed'. The meaning of the phrase 'he believed' is open to discussion. It would be better, then, to avoid altogether the term 'proof' in our Easter sermons, the function of which is not to prove but to proclaim and to witness to our resurrection faith.

How then can we present the account of the tomb in a homily? Since the unity of the narrative seems to be supplied by the women, and Mark seems to invite the reader or hearer to identify with them, the behaviour of the women may be used to unify the preaching. They go to the tomb because of their loyalty to Jesus (Mk 16:1–2); but their gesture of gratitude is intended for a dead man. Jesus has become a memory; he belongs to the past; they have to come to terms with his death. The stone which closes the entrance to the tomb symbolizes the dividing line by which the dead are severed from the living (Mk 16:3). Obsessed by their idea of entering the tomb to anoint the corpse, the women do not halt when they find the stone removed. They have no eyes for signs (Mk 16:4). It is not until the young man distracts them from their plans and reveals the absence of Jesus that they are amazed and disconcerted (Mk 16:5). They are confronted with a new reality and Mark brings his reader face to face with the mystery of God's power. From within the tomb, the place of death, God reveals to them the significance of the event by means of his messenger. We are nowhere told that the women try to verify whether the tomb was really empty. It is the angel who tells them that Jesus is risen and is not there (Mk 16:6). The risen Christ is the same person as the Jesus who was crucified. Cross and resurrection cannot be separated and the risen Christ does not disown his physical history. This too is emphasized by the reference to the empty tomb. But with this message the function of the tomb is ended and it would be pointless to give it any further attention. In fact, the angel turns the women's attention from the tomb to the encounter with the risen Christ. They are to announce to the disciples and Peter that this encounter is to take place in Galilee where they will see him (Mk 16:7). The women react to the news of the resurrection with fear and trembling and flee without saying anything to anybody (Mk 16:8). Their terror is apparently caused by the fact that, while they can still cope with Jesus' death, however hard it may be, they are now faced with something altogether new which they do not know how to cope with. The audience should be invited to follow the course adopted by the women: one may look back to the past as they did, but only to find a greater driving-power towards the future. Easter rehabilitates the disciples and sends them to proclaim God's saving act in Christ in the latter's death and resurrection. The Church continues this mission today. In the context of the passion story, Mk 16:1–8 has the function of marking

> God's response to the blasphemous actions of men against his representative, and it is simultaneously an answer to the question about God's whereabouts in view of his suffering. Where the Psalms about suffering speak of the final saving of the suffering Just One by God's help, at the end of the story of the Passion of Jesus, the Just One, the divine messenger of God proclaims Christ's resurrection as his saving through God's mighty act.[26]

To understand the special Matthean emphases in the account of the empty tomb, one must see it in the context of Mt 27:62–66 and Mt 28:11–15, the story of the guards at the tomb. An indication of Matthew's main concern is found in the women's coming 'to see the sepulchre' (Mt 28:1), unlike Mark and Luke, where they come to bring spices. In Matthew's version, therefore, our attention is drawn to the tomb itself. This is due to the fact that, by the time the gospel was written, the empty tomb was the object of controversy. Matthew insists on the fact that the Jews themselves 'made the sepulchre secure by sealing the stone and setting a guard' (Mt 27:66; cf. 27:64–65) and that the Jewish accusations were totally fabricated (Mt 28:11–15). Matthew's version is largely determined by apologetic interests. It counteracts Jewish polemic against a later resurrection kerygma which made use of the empty tomb. The great earthquake and the angel's descent from heaven (Mt 28:2–3) underline the decisive (eschatological) character of Jesus' resurrection. The account (cf. Mt 28:7, 10) also points towards the commission in Galilee (cf. Mt 28:16–20). To Matthew's contemporaries, the tomb was not just the 'final dwelling place': it symbolized the power of death. Closed by a stone, it symbolized death's triumph over life, but opened, it became a sign of victory over death, and the 'angel of the Lord' who 'rolled back the stone, and sat upon it' is the sign of God's final victory over death.

Luke draws attention to the contrast between what the women found, i.e., an empty tomb, and what they failed to find, i.e., 'the body of the Lord Jesus' (Lk 24:3). For people who would reduce the appearances of the risen Christ to that of a spirit or a ghost (cf. Lk 24:37), Luke emphasizes the bodily reality of the risen Christ, although this bodily reality is at the same time so different from Jesus' mode of existence during his earthly ministry that he is not recognized by the natural eye (Lk 24:16, 37). Next we could concentrate on the message of the angel. Resurrection is a transformation into an entirely new mode of existence which takes place at the point of intersection between time and eternity. Only the 'negative' aspect of this transformation can be observed: 'He is not here' (Lk 24:5). However, in itself, this observation is susceptible of diverse interpretations. The positive aspect, 'He is risen', can only be revealed by God (through angels). Where is the risen Christ and where can we experience him? We should not 'seek him among the dead' (Lk 24:5), trying to found our resurrection faith on the empty tomb. We will meet him instead when he speaks to us in a Christological interpretation of the scriptures, in the eucharistic celebration (Lk 24:13–35), and wherever forgiveness is experienced (cf. Lk 24:47) and the resulting witnessing love is lived in community (cf. Acts).

Mt 28:16–20

This pericope is read on Ascension Day of year A and Trinity Sunday of year B. As can be seen from Chapter Five of this book, there is a wealth of materials in this text. The homilist will have to select some of them with an eye to the conditions of the community being addressed. We will develop only a few points here and refer the reader to our detailed explanation in Chapter Five for other possibilities.

Two cautionary remarks should be made. Firstly, we should avoid speaking of the final scene of Matthew's gospel in anachronistic and historically altogether incorrect terms as, e.g., 'Jesus said in fact to the disciples, already constitutionally erected in an apostolic and ecclesiastical hierarchy: "Go and teach" (Mt 28:19)'. It is true that Matthew repeatedly refers to the institutional element in the Christian community, but this does not mean that we should read a Vatican I image of the Church into his gospel!

Secondly, we should recall that, except for Luke in the Acts of the Apostles, the New Testament considers the ascension as an integral part of the Easter event. Therefore, Ascension Day should not be presented as an historical commemoration, and we should certainly not attempt to describe the 'historical circumstances' of the ascension. Almost all Easter accounts, including Mt 28:16–20, present the appearances as manifestations of the risen Christ from heaven, i.e., as manifestations of the already ascended One. In fact, Christ's words, 'All authority in heaven and on earth has been given to me' (Mt 28:18), have the same meaning as 'So then the Lord Jesus . . . sat down at the right hand of God' (Mk 16:19; cf. Acts 2:33; 5:31; 7:55–56; Rom 8:34).

A first indication for a homily can be found in the location of this appearance on a mountain. This location is usually related to the mountain of the Sermon (Mt 5:1), a possibility we will discuss below, and the mountain of the transfiguration (Mt 17:1). But we can also relate it to the mountain on which Matthew situates the third temptation (Mt 4:8). In the account of his baptism, Jesus has been designated 'Son of God' or Messiah in words reminiscent of Isa 42:1 and Ps 2:7, which describe his role as that of a Servant-Messiah. This understanding of his messianic role is challenged by the devil (cf. the twice-repeated 'If you are the Son of God', Mt 4:3, 6), who finally offers him power over all the kingdoms of the earth: 'All these I will give you . . .' (Mt 4:9). Jesus categorically rejects this proposal. He will remain faithful to his role of Servant-Messiah, even if it entails being 'obedient unto death, even death on a cross' (Phil 2:8). As a seal of approval on the life of his Messiah, God raised Jesus from the dead. And now the risen Christ stands again on a mountain and says: 'All authority in heaven and on earth has been given to me (by God)' (Mt 28:18). The power and authority Jesus refused to seize in collusion with the devil, and much more ('all authority in heaven and on earth'), is now given to him by God. As Messiah and embodiment of the true people of God (both baptism and temptation accounts recall the Exodus), Jesus said 'No' to the alluring offer of power. If he said 'No', he wants his people, the Church, to say 'No'. He wants his Church to reject the temptation of joining any kind of power play. Wherever the Church does get involved in it – and who would dare to say that it never has, in the remote as well as in the recent past; and the universal as well as the local Church – it cannot count on God's blessing. Whatever immediate gain may seem the result of the 'deal', in the long run it will be detrimental to the real good of the people of God. Only when the Church is ready to be a Servant-Church and time and again to die with Christ will it ultimately receive God's seal of approval.

Another possibility is the explanation of the words spoken by the risen Christ. The opening words about his authority echo what is said of the Son of man in Dan 7:14LXX. This statement of authority is followed by a missionary charge in three parts: Firstly, to 'make disciples' of all nations, which is apparently Matthew's rewording of the earlier expression 'to preach the gospel' (cf. Mk 16:15). From the very beginning of Christianity there was a close relation between the appearances and the command of mission, as can be seen in the use of the word 'apostle', and the terms in which Paul speaks of his own call on the road to Damascus (Gal 1:16). Secondly, the call to mission comprises the charge to baptize. Those who had not had an immediate encounter with the risen Christ were brought into the sphere of the Easter experience through baptism. The earliest Christian communities administered baptism in the name of Jesus. But the use of Jesus' name alone as a baptismal formula can be said to imply the threefold name. For baptism in the name of Jesus includes the confession of him as the Messiah; in Jewish thought Messiah means the agent of God's (the Father's) decisive intervention in salvation history; and the outpouring of the Spirit is the first and foremost gift of the messianic times. We may say, therefore, that from the very beginning Christians understood baptism in an *implicitly* trinitarian sense. This was then later made explicit. Thirdly, the command to baptize is accompanied by a charge to teach, which may refer to catechetical instruction. This will be developed further in the third suggestion for a homily. The threefold charge is then followed by a final promise of the permanent presence of the glorified Christ. The most typical element of Matthew's final pericope is certainly the great missionary charge. The homilist may try to show how this divine imperative can and must be obeyed in an age of dialogue with other religions.

Our third suggestion focuses on the words 'teaching them to observe *all that I have commanded you*' (Mt 28:20). The Eleven are told to make disciples of all nations, baptizing them and teaching them the way of discipleship as Jesus has expounded it previously in the gospel. It has long been recognized that the phrase 'all that I have commanded you' refers in the first place to the Sermon on the Mount (think of the setting of both scenes on a mountain), and further also to the other four great discourses, especially the Church or Community Discourse (Mt 18). The homilist may try to develop the characteristics of the true people of God, the Church, which Jesus orders the Eleven to build up, as these characteristics are found in Mt 5 – 7 and 18. While the Sermon on the Mount deals especially, though not exclusively (cf.

Mt 5:13–16 which certainly has a communitarian meaning), with demands of discipleship for the individual, Mt 18 describes the Church as a community of disciples who are not motivated by ambitions (who is the greatest?), and a brotherhood in which everyone is equally in need of forgiveness (Mt 18:21–35).

Lk 24:13–35

Emmaus

This pericope is read on the Third Sunday of Easter of year A and on Wednesday of the Octave of Easter.

As in our comments on the accounts of the finding of the empty tomb, we would like to start by pointing out some errors which should definitely be avoided. Again writers and homilists try to 'get beyond' the pericope itself by adding imaginative details of their own making, especially as regards their description of the characters of the story.

First, the risen Christ is often described in the most fanciful way. He is made to smile at the two disciples, there is a musical quality in his voice, and the risen Christ is recognized not only by the breaking of the bread, but by the distribution of Easter eggs as well! The risen Lord is made to exhibit the threefold art of coming close to people, conversing with them, and making them happy. It is asked what was so typical in Jesus' way of breaking the bread that it led the disciples to recognition, etc. These are all mistaken emphases caused by the failure to pay due attention to the literary form of the pericope. Furthermore, under the influence of dogmatic preoccupations, the whole account is sometimes interpreted in terms of the real presence of Christ in the offerings of bread and wine over which the 'exact words' of the consecration have been pronounced, to come to the conclusion that the meal at Emmaus was not a eucharistic celebration!

Secondly, the two disciples are made to walk in the bright sun and the temperature outside warms them inside as well: 'Did not our hearts burn within us?' (Lk 24:32). The invitation 'Stay with us, for it is toward evening' (Lk 24:29) is taken as a starting-point for considerations on evening prayer. Thus particular clauses are taken out of their context and used as pegs for the homilist's own ideas. A special interest is shown in the question why the two disciples did not recognize the risen Lord. The answers range from disappointment and anxiety to deficient theology. While these 'deficiencies' of the Emmaus disciples are condemned and lead to a series of warnings and irrelevant moralizings, their warm-heartedness and hospitality are often praised. Whatever importance may be attached to hospitality elsewhere in the Bible, it is not the primary subject of the Emmaus account.

How, then, can we develop a homily which does justice to the literary form and the true message of the pericope? Whatever may be the origin of the account, in its present form it certainly expresses the experience of early Christian worship in which the risen Christ manifests himself through the Christological interpretation of the scriptures and the breaking of the bread. The homilist could relate both points of the eucharistic liturgy to the revelation of the risen Christ and show how word and sacrament are two integral aspects of one and the same presence of Christ among the faithful. Thus the homilist may be of real help to Christians who are sometimes puzzled by the various ways in which Christ is said to be present: in the proclamation of the word, in every sacrament, and then in a very special way in the Eucharist. At the same time he can bring to the fore the chief emphasis of our resurrection faith which is not so much an event of the past as the risen Christ's abiding presence among us.

Apparently, the discouraged disciples are not prepared for any manifestation of the risen Christ. Whatever hopes they might have had belong to the past. Jesus approaches and accompanies them, but they fail to recognize him. They tell him what has happened in Jerusalem. They even know the news about the empty tomb and that angels told the women that Jesus was alive. But all this knowledge serves no purpose so long as they do not see Jesus (cf. Lk 24:24). A first decisive development takes place when Jesus refers to the scriptures and shows how the events which puzzle them so much are part of God's plan (Lk 24:25–27). But by themselves the scriptures are not enough to make the disciples recognize the risen Christ. They ask their companion to stay and during the meal the second, decisive development takes place: 'he took the bread and blessed, and broke it, and gave it to them' (Lk 24:30). At this very moment their eyes are opened by God. Through divine revelation they recognize the risen Lord in the meal they share with him. This recognition in the meal has, however, been prepared during the explanation of the scriptures: 'Did not our hearts burn within us . . . while he opened to us the scriptures?' (Lk 24:32). This experience impels them to return to Jerusalem and to witness to the risen One. But before they actually do so they are met by the confession of the Easter faith of the community: 'The Lord has risen indeed, and has appeared to Simon' (Lk 24:34).

Unlike the impression we get from some homilies which dwell extensively on the character of the two disciples, their anonymity serves to underline the importance of the event apart from the particular persons involved. Even if one of them is called Cleopas, no one is quite sure who he is. The two disciples represent everyone or, better, every disciple or aspirant disciple. The account has indeed a bearing upon the situation in which Christians of all times and places stand. It tells us that real faith is born not through any knowledge of past events or the scriptures as such, but in a meeting with the risen Christ. In many ways he meets us on our way through life, even when we fail to recognize him for a long time. We too are often still walking along speaking of shaken or lost hopes, trying to make sense of it. And then he stands besides us in one way or another. He meets us in people who live his 'new commandment', where two or three are gathered in his name, and he is 'in the midst of them' (cf. Mt 18:20), but especially in the liturgical event of the Christological interpretation of the scriptures and the breaking of the bread.

The situation of the two disciples is that of all those who have not yet received the grace of Easter faith, those who are instructed about the facts, but cannot yet see the true meaning of these facts. Whatever is said of the two disciples on the road to Emmaus is true of the 'road' every Christian has to go, perhaps more than once in a lifetime, for every step of growth contains the possibility of closing oneself to the meaning of the facts, which is then called loss of faith.

Lk 24:36–49

Lk 24:35–48 is read on the Third Sunday of Easter of year B and on Thursday of the Octave of Easter. While it is relatively easy to see that the last verse of the Emmaus account (Lk 24:35) is included in the reading to clarify the meaning of Lk 24:36, 'As they were saying this . . .', it is more difficult to understand why the lectionary omits verse 49, 'And behold I send the promise of my Father upon you . . .'. The Lutheran, Presbyterian, Methodist and United Church of Christ lectionaries all include the verse in the reading.

As shown in Chapter Seven, this gospel reading consists of a largely pre-Lucan tradition regarding an appearance of the risen Christ (Lk 24:36–43) and another pericope in which Luke succeeds in adapting the formulation of the early Christian kerygma to his own theological concerns. In Luke's redaction the appearance provides the setting for the very important words of the risen Christ (Lk 24:44–49).

The appearance account seems to be concerned with possible 'spirit-interpretations' (cf. Lk 24:27) of the revelation of the risen Christ. Belief in the *reality* of the resurrection is expressed in *real*istic terms. These realistic details, therefore, should not be taken literally, and should not be dwelt upon or expanded in the homily. It is much more important to show that the risen Christ is not just a 'spirit' or a 'soul', but that his whole person is glorified and lives on among us. In other words, the scene demonstrates the continuing identity between the Jesus whom the disciples have known and his present appearance as the Christ. The meal context suggests the association of the experience of the resurrection with the Eucharist.

Luke's real interest seems to be found in the second half of the reading (Lk 24:44–49), in which we find a unique emphasis on the scriptures and on making them an 'open book' in an altogether new way. In fact, the verb 'to open' is used three times in Luke's final chapter: in the first instance, 'their eyes were opened' (Lk 24:31), in the second, the disciples reflect on what happened to them 'while he opened to us the scriptures' (Lk 24:32), and in the third the two motifs are brought together when 'he opened their minds to understand the scriptures' (Lk 24:45). The specific character of this interpretation of scripture is expressed in three infinitives (in Greek) which indicate a continuity between the Christ who had to *suffer* and to *rise* from the dead so that repentance and forgiveness of sins could be *preached* in his name to all nations, beginning from Jerusalem (Lk 24:45–46). The middle of the three infinitives, 'to rise', binds the other two together, suggesting that only the risen Christ opens eyes (Lk 24:31) and minds (Lk 24:45), so that hesitating disciples are transformed into effective witnesses. But scripture, thus understood, is not their only guide. They will also receive the power of the Spirit, the power of God himself. Thus the end of the present gospel reading allows us to refer to Pentecost.

It may also be pointed out that in the three accounts of the tomb, the disciples on the road to Emmaus, and the group appearance, the significance of the *plan of God* in the suffering of the Messiah and his rising from the dead come repeatedly to the fore.

Lk 24:50–53

Lk 24:46–53 is read on Ascension Day of year C. We would prefer the reading to begin with verse 44. As we have discussed the first half of this reading in the preceding section we confine ourselves here to the second half, Lk 24:50–53, which deals with the ascension. We simply recall that in Lk 24:44–49 the evangelist has Jesus explain that God's saving plan expressed in the scriptures climaxes in his death and resurrection, and that its purpose is to establish a worldwide mission of the Church to offer to all men 'repentance and forgiveness of sins'. Hereby the risen Christ commissions his disciples, but before their missionary task can begin they must wait for the outpouring of the Spirit at Pentecost.

While in Acts 1 the ascension narrative is presented as inaugurating the period of the Church and looks forward to the mission of the same Church, the present account of the ascension looks backward and is presented as the conclusion of the earthly ministry of Jesus. This is the last of Jesus' appearances and a farewell scene, as can be gathered from the fact that Jesus leaves the disciples while blessing them. He, so to say, departed from them and was taken up into heaven in his attitude of blessing them. In other words, it was a lasting blessing. That is the reason why, unlike most partings, this one does not leave the disciples sad but rejoicing.

In fact, far from taking leave of the world, Jesus is now enthroned as the Lord of the world and draws near to it in a new way. The disciples, then, are by no means called to an out-of-the-world spirituality, but rather to a mission in the world. Any tendency to heavengazing is discouraged: 'Men of Galilee, why do you stand looking into heaven?' (Acts 1:11). The disciples of all times and places are called to active witness: 'you shall be my witnesses . . . to the end of the earth' (Acts 1:8). This witness may and should take on different forms in different times and situations, but it should always be the characteristic of the true disciple who knows that the Lord is present and wants us to make this presence known and experienced by all men.

Mk 16:15–20

This pericope is read on Ascension Day of year B. The gospel pericope in reality begins with verse 14, but it is understandable that the lectionary omits this verse, which says that Jesus 'upbraided them for their unbelief and hardness of heart' and therefore does not fit the occasion so well.

Again a number of things should be avoided in a homily on this text. First, concerning the presentation of Jesus' ascension itself, we should try to avoid the kind of emotional description which we find in not a few homilies. In some of them Jesus is said to make a little detour to go by Bethany in order to pay a last visit to Lazarus and his sisters. He is made to take leave of the scenes of his life either upon his arrival at the Mount of Olives, or while 'soaring' already above it, changing his look from tender and thankful when he turns to Bethlehem to stern when he directs it toward Jerusalem. He is overheard saying farewell to the world which gave him such a hard time. While he ascends he is accompanied by invisible hosts of redeemed souls and by legions of angels who do homage to him. The cloud which takes Jesus out of sight (cf. Acts 1:9; not mentioned in Mark) is situated at a height of about six hundred metres. Some homilists list the differences between Jesus' ascension and a journey into space.

Secondly, a number of homilies are occupied with the Christian's longing for heaven. The eleven disciples are represented as standing at the Mount of Olives with shining eyes looking upwards to another world there above. There often follows a moralizing rhetorical question like, e.g., whether it is too much to turn our eyes once a year away from the mundane affairs of life to the mountain of the ascension. The earth is still often considered as a place of exile where we have to earn our ticket to heaven, and the Church as a kind of travel agency helping us to prepare for the journey. In short, many a homily still encourages a flight-from-the-world piety. This approach cannot claim the ascension in its support, because the ascension of Christ does not mean his taking leave of the world, but rather his enthronement as the Lord of the world. The ascension does not remove Christ from this world, but brings him near in a new way.

How, then, can we appropriately present the message of this text? As said in Chapter Eight, the canonical ending of Mark's gospel (Mk 16:9–20) is more or less a summary of the Easter accounts found in the other gospels. Since various traditions are combined here in a rather loose sequence the passage contains several possibilities, and almost every verse could serve as a starting-point for a homily. But since we read this passage on the feast of the Ascension it seems best to start from verse 19, which does not exactly *describe* the ascension itself, but *refers to* it by means of implicit quotations from II Kgs 2:11, the assumption of Elijah, and Ps 110(109):1.

Mk 16:19 is obviously formulated according to the contemporary conception of the world. Rather than give support to an outdated cosmology, the homilist should proclaim the theological and salvific meaning of the ascension. The fact that Jesus' enthronement as king of the world is expressed in spatial categories does not mean that the homilist should present it as an immediately observable fact. He may, if need be, briefly compare the ascension and a journey into space, but only to point out that the latter is totally different from the former.

> Heaven is not a place beyond the stars. It is something much vaster and more breath-taking: it means that there is a place for man in God. This has its basis in the interpenetration of the human and divine natures in Jesus the man who was crucified and exalted ... What we call 'heaven', therefore, is actually himself. For heaven is not a space or sphere but a person, the person of him in whom God and man are for ever indivisibly one. And we are going to heaven, are indeed entering into heaven to the extent that we go to Jesus and enter into him. To that extent the term 'ascension' can be applied to a process that takes place in the midst of our everyday lives.[27]

The homilist should first of all situate the ascension in the Easter event as a whole: the risen Lord is revealed as the glorified Lord. The disciples experience first that Jesus is alive, and then that he is Lord: he is sitting at the right hand of God. In other words, the feast of the Ascension is the real feast of Christ the King, and one may wonder about the appropriateness of another feast of Christ the King on the last Sunday of the liturgical year.

Then, the homilist should radically desist from presenting the ascension in spatial categories in order not to give the impression that Jesus is now far away from us. On the contrary, it should be explained that his kingship consists in the fact that his glorified presence pervades all things. Therefore, the disciples then and now are told not to spend their time 'looking into heaven' (Acts 1:11), but to take up their mission to the world which belongs already basically to Christ, but has still to be made aware of Christ's claim.

This claim is accepted in faith or rejected in unbelief (Mk 16:16). Its proclamation by those who believe will be accompanied by signs

(Mk 16:17), which, however, should never be considered independently from faith, or used as supernatural advertisements. They are powerful acts of Christ who is the redeemer of the whole of creation and whose saving intervention affects our whole existence.

Notes

1. Richard J. Dillon, *From Eye-Witnesses to Ministers of the Word* (Analecta Biblica 82; Rome: Biblical Institute Press, 1978), pp. 18, 19–20.
2. R. J. Dillon, *ibid.*, p. 24.
3. P. F. Ellis, *Matthew: His Mind and his Message* (Collegeville, Minn.: The Liturgical Press, 1974), p. 24.
4. J. E. Alsup, *The Post-Resurrection Appearance Stories of the Gospel Tradition* (Stuttgart: Calwer Verlag/London: SPCK, 1975), pp. 159, 161.
5. J. P. Meier, 'Nations or Gentiles in Matthew 28:19?', *The Catholic Biblical Quarterly* 39 (1977), 102.
6. J. Schaberg, *The Father, the Son and the Holy Spirit: The Triadic Phrase in Matt. 28:19b* (Chico, Cal.: Scholars Press, 1982). pp. 335–6.
7. *(Midrash) Halachah*: an exposition of the Pentateuch, deriving legal principles and rules for conduct from the text.
8. G. Schrenk, '*entellomai, entolē*' in *Theological Dictionary of the New Testament* II (ed. G. Kittel; Grand Rapids: Eerdmans/London: SCM Press, 1964), p. 545.
9. Cf. *Pirke Aboth* 3, 2: 'But, when two sit and there are between them words of Torah, the Shekhinah rests between them . . .'.
10. Gen 11:28 – 12:4a; 15:1–6; 17:1–14; 17:15–27; 24:1–9; 26:1–6; 26:23–25; 28:10–22; 35:9–15; 41:37–45; 46:1–5a; Ex 3:1 – 4:16; 6:2–13; 7:1–6; Num 22:22–35; Deut 31:14–23; Jos 1:1–11; Judg 4:4–10; 6:11–24; I Sam 3:1 – 4:1a; I Kgs 19:1–19a; Isa 6; Jer 1:1–10; Ez 1:1 – 3:15; Isa 49:1–6; I Chron 22:1–16; Ezra 1:1–5.
11. Mt 14:22–33; 17:1–8; 28:1–8; 28:9–10; 28:11–15; 28:16–20; Mk 11:1–10; Ps.-Mk 16:9–20; Lk 1:5–25; 1:26–38; 2:8–18; 5:1–11; 7:20–28; 10:1–17; 15:11–31; 22:7–13; 22:14–38; 24:36–53; Acts 1:1–12; 7:30–36; 9:1–8; 9:9–18; 10:1–8; 10:9–29; 10:30–33; 11:4–17; 12:6–11; 13:1–3; 16:24–34; 22:6–11; 22:12–16; 22:17–21; 23:11; 26:12–20; 27:21–26; Jn 20:19–21; Rev 1:10–20.
12. R. J. Dillon, *From Eye-Witnesses to Ministers of the Word*, p. 122.
13. R. J. Dillon, *ibid.*, pp. 133, 138.
14. R. J. Dillon, *ibid.*, p. 107.
15. R. J. Dillon, *ibid.*, p. 93.
16. R. J. Dillon, *ibid.*, pp. 152–3.
17. G. Lohfink, *Die Himmelfahrt Jesu. Untersuchungen zu den*

Himmelfahrts- und Erhöhungstexten bei Lukas (Munich: Kösel-Verlag, 1971), pp. 147–51.

18. R. J. Dillon, *From Eye-Witnesses to Ministers of the Word*, p. 224.
19. J. E. Alsup, *The Post-Resurrection Appearance Stories*, p. 121.
20. R. E. Brown, *The Virginal Conception and Bodily Resurrection of Jesus* (New York: Paulist Press, 1973/London: Geoffrey Chapman, 1974), p. 71 n. 123.
21. R. E. Brown, *ibid.*, p. 75 n. 128.
22. N. Perrin, *The Resurrection Narratives. A New Approach* (London: SCM Press, 1977), p. 81.
23. N. Clark, *Interpreting the Resurrection* (London: SCM Press/ Philadelphia: The Westminster Press, 1967), p. 9.
24. N. Clark, *ibid.*, pp. 104–5.
25. N. Clark, *ibid.*, p. 104.
26. U. Wilckens, *Resurrection. Biblical Testimony to the Resurrection: An Historical Examination and Explanation* (Edinburgh: The Saint Andrew Press, 1977/Atlanta: John Knox Press, 1978), p. 43.
27. J. Ratzinger in *Geist und Leben* 40 (1967), 83; as quoted in translation in F. Kamphaus, *The Gospels for Preachers and Teachers* (London: Sheed and Ward, 1974), p. 110.

For Further Reading

Boff, L., *The Question of Faith in the Resurrection of Jesus* (Synthesis Series; Chicago: Franciscan Herald Press, 1972).

Brown, R. E., *The Virginal Conception and Bodily Resurrection of Jesus* (New York: Paulist Press, 1973/London: Geoffrey Chapman, 1974).

Clark, N., *Interpreting the Resurrection* (London: SCM Press/ Philadelphia: The Westminster Press, 1967).

Flood, E., *The Resurrection* (New York: Paulist Press, 1973).

Hagerman, H. G., and Beher, J. C., *Easter* (Proclamation: Aids for Interpreting the Lessons of the Church Year. Series C; Philadelphia: Fortress Press, 1974).

Léon-Dufour, X., *Resurrection and the Message of Easter* (London: Geoffrey Chapman, 1974/New York: Holt, Rinehart & Winston, 1975).

O'Collins, G., *The Resurrection of Jesus Christ* (Valley Forge, Pa.: The Judson Press, 1973)/*The Easter Jesus* (London: Darton, Longman and Todd, 1973).

O'Collins, G., *What Are They Saying about the Resurrection?* (A Deus Book; New York: Paulist Press, 1978).

Perrin, N., *The Resurrection Narratives. A New Approach* (London: SCM Press, 1977)/*The Resurrection According to Matthew, Mark, and Luke* (Philadelphia: Fortress Press, 1977).

Ramsey, A. M., *The Resurrection of Christ* (Fontana Books; London: Collins, 1961).

Rice, C., and Martyn, J. C., *Easter* (Proclamation: Aids for Interpreting the Lessons of the Church Year. Series B; Philadelphia: Fortress Press, 1975).

Richards, H. J., *The First Easter. What Really Happened?* (Fontana Books; London: Collins, 1976).

Snow, J. H., and Furnish, V. P., *Easter* (Proclamation: Aids for Interpreting the Lessons of the Church Year. Series A; Philadelphia: Fortress Press, 1975).

Wilckens, U., *Resurrection. Biblical Testimony to the Resurrection: An Historical Examination and Explanation* (Edinburgh: The

Saint Andrew Press, 1977/Atlanta: John Knox Press, 1978).
Williams, R., *Resurrection. Interpreting the Easter Gospel* (London: Darton, Longman and Todd, 1982).

General Bibliography

Ahern, B., 'Of Resurrection Theology', *Worship* 35 (1961), 293–8.

Aland, K., 'Der Schluss des Markusevangeliums' in *L'Évangile selon Marc. Tradition et rédaction* (ed. M. Sabbe; Bibliotheca Ephemeridum Theologicarum Lovaniensium 34; Louvain: Leuven University Press, 1974), pp. 435–70.

Allen, D., 'Resurrection Appearances as Evidence', *Theology Today* 30 (1973), 6–13.

Alsup, J. E., *The Post-Resurrection Appearance Stories of the Gospel Tradition* (Calwer theologische Monographien 5; Stuttgart: Calwer Verlag/ London: SPCK, 1975).

Anderson, C., 'The Resurrection of Jesus' in *The Historical Jesus: A Continuing Quest* (Grand Rapids: Eerdmans, 1972), pp. 156–78.

Anderson, H., 'The Easter Witness of the Evangelists' in *The New Testament in Historical and Contemporary Perspective. Essays in Memory of G. H. C. Macgregor* (ed. H. Anderson and W. Barclay; Oxford: Blackwell, 1965), pp. 35–55.

Anderson, T., 'Resurrection and Radical Faith', *Religious Studies* 9 (1973), 101–12.

Annand, R., '"He was seen of Cephas", a Suggestion about the First Resurrection Appearance to Peter', *Scottish Journal of Theology* 11 (1958), 180–7.

Audet, L., 'What is the Risen "Spiritual Body"?', *Theology Digest* 21 (1973), 4–7.

Barth, G., 'Matthew's Understanding of the Law' in G. Bornkamm, G. Barth and H. J. Held, *Tradition and Interpretation in Matthew* (Philadelphia: The Westminster Press/London: SCM Press, 1963), pp. 58–164.

Bartsch, H.-W., *Das Auferstehungszeugnis. Sein historisches und sein theologisches Problem* (Theologische Forschung. Wissenschaftliche Beiträge zur kirchlich-evangelische Lehre 41; Hamburg–Bergstedt: Herbert Reich, 1965).

Bartsch, H.-W., 'Das ursprüngliche Schluss der Leidensgeschichte. Überlieferungsgeschichtliche Studien zum Markus-Schluss' in *L'Évangile selon Marc. Tradition et rédaction* (ed. M. Sabbe; Bibliotheca Ephemeridum Theologicarum Lovaniensium 34; Louvain: Leuven University Press, 1974), pp. 411–33.

Bartsch, H.-W., 'Inhalt und Funktion des urchristlichen Osterglaubens', *New Testament Studies* 26 (1979–80), 180–96.

Basset, J.-C., 'Dernières paroles du ressuscité et mission de l'Église aujourd'hui (A propos de Mt 28, 18–20 et parallèles)', *Revue de Théologie et Philosophie* 114 (1982), 349–67.

Bater, R. R., 'Toward a More Biblical View of the Resurrection', *Interpretation* 23 (1969), 47–65.

Baumann, R., 'Was heisst Auferstehung Jesu? Zum Stand ihrer theologischen Interpretation', *Herder Korrespondenz* 27 (1973), 190–6.

Bavel, T. J. van, 'Verrijzenis: Grondslag of object van het geloof in Christus? (The Resurrection Foundation or Object of our Faith?)', *Tijdschrift voor Theologie* 13 (1973), 133–44.

Beare, F. W., 'Sayings on the Risen Jesus in the Synoptic Tradition: an Inquiry into their Origin and Significance' in *Christian History and Interpretation. Studies presented to John Knox* (ed. W. R. Farmer *et al.*; Cambridge: University Press, 1967), pp. 161–81.

Benoit, P., *The Passion and Resurrection of Jesus Christ* (New York: Herder and Herder/London: Darton, Longman and Todd, 1969).

Benzerath, M., Schmid, A., and Guillet, J. (eds), *La Pâque du Christ. Mystère du salut. Mélanges offerts au P. F. X. Durrwell pour son 70ᵉ anniversaire* (Lectio Divina 112; Paris: Éditions du Cerf, 1982).

Berger, K., *Die Auferstehung des Propheten und die Erhöhung des Menschensohnes. Traditionsgeschichtliche Untersuchungen zur Deutung des Geschickes Jesu in frühchristlichen Texten* (Studien zur Umwelt des Neuen Testaments 13; Göttingen: Vandenhoeck & Ruprecht, 1976).

Berghe, P. van den, 'Het Pasen van de Heer volgens de Schriften', *Tijdschrift voor Liturgie* 64 (1980), 10–21.

Betz, H. D., 'The Origin and Nature of Christian Faith According to the Emmaus Legend (Luke 24:13–32)', *Interpretation* 23 (1969), 32–46.

Beuken, W., 'De opstanding in de oudste prediking', *Verbum* 28 (1961), 270–5.

Bligh, J., 'Scripture Reading. Matching Passages, 3: The Resurrection Narratives', *The Way* 9 (1969), 148–61.

Bode, E. L., 'A Liturgical Sitz im Leben for the Gospel Tradition of the Women's Easter Visit to the Tomb of Jesus?', *The Catholic Biblical Quarterly* 32 (1970), 237–42.

Bode, E. L., *The First Easter Morning. The Gospel Accounts of the Women's Visit to the Tomb of Jesus* (Analecta Biblica 45; Rome: Biblical Institute Press, 1970).

Bode, E. L., 'On the third day according to the Scriptures', *The Bible Today* no. 48 (April 1970), 3297–303.

Bode, E. L., 'Life, Peace, Forgiveness – The Resurrection Message', *The Bible Today* no. 83 (March 1976), 718–24.

Boomershine, T. E., 'Mark 16:8 and the Apostolic Commission', *Journal of Biblical Literature* 100 (1981), 225–39.

Boomershine, T. E., and Bartholomew, G. L., 'The Narrative Technique of Mark 16:8', *ibid.*, 213–23.

Bornkamm, G., 'Der Auferstandene und der Irdische, Mt 28:16–20' in G. Bornkamm, G. Barth and H. J. Held, *Überlieferung und Auslegung im Matthäusevangelium* (6th ed.: Neukirchen-Vluyn: Neukirchener Verlag, 1970), pp. 289–310.

Bornkamm, G., Barth, G., and Held, H. J., *Tradition and Interpretation in Matthew* (New Testament Library; Philadelphia: The Westminster

Press/London: SCM Press, 1963) (trans. of earlier ed. of the preceding).

Bowman, D. J., 'The Resurrection in Mark', *The Bible Today* no. 11 (March 1964), 709–13.

Brändle, M., 'Early Christian Understanding of the Resurrection', *Theology Digest* 16 (1968), 14–17.

Brändle, M., 'Did Jesus' Tomb Have to be Empty?', *ibid.*, 18–21.

Brändle, M., 'Narratives of the Synoptics about the Tomb', *ibid.*, 22–6.

Broer, I., 'Zur heutigen Diskussion der Grabesgeschichte', *Bibel und Leben* 10 (1969), 40–52.

Broer, I., *Die Urgemeinde und das Grab Jesu: Eine Analyse der Grablegungsgeschichte im Neuen Testament* (Studien zum Alten und Neuen Testament 31; Munich: Kösel-Verlag, 1972).

Brooks, O. S., 'Matthew XXVIII. 16–20 and the Design of the First Gospel', *Journal for the Study of the New Testament* 10 (1981), 2–18.

Brown, R. E., 'The Resurrection and Biblical Criticism' in *God, Jesus, and Spirit* (ed. D. Callahan; New York: Herder and Herder/London: Geoffrey Chapman, 1969), pp. 110–22.

Brown, R. E., Donfried, K. P., and Reumann, J. (eds), *Peter in the New Testament* (New York: Paulist Press, 1973/London: Geoffrey Chapman, 1974).

Brown, S., *Apostasy and Perseverance in the Theology of Luke* (Analecta Biblica 36; Rome: Pontifical Biblical Institute, 1969).

Brown, S., 'Resurrection of Jesus in the Life of the Christian', *Worship* 45 (1971), 514–28.

Bruns, J. E., 'A Note on Mk 16:9–20', *The Catholic Biblical Quarterly* 9 (1947), 358–9.

Burkill, T. A., *Mysterious Revelation. An Examination of the Philosophy of Mark's Gospel* (Ithaca: Cornell University Press, 1963).

Campenhausen, H. von, 'The Events of Easter and the Empty Tomb' in *Tradition and Life in the Church* (Philadelphia: Fortress Press/London: Collins, 1968), pp. 42–89.

Cantinat, J., *Réflexions sur la résurrection de Jésus d'après saint Paul et saint Marc* (Paris: Gabalda, 1979).

Catchpole, D., 'The Fearful Silence of the Women at the Tomb: A Study in Markan Theology', *Journal of Theology for Southern Africa* 18 (1977), 3–10.

Clark, K. W., 'The Gentile Bias in Matthew', *Journal of Biblical Literature* 66 (1947), 165–72.

Clark, W. R., 'Jesus, Lazarus, and Others: Resuscitation or Resurrection', *Religion in Life* 49 (1980), 230–41.

Clévenot, M., 'Auferstehung – Aufstand. Lektüre von Mk 16, 1–8 und Apg 17, 1–10' in *Die Bibel als politisches Buch* (ed. D. Schirmer; Urban-Taschenbücher; Stuttgart: Kohlhammer, 1982), pp. 57–64.

Coetzee, J. C., 'De Betekenis van Kruis en Opstanding bij Rudolf Bultmann', *Neotestamentica* 4 (1970). 108–31.

Collins, J. J., 'Resurrection as Model for Christian Life', *The Bible Today* no. 83 (March 1967), 732–7.

Comblin, J., *The Resurrection in the Plan of Salvation* (Notre Dame, Ind.: Fides Publishers, 1966).

Conzelmann, H., *The Theology of St Luke* (London: Faber and Faber, 1960/New York: Harper and Row, 1961).

Coppens, J., 'Pour mieux situer et comprendre la résurrection du Christ', *Ephemerides Theologicae Lovanienses* 48 (1972), 131–8.

Cousin, H., 'Les récits de Pâques', *Lumière et Vie* 23 (no. 119; 1974), 18–34.

Crehan, J. H., 'St Peter's Journey to Emmaus', *The Catholic Biblical Quarterly* 15 (1953), 418–26.

Crossan, J. D., 'Mark and the Relatives of Jesus', *Novum Testamentum* 15 (1973), 81–113.

Crossan, J. D., 'Empty Tomb and Absent Lord (Mark 16:1–8)' in *The Passion in Mark* (ed. W. H. Kelber; Philadelphia: Fortress Press, 1976), pp. 135–52.

Cullmann, O., 'Immortality and Resurrection', *Theology Digest* 5 (1957), 86–7.

Cullmann, O., 'The Resurrection: Event and Meaning', *Christ Today* 9 (1965), 660–1.

Culpepper, R. A., 'The Passion and Resurrection in Mark', *Review and Expositor* 75 (1978), 583–600.

Curtis, K. P. G., 'Luke XXIV.12 and John XX.3–10', *Journal of Theological Studies* N.S. 22 (1971), 512–15.

Curtis, K. P. G., 'Three Points of Contact Between Matthew and John in the Burial and Resurrection Narratives', *Journal of Theological Studies* N.S. 23 (1972), 440–4.

Dache, M., 'The Lord's Apparitions and the Resurrection. Research into the Attitudes of Adolescents Receiving Religious Instruction', *Lumen Vitae* 26 (1971), 461–8.

Davies, J. G., 'Factors Leading to the Emergence of Belief in the Resurrection of the Flesh', *Journal of Theological Studies* N.S. 23 (1972), 448–55.

Davis, C., 'The End of the World: the Resurrection', *Worship* 34 (1960), 185–8.

Davis, C., 'The Resurrection of the Body', *Theology Digest* 8 (1960), 99–103.

Delorme, J., 'The Resurrection and Jesus' Tomb: Mark 16, 1–8 in the Gospel Tradition' in *The Resurrection and Modern Biblical Thought* (ed. P. de Surgy; New York: Corpus Books, 1970), pp. 74–106.

Derrett, J. D. M., *The Anastasis: The Resurrection of Jesus as an Historical Event* (Shipston-on-Stour, Warwickshire: P. Drinkwater, 1982).

Descamps, A., 'La structure des récits évangéliques de la résurrection', *Biblica* 40 (1959), 726–41.

Desreumaux, J., 'Les disciples d'Emmaüs', *Bible et Vie Chrétienne* 56 (1964), 45–56.

Dhanis, E., 'L'ensevelissement de Jésus et la visite au tombeau dans l'évangile de Marc (Mc XV, 40 – XVI, 8)', *Gregorianum* 39 (1958), 367–410.

Dillon, R. J., *From Eye-Witnesses to Ministers of the Word* (Analecta Biblica 82; Rome: Biblical Institute Press, 1978).

Dillon, R. J., 'Easter Revelation and Mission Program in Luke 24:46–48' in *Sin, Salvation and the Spirit* (ed. D. Durken; Collegeville, Minn.: The Liturgical Press, 1980), pp. 240–70.

Dodd, C. H., 'The Appearances of the Risen Christ: a Study in Form-Criticism of the Gospels' in *More New Testament Studies* (Manchester: University Press/Grand Rapids: Eerdmans, 1968), pp. 102–33.

Donne, B. K., 'The Significance of the Ascension of Jesus Christ in the New Testament', *Scottish Journal of Theology* 30 (1977), 555–68.

Doré, J., 'Croire en la résurrection de Jésus-Christ', *Études* no. 356 (1982), 525–42.

Drane, J. W., 'Some Ideas of Resurrection in the New Testament Period', *Tyndale Bulletin* 24 (1973), 99–110.

Dumm, D., 'Luke 24:44–49 and Hospitality' in *Sin, Salvation and the Spirit* (ed. D. Durken; Collegeville, Minn.: The Liturgical Press, 1980), pp. 231–9.

Dummett, M., 'Biblical Exegesis and the Resurrection', *New Blackfriars* 58 (no. 681; 1977), 56–72.

Dunlop, L., 'The Resurrection and a Modern Theory', *Australasian Catholic Record* 50 (1973), 101–12.

Dupont, J., 'Ressuscité "le troisième jour"', *Biblica* 40 (1959), 742–61.

Dupont, J., 'The Meal at Emmaus' in *The Eucharist in the New Testament* (ed. J. Delorme; London: Geoffrey Chapman, 1964/Baltimore: Helicon Press, 1965), pp. 105–21.

Dupont, J., 'Les discours de Pierre dans les Actes et le chapitre XXIV de l'évangile de Luc' in *L'Évangile de Luc. Problèmes littéraires et théologiques* (ed. F. Neirynck; Bibliotheca Ephemeridum Theologicarum Lovaniensium 32; Gembloux: Éditions J. Duculot, 1973), pp. 329–74.

Dupont, J., 'La portée christologique de l'évangelisation des nations d'après Luc 24,47' in *Neues Testament und Kirche* (ed. J. Gnilka; Freiburg: Herder, 1974), pp. 125–43.

Dupont, J., 'Les disciples d'Emmaüs' in *La Pâque du Christ. Mystère de salut* (ed. M. Benzerath, A. Schmid and J. Guillet; Lectio Divina 112; Paris: Éditions du Cerf, 1982), pp. 167–95.

Durrwell, F. X., *The Resurrection: A Biblical Study* (London/New York: Sheed and Ward, 1960).

Ebert, H., 'Die Krise des Osterglaubens. Zur Diskussion über die Auferstehung Jesu', *Hochland* 60 (1968), 305–31.

Ehrhardt, A., 'The Disciples of Emmaus', *New Testament Studies* 10 (1963–64), 182–201.

Ellis, I. P., 'But Some Doubted', *New Testament Studies* 14 (1967–68), 547–80.

Ernst, J., 'Schriftauslegung und Auferstehungsglaube bei Lukas', *Theologie und Glaube* 60 (1970), 360–74.

Evans, C. F., 'I will go before you into Galilee', *Journal of Theological Studies* N.S. 5 (1954), 3–18.

Evans, C. F., *Resurrection and the New Testament* (Studies in Biblical Theology, 2nd series, 12; London: SCM Press/Naperville, Ill.: A. R. Allenson, 1970).

Farmer, W. R., *The Last Twelve Verses of Mark* (Society for New Testament Studies Monograph Series 25; Cambridge University Press, 1974).

Feehan, M., 'The Meaning of the Resurrection: A Personal Inquiry', *The Bible Today* no. 84 (April 1976), 813–19.

Feuillet, A., 'Les pèlerins d'Emmaüs (Lc 24, 13–35)', *Nova et Vetera* 47 (1972), 89–98.

Feuillet, A., 'La découverte du tombeau vide en Jean 20, 3–10 et la Foi au Christ Ressuscité', *Esprit et Vie* 87 (18; 1977), 257–66.

Feuillet, A., 'L'Apparition du Christ à Marie-Madeleine, Jean 20, 11–18. Comparaison avec l'apparition aux disciples d'Emmaüs, Luc 24, 13–35', *Esprit et Vie* 88 (12–13; 1978), 193–204; (14; 1978), 209–23.

Fischer, B., 'The Risen Christ and the Liturgy', *Theology Digest* 8 (1960), 123–6.

Fischer, K. M., *Das Ostergeschehen* (Aufsätze und Vorträge zur Theologie und Religionswissenschaft 71; Berlin: Evangelische Verlagsanstalt, 1978).

Flanagan, N. M., 'Preaching Easter – Body, Bread, Brethren', *The Bible Today* no. 83 (March 1976), 725–31.

Ford, L. S., 'The Resurrection as the Emergence of the Body of Christ', *Religion in Life* 42 (1973), 466–77.

Frankemölle, H., 'Amtskritik im Matthäus-Evangelium?', *Biblica* 54 (1973), 247–62.

Frankemölle, H., *Jahwebund und Kirche Christi. Studien zur Form- und Traditionsgeschichte des 'Evangeliums' nach Matthäus* (Neutestamentliche Abhandlungen, N.F. 10; Münster: Aschendorff, 1974).

Franklin, E., *Christ the Lord. A Study in the Purpose and Theology of Luke-Acts* (London: SPCK/Philadelphia: The Westminster Press, 1975).

Freudenberg, W., *Ist er wirklich auferstanden? Eine Untersuchung der biblischen Auferstandungsberichte* (Wuppertal: Brockhaus, 1977).

Freyne, S., 'Some Recent Writing on the Resurrection', *Irish Theological Quarterly* 38 (1971), 144–63.

Friedrich, G., 'The Meaning of Jesus Being Raised', *Theology Digest* 21 (1973), 12–16.

Fuchs, E., and Künneth, W., *Die Auferstehung Jesu Christi von den Toten. Dokumentation eines Streitgesprächs* (Neukirchen-Vluyn: Neukirchener Verlag, 1973).

Füssel, K., 'Auferstehung – Einstieg in die unendliche Geschichte' in *Die Bibel als politisches Buch* (ed. D. Schirmer; Urban-Taschenbücher; Stuttgart: Kohlhammer, 1982), pp. 65–72.

Fuller, D. P., 'The Resurrection of Jesus and the Historical Method', *Journal of Bible and Religion* 34 (1966), 18–24.

Fuller, D. P., *Easter Faith and History* (Grand Rapids: Eerdmans, 1973).

Fuller, R. H., *The Formation of the Resurrection Narratives* (New York: The Macmillan Company, 1971/London: SPCK, 1972).

Fuller, R. H., *Preaching the New Lectionary: The Word of God for the Church Today* (Collegeville, Minn.: The Liturgical Press, 1974).

Galvin, J. P., 'Resurrection as Theologia Crucis Jesu: The Foundational Christology of Rudolf Pesch', *Theological Studies* 38 (1977), 513–25.

Galvin, J. P., 'The Resurrection of Jesus in Contemporary Catholic Systematics', *Heythrop Journal* 20 (1979), 123–45.

Galvin, J. P., 'A Recent Jewish View of the Resurrection', *Expository Times* 91 (1979–80), 277–9.

Gatzweiler, K., 'La Résurrection de Jésus, ses Répercussions dans l'Histoire', *Revue Ecclésiastique de Liége* 53 (1967), 257–84.

Geering, L., *Resurrection: A Symbol of Hope* (London/Toronto: Hodder and Stoughton, 1971).

Geffré, C., 'Die Auferstehung Christi in heutiger Theologie', *Theologie der Gegenwart* 16 (1973), 39–46.

George, A., 'The Accounts of the Appearances to the Eleven from Luke 24, 36–53' in *The Resurrection and Modern Biblical Thought* (ed. P. de Surgy; New York: Corpus Books, 1970), pp. 49–73.

Gerits, H., 'Le message pascal au tombeau (Lc 24,1–12). La résurrection selon la présentation de Luc', *Estudios Teológicos* 8 (1981), 3–63.

Gesché, A., 'De Verrijzenis van Jesus en de Heilsgeschiedenis', *Getuigenis* 13 (1969), 153–61.

Gibbs, J. M., 'Luke 24:13–33 and Acts 8:26–39: The Emmaus Incident and the Eunuch's Baptism as Parallel Stories', *Bangalore Theological Forum* 7 (1975), 17–30.

Gibert, P., *La résurrection du Christ. Le témoignage du Nouveau Testament. De l'histoire à la foi: Croire aujourd'hui* (Paris/Montreal: Desclée de Brouwer/Bellarmin, 1975).

Giblin, C. H., 'Structural and Thematic Correlations in the Matthean Burial-Resurrection Narrative (Matt. XXVII. 57 – XXVIII. 20)', *New Testament Studies* 21 (1974–75), 406–20.

Giblin, C. H., 'A Note on Doubt and Reassurance in Mt 28:16–20', *The Catholic Biblical Quarterly* 37 (1975), 68–75.

Gils, F., 'Pierre et la foi au Christ ressuscité', *Ephemerides Theologicae Lovanienses* 38 (1962), 5–43.

Gisel, P., 'La résurrection ou l'irruption de la souveraineté de Dieu. Remarques à partir de E. Käsemann', *Quatre Fleuves* 15–16 (1982), 131–44.

Gnilka, J., 'Der Missionsauftrag des Herrn nach Mt 28 und Apg 1', *Bibel und Leben* 9 (1968), 1–9.

Gollwitzer, H., *Jesu Tod und Auferstehung nach dem Bericht des Lukas* (Kaiser Traktate 44; Munich: Kaiser Verlag, 1979).

González-Ruíz, J.-M., 'Redemption and Resurrection', *Concilium* no. 11 (I.2; 1966), 66–87.

Goppelt, L., 'Das Osterkerygma heute' in *Christologie und Ethik. Gesammelte Aufsätze* (Göttingen, 1968), pp. 79–101.

Goppelt, L., 'Die Auferstehung Jesu in der Kritik, ihr Sinn und ihre Glaubwürdigkeit' in *Grundlagen des Glaubens* (ed. P. Rieger and J. Strauss; Tutzinger Texte; Munich: Kösel-Verlag, 1970), pp. 55–74.

Goulder, M. D., 'The Empty Tomb', *Theology* 79 (no. 670; 1976), 206–14.

Goulder, M. D., 'Mark XVI.1–8 and Parallels', *New Testament Studies* 24 (1977–78), 235–40.

Gourgues, M., *A la droite de Dieu. Résurrection de Jésus et actualisation du psaume 110:1 dans le Nouveau Testament* (Paris: Gabalda, 1978).

Gourgues, M., 'A propos du symbolisme christologique et baptismal de Marc 16,5', *New Testament Studies* 27 (1981), 672–8.

Grabner-Haider, A., 'Leibliches Dasein und neue Auferstehungsleiblichkeit in der Katechese', *Katechetische Blätter* 93 (1968), 143–7.

Grabner-Haider, A., 'The Biblical Understanding of "Resurrection" and "Glorification"', *Concilium* no. 41 (I.5; 1969), 66–81.

Grass, H., *Ostergeschehen und Osterberichte* (Göttingen: Vandenhoeck & Ruprecht, 1962).

Grassi, J. A., 'Emmaus Revisited (Luke 24, 13–35 and Acts 8, 26–40)', *The Catholic Biblical Quarterly* 26 (1964), 463–7.

Grassi, J. A., 'The Resurrection and the Ezechiel Panel of the Dura-Europos Synagogue', *The Bible Today* no. 11 (March 1964), 721–6.

Grelot, P., 'La résurrection de Jésus et l'histoire. Historicité et historialité', *Quatre Fleuves* 15–16 (1982), 145–79.

Guillaume, J. M., *Luc. Interprète des anciennes traditions sur la résurrection de Jésus* (Paris: Gabalda, 1977).

Guillet, J., 'Die Mitte der Botschaft: Jesu Tod und Auferstehung', *Internationale Katholische Zeitschrift/Communio* 2 (1973), 225–38.

Guillet, J., 'Die Bezeugung der Auferstehung nach der Apostelgeschichte', *Internationale Katholische Zeitschrift/Communio* 11 (1982), 21–31.

Guillet, J., 'Les récits évangéliques de la résurrection', *Quatre Fleuves* 15–16 (1982), 7–21.

Gutwenger, E., 'The Narration of Jesus' Resurrection', *Theology Digest* 16 (1968), 8–13.

Hahn, F., *Mission in the New Testament* (Studies in Biblical Theology 47; London: SCM Press/Naperville, Ill.: A. R. Allenson, 1965).

Hamilton, N. Q., 'Resurrection Tradition and the Composition of Mark', *Journal of Biblical Literature* 84 (1965), 415–21.

Hare, D., and Harrington, D., ' "Make Disciples of All Nations" (Matthew 28: 19)', *The Catholic Biblical Quarterly* 37 (1975), 359–69.

Hebblethwaite, P., 'Theological Themes in the Lucan Post-Resurrection Narratives', *The Clergy Review* 50 (1965), 360–9.

Hengel, M., 'Ist der Osterglaube noch zu retten?', *Theologische Quartalschrift* 153 (1973), 252–69.

Hilger, G., 'Der Herr ist wirklich auferstanden. Lk 24,13–35 und 36–49 in der Katechese des 3. und 4. Schuljahres', *Katechetische Blätter* 94 (1969), 129–43.

Holtz, F., 'La valeur sotériologique de la Résurrection du Christ', *Ephemerides Theologicae Lovanienses* 29 (1953), 609–45.

Holtz, F., 'The Soteriological Value of the Resurrection of Christ', *Theology Digest* 3 (1955), 101–6.

Hooke, S. H., *The Resurrection of Christ as History and Experience* (London: Darton, Longman and Todd, 1967).

Horst, P. W. van der, 'Can a Book end with gar? A Note on Mark XVI, 8', *Journal of Theological Studies* N.S. 23 (1972), 121–4.

Horvath, T., 'The Early Markan Tradition on the Resurrection', *Revue de l'Université d'Ottawa* 43 (1973), 445–8.

Hoskyns, E. C., and Davey, N., *Crucifixion – Resurrection. The Pattern of Theology and Ethics of the New Testament* (London: SPCK, 1981).

Howe, E. M., ' "But Some Doubted" (Matt. 28:17). A Re-Appraisal of Factors Influencing the Easter Faith of the Early Christian Community', *Journal of the Evangelical Theological Society* 18 (1975), 173–80.

Hubbard, B. J., *The Matthean Redaction of a Primitive Apostolic Commissioning: An Exegesis of Matthew 28:16–20* (Society of Biblical Literature Dissertation Series 19; Missoula, Mont.: University of Montana, 1974).

Huffman, N., 'Emmaus among the Resurrection Narratives', *Journal of Biblical Literature* 64 (1945), 205–26.

Hug, J., *La finale de l'évangile de Marc (Mc 16, 9–20)* (Paris: Gabalda, 1978).

Iersel, B. van, 'Terug van Emmaüs: Bijdragen tot een structurele tekstanalyse van Lc 24, 13–35', *Tijdschrift voor Theologie* 18 (1978), 294–323.

Iersel, B. van, ' "To Galilee" or "in Galilee" in Mark 14,28 and 16,7', *Ephemerides Theologicae Lovanienses* 58 (1982), 365–70.

Jansen, J. F., *The Resurrection of Jesus Christ in New Testament Theology* (Philadelphia: The Westminster Press, 1979).

Janssen, J., 'De verrijzenisverhalen in Lucas 24', *Getuigenis* 27 (1983), 99–106.

Jeanne d'Arc, Soeur, *Les pèlerins d'Emmaüs* (Lire la Bible 47; Paris: Éditions du Cerf, 1977).

Jeanne d'Arc, Soeur, 'Catechesis on the Road to Emmaus', *Lumen Vitae* 32 (1977), 143–56.

Jeanne d'Arc, Soeur, 'Un grand jeu d'inclusions dans "les pèlerins d'Emmaüs"', *Nouvelle Revue Théologique* 99 (1977), 62–76.

Jeremias, J., 'Die Drei-Tage-Worte der Evangelien' in *Tradition und Glaube* (ed. G. Jeremias, H. W. Kuhn and H. Stegemann; Göttingen: Vandenhoeck & Ruprecht, 1971), pp. 221–9.

Joseph, M. J., 'Risen Christ in the Theology of St Paul', *BibleBhashyam* 3 (1977), 116–30.

Kahmann, J., '"Il est ressuscité, le crucifié", Marc 16,6a et sa place dans l'évangile de Marc' in *La Pâque du Christ. Mystère de salut* (ed. M. Benzerath, A. Schmid and J. Guillet; Lectio Divina 112; Paris: Éditions du Cerf, 1982), pp. 121–30.

Kamphaus, F., *The Gospels for Preachers and Teachers* (London: Sheed and Ward, 1974).

Kannengieser, C., *Foi en la résurrection: résurrection de la foi* (Le point théologique 9; Paris: Beauchesne, 1974).

Kelber, W., *The Kingdom in Mark. A New Place and a New Time* (Philadelphia: Fortress Press, 1974).

Kerr, F., 'Recent Catholic Writing on the Resurrection: (1) The Empty Tomb Story; (2) The Appearance Stories', *New Blackfriars* 58 (1977), 453–61, 506–15.

Kesich, V., *The First Day of the New Creation: The Resurrection and the Christian Faith* (Crestwood, N.Y.: St Vladimir's Seminary Press, 1982).

Kienzler, K., *Logik der Auferstehung. Eine Untersuchung zu R. Bultmann, G. Ebeling, und W. Pannenberg* (Freiburger theologische Studien 100; Freiburg/Basel/Vienna: Herder, 1976).

Kingsbury, J. D., 'The Composition and Christology of Matt 28:16–20', *Journal of Biblical Literature* 93 (1974). 573–84.

Kingsbury, J. D., *Matthew: Structure, Christology, Kingdom* (Philadelphia: Fortress Press, 1975/London: SPCK, 1976).

Kingsbury, J. D., 'Expository Article. Luke 24:44–49', *Interpretation* 35 (1981), 170–4.

Klappert, B., 'Legitimationsformel und Erscheinungsüberlieferung. Zur Formkritik der neutestamentliche Auferstehungstraditionen. Eine Anfrage an U. Wilckens', *Theologische Beiträge* 5 (1974), 67–81.

Knackstedt, H. O., 'Die Geschichte vom leeren Grab in der Katechese', *Katechetische Blätter* 93 (1968), 135–42.

Knoch, O., ' "Machet alle Völker zu meinen Jünger!" Die Botschaft des Evangeliums nach Matthäus', *Bibel und Kirche* 26 (1971), 65–9.

Kolping, A., 'Zur Entstehung des Glaubens an die Auferstehung Jesu', *Münchener Theologische Zeitschrift* 26 (1971), 56–69.

Kolping, A., 'Um den Realitätscharacter der Ostererscheinungen', *Theologische Revue* 73 (1977), 441–50.

Kratz, R., *Auferweckung als Befreiung. Eine Studie zur Passions- und Auferstehungstheologie des Matthäus (besonders Mt 27:65–28:15)* (Stuttgarter Bibelstudien 65; Stuttgart: KBW Verlag, 1973).

Kremer, J., *Die Osterbotschaft der vier Evangelien. Versuch einer Auslegung der Berichte über das leere Grab und die Erscheinungen des Auferstandenen* (Stuttgarter Bibelstudien; Stuttgart: KBW Verlag, 1968).

Kremer, J., 'Ist Jesus wirklich von den Toten auferstanden?', *Stimmen der Zeit* 94 (1969), 310–20.

Kremer, J., *Die Osterevangelien – Geschichten um Geschichte* (Stuttgart: Katholisches Bibelwerk, 1977).

Kremer, J., 'Auferstanden – auferweckt', *Biblische Zeitschrift* 23 (1979), 97–8.

Kress, R., 'Resurrection Faith: Life or Fuga Mundi?', *Review for Religious* 32 (1973), 97–101.

Küng, H., 'The Origins of Resurrection Belief', *Theology Digest* 23 (1975), 136–42.

Lacoste, J.-Y., 'Du droit de l'histoire au droit de Dieu: sur la résurrection de Jésus', *Nouvelle Revue Théologique* 104 (1982), 495–531.

Ladd, G. E., *I Believe in the Resurrection of Jesus* (Grand Rapids: Eerdmans/ London: Hodder and Stoughton, 1975).

Lambrecht, J., 'The Events surrounding the Resurrection of Jesus', *Revue Africaine de Théologie* 5 (1981), 183–95.

Lambrecht, J., *Daar komt toch eens . . . Opstellen over verrijzenis en eeuwig leven* (Nike-reeks. Theologische en pastorale publicaties. Faculteit van Godgeleerdheid; Leuven: Acco, 1981).

Lambrecht, J., 'De betekenis van Jezus' verrijzenis voor de christen nu', *Internationaal Katholiek Tijdschrift/Communio* 7 (1982), 16–25.

Lampe, G., 'The Resurrection', *Epworth Review* 3 (1976), 88–99.

Lange, J., *Das Erscheinen des Auferstandenen im Evangelium nach Matthäus. Eine traditions- und redaktionsgeschichtliche Untersuchung zu Mt 28, 16–20* (Forschung zur Bibel 11; Würzburg: Echter Verlag, 1973).

Langkammer, H., 'Tod und Auferweckung Jesu Christi im urchristlichen Kerygma', *Münchener Theologische Zeitschrift* 33 (1982), 44–53.

Lapide, P., *Auferstehung. Ein jüdisches Glaubenserlebnis* (Munich: Kösel-Verlag, 1977).

LaVerdiere, E. A., 'The Ascension of the Risen Lord', *The Bible Today* no. 95 (March 1978), 1553–9.

Leaney, A. R. C., 'Jesus and Peter. The Call and Postresurrection Appearance (Lk V, 1–11 and XXIV, 34)', *Expository Times* 65 (1954), 381–2.

Leaney, A. R. C., 'The Resurrection Narratives in Luke (XXIV.12–53)', *New Testament Studies* 2 (1955–56), 110–14.

Legault, A., 'Christophanies et Angélophanies dans les récits évangéliques de la Résurrection', *Science et Esprit* 21 (1969), 443–57.

Legrand, L., 'The Resurrection of Christ', *BibleBhashyam* 1 (1975), 247–55.

Legrand, L., 'Christ the Fellow Traveller. The Emmaus Story in Luke 24·13–35', *Indian Theological Studies* 19 (1982), 33–44.

Lehmann, K., *Auferweckt am dritten Tage nach der Schrift* (Quaestiones Disputatae 38; Freiburg: Herder, 1968).

Lehmann, K., 'Die Erscheinungen des Herrn. Thesen zur hermeneutisch-theologischen Struktur der Ostererzählungen' in *Theologisches Jahrbuch 1976* (ed. W. Ernst; Leipzig: St. Benno Verlag, 1976), pp. 145–58.

Lehmann, K., 'Het Emmaüsverhaal, een toegang tot het Paasgebeuren van-daag', *Internationaal Katholiek Tijdschrift/Communio* 7 (1982), 54–60.

Léon-Dufour, X., 'Bulletin d'Exégèse du Nouveau Testament. II. Sur la résurrection de Jésus', *Recherches de Science Religieuse* 57 (1969), 583–622.

Léon-Dufour, X., 'Resurrection as Victory of Love', *Theology Digest* 21 (1973), 111–12.

Liefeld, W. L., 'Exegetical Notes: Luke 24:13–35', *Trinity Journal* 2 (1981), 223–9.

Lindemann, A., 'Die Osterbotschaft des Markus. Zur theologischen Interpretation von Mark. 16.1–8', *New Testament Studies* 26 (1979–80), 298–317.

Lindijer, C. H., 'Two Creative Encounters in the Work of Luke (Lk XXIV, 13–35 and Acts VIII, 26–40)' in *Miscellanea Neotestamentica II* (ed. T. Baarda, A. F. J. Klijn and W. C. van Unnik; Leiden: Brill, 1978), pp. 77–86.

Loewe, W., 'The Appearances of the Risen Lord: Faith, Fact, and Objectivity', *Horizons* 6 (1979), 177–92.

Loewen, H., 'The Great Commission', *Direction* 7 (1978), 33–5.

Lohfink, G., 'The Resurrection of Jesus and Historical Criticism', *Theology Digest* 17 (1969), 110–14.

Lohfink, G., *Die Himmelfahrt Jesu. Untersuchungen zu den Himmelfahrts- und Erhöhungstexten bei Lukas* (Studien zum Alten und Neuen Testament 24; Munich: Kösel-Verlag, 1971).

Lohfink, G., 'Der Ablauf der Osterereignisse und die Anfänge der Urgemeinde', *Theologische Quartalschrift* 160 (1980), 162–76.

Lohr, C. H., 'Oral Techniques in the Gospel of Matthew', *The Catholic Biblical Quarterly* 23 (1961), 403–35.

Lohse, E., *Die Auferstehung Jesu Christi im Zeugnis des Lukasevangeliums* (Neukirchen-Vluyn: Neukirchener Verlag, 1961).

Longstaff, T. R. W., 'The Women at the Tomb: Matthew 28:1 Re-examined', *New Testament Studies* 27 (1980–81), 277–82.

Lubsczyk, H., 'Kyrios Jesus. Beobachtungen und Gedanken zum Schluss des Markusevangeliums' in *Die Kirche des Anfangs. Festschrift für H. Schürmann* (ed. R. Schnackenburg, J. Ernst and J. Wanke; Leipzig: St Benno Verlag, 1977), pp. 133–74.

Luz, U., 'Die Jünger im Matthäusevangelium', *Zeitschrift für die neutestamentliche Wissenschaft* 66 (1971), 141–71.

Lyonnet, S., 'Redemptive Value of the Resurrection', *Theology Digest* 8 (1960), 89–93.

Lyonnet, S., 'Redemption through Death and Resurrection', *Worship* 35 (1961), 281–7.

McArthur, H. K., 'On the Third Day', *New Testament Studies* 18 (1971–72), 81–6.

McConnell, R. S., *Law and Prophecy in Matthew's Gospel. The Authority and Use of the Old Testament in the Gospel of St Matthew* (Basel: Reinhardt Kommissionsverlag, 1969).

McGovern, J. J., 'Mission Commands – Programs for Humanity', *The Bible Today* no. 73 (November 1974), 36–46.

McHugh, J., 'The Origins and Growth of the Gospel Traditions. III. The Resurrection', *The Clergy Review* 58 (1973), 162–75.

Mackowski, R. M., 'Where is Biblical Emmaus?', *Science et Esprit* 32 (1980), 93–103.

McNulty, T. M., 'The "Secular" Meaning of Easter', *Theology Digest* 22 (1974), 114–16.

Mahoney, R., *Two Disciples at the Tomb. The Background and Message of John 20.1–10* (Theologie und Wirklichkeit 6; Berne/Frankfurt am Main: H. Lang/P. Lang, 1974).

Malina, B., 'The Literary Structure and Form of Matt. XXVIII.16–20', *New Testament Studies* 17 (1970–71), 87–103.

Mangatt, G., 'At the Tomb of Jesus', *BibleBhashyam* 3 (1977), 91–6.

Marin, L., 'Die Frauen am Grabe. Versuch einer Strukturanalyse an einem Text des Evangeliums' in *Erzählende Semiotik nach Berichten der Bibel* (ed. C. Chabrol and L. Marin; Munich: Kösel-Verlag, 1973) pp. 67–85.

Marshall, I., 'The Resurrection of Jesus in Luke', *Tyndale Bulletin* 24 (1973), 55–98.

Martini, C. M., 'The Witness concerning the Resurrection', *Theology Digest* 22 (1974), 109–13.

Marxsen, W., *Die Auferstehung Jesu als historisches und als theologisches Problem* (Gütersloh: Verlagshaus Gerd Mohn, 1964).

Marxsen, W., *Mark the Evangelist* (trans. R. A. Harrisville *et al.*; Nashville, Tenn.: Abingdon, 1969).

Marxsen, W., *The Resurrection of Jesus of Nazareth* (Philadelphia: Fortress Press/London: SCM Press, 1970) (trans. of *Die Auferstehung* above).

Matthey, J., 'The Great Commission according to Matthew', *International Review of Mission* 69 (247; 1980), 161–73.

Meier, J. P., *Law and History in Matthew's Gospel* (Analecta Biblica 71; Rome: Biblical Institute Press, 1976).

Meier, J. P., 'Nations or Gentiles in Matthew 28:19?', *The Catholic Biblical Quarterly* 39 (1977), 94–102.

Meier, J. P., 'Two Disputed Questions in Matt. 28:16–20', *Journal of Biblical Literature* 96 (1977), 407–24.

Menoud, P., 'Observations on the Ascension in Luke-Acts' in *Jesus Christ and the Faith. A Collection of Studies by Ph. H. Menoud* (Pittsburgh: The Pickwick Press, 1978), pp. 107–20.

Merklein, H., 'Die Auferstehung Jesu und die Anfänge der Christologie', *Zeitschrift für die neutestamentliche Wissenschaft* 72 (1981), 1–26.

Meye, R. P., *Jesus and the Twelve. Discipleship and Revelation in Mark's Gospel* (Grand Rapids: Eerdmans, 1968).

Meynet, R., 'Comment établir un chiasme. A propos des "Pèlerins d'Emmaüs"', *Nouvelle Revue Théologique* 100 (1978), 233–49.

Michiels, R., 'Notre foi dans le Seigneur ressuscité', *Collectanea Mechliniensia* 55 (1970), 227–53.

Minear, P. S., *To Heal and to Reveal. The Prophetic Vocation according to Luke* (New York: The Seabury Press, 1976).

Minear, P. S., *To Die and to Live: Christ's Resurrection and Christian Vocation* (New York: The Seabury Press, 1977).

Moore, S., 'The Resurrection: A Confusing Paradigm-Shift', *Downside Review* 98 (333, 1980), 257–66.

Morlet, M., 'La Résurrection du Christ. Où en est la recherche exégétique actuelle?', *Esprit et Vie. Ami du Clergé* 79 (1969), 601–6.

Moule, C. F. D., 'St Mark XVI.8, Once More', *New Testament Studies* 2 (1955–56), 58–59.

Moule, C. F. D., 'The Post-Resurrection Appearances in the Light of Festival Pilgrimages', *New Testament Studies* 4 (1957–58), 58–61.

Moule, C. F. D. (ed.), *The Significance of the Message of the Resurrection for Faith in Jesus Christ* (Studies in Biblical Theology, 2nd series, 8; London: SCM Press/Naperville, Ill.: A. R. Allenson, 1968).

Mouson, J., *et al.*, *De Verrezen Heer. Een exegetische, theologische en catechetische benadering* (Antwerp: Patmos, 1969).

Muddiman, J., 'A Note on Reading Luke XXIV, 12', *Ephemerides Theologicae Lovanienses* 48 (1972), 542–8.

Mullins, T. Y., 'New Testament Commission Forms, Especially in Luke-Acts', *Journal of Biblical Literature* 95 (1976), 603–14.

Mussner, F., *Die Auferstehung Jesu* (Biblische Handbibliothek 7; Munich: Kösel-Verlag, 1969).

Nauck, W., 'Die Bedeutung des leeren Grabes für den Glauben an den Auferstandenen', *Zeitschrift für die neutestamentliche Wissenschaft* 47 (1956), 243–76.

Navone, J., *Themes of St Luke* (Rome: Gregorian University Press, 1970).

Neirynck, F., 'La rédaction matthéenne et la structure du premier Évangile' in *De Jésus aux Évangiles. Tradition et rédaction dans les Évangiles synoptiques* (ed. I. de la Potterie; Bibliotheca Ephemeridum Theologicarum Lovaniensium 25; Gembloux: Éditions J. Duculot, 1967), pp. 41–73.

Neirynck, F., 'Les femmes au tombeau: Étude de la rédaction matthéenne (Mt 28, 1–10)', *New Testament Studies* 15 (1968–69), 168–90.

Neirynck, F., 'The Uncorrected Historic Present in Lk XXIV.12', *Ephemerides Theologicae Lovanienses* 48 (1972), 548–53.

Neirynck, F., 'Le récit du tombeau vide dans l'évangile de Luc (Lc 24, 1–12)' in *Miscellanea J. Vergote. Orientalia Lovaniensia Periodica* 6–7 (1975–76), pp. 427–41.

Neirynck, F., '*Parakupsas blepei*. Lc 24, 12 et Jn 20, 5', *Ephemerides Theologicae Lovanienses* 53 (1977), 113–52.

Neirynck, F., '*Anateilantos tou hēliou* (Mc 16, 2)', *Ephemerides Theologicae Lovanienses* 54 (1978), 70–103.

Neirynck, F., '*Apēlthen pros heauton* (Lc. 24, 12 et Jn 20, 10)', *ibid.*, 104–18.

Neirynck, F., 'Lc XXIV. 12. Les témoins du texte occidental' in *Miscellanea Neotestamentica* I (ed. T. Baarda, A. F. J. Klijn and W. C. van Unnik; Leiden: Brill, 1978), pp. 45–60.

Neirynck, F., 'Marc 16, 1–8. Tradition et rédaction. Tombeau vide et angélophanie', *Ephemerides Theologicae Lovanienses* 56 (1980), 56–88.

Newman, J., 'The Resurrection', *The Furrow* 33 (1982), 531–9.

Nicolas, M.-J., 'La Résurrection du Christ', *Revue Thomiste* 77 (1977), 94–129.

Niemann, F.-J., 'Die Erzählung vom leeren Grab bei Markus', *Zeitschrift für katholische Theologie* 101 (1979), 188–99.

Nötscher, F., 'Zur Auferstehung nach drei Tagen', *Biblica* 35 (1954), 313–19.

Nyamiti, C., 'Christ's Resurrection in the Light of African Tribal Initiation Ritual', *Revue Africaine de Théologie* 3 (1979), 171–84.

Oberlinner, L., 'Die Verkündigung der Auferstehung Jesu im geöffneten und leeren Grab. Zu einem vernachlässigten Aspekt in der Diskussion um das Grab Jesu', *Zeitschrift für die neutestamentliche Wissenschaft* 73 (1982), 159–82.

O'Brien, P. T., 'The Great Commission of Matthew 28:18–20. A Missionary Mandate or Not?', *Reformed Theological Review* 35 (1976), 66–78.

O'Collins, G., 'Peter as Easter Witness', *Heythrop Journal* 22 (1981), 1–18.

O'Neill, J. C., 'On the Resurrection as a Historical Question' in *Christ, Faith and History. Cambridge Studies in Christology* (ed. S. W. Sykes and J. P. Clayton; Cambridge: University Press, 1972), pp. 205–19.

Orlett, R., 'An Influence of the Early Liturgies upon the Emmaus Account', *The Catholic Biblical Quarterly* 21 (1959), 212–19.

O'Toole, R. F., 'Luke's Understanding of Jesus' Resurrection – Ascension – Exaltation', *Biblical Theology Bulletin* 9 (1979), 106–14.

Pamment, M., 'Empty Tomb and Resurrection', *New Blackfriars* 62 (1981), 488–93.

Pannenberg, W., 'A Theology of Death and Resurrection', *Theology Digest* 23 (1975), 143–8.

Parkhurst, L. G., 'Matthew 28:16–20 Reconsidered', *Expository Times* 90 (1978–79), 179–80.

Paulsen, H., 'Mk. XVI. 1–8', *Novum Testamentum* 22 (1980), 138–75.

Pelletier, A., 'Les apparitions du Ressuscité en termes de la Septante', *Biblica* 51 (1970), 76–9.

Perrot, C., 'Paul et la résurrection de Jésus', *Quatre Fleuves* nos 15–16 (1982), 23–33.

Perrot, C., 'Emmaüs ou la rencontre du Seigneur (Lc 24, 13–35)' in *La Pâque du Christ. Mystère du salut* (ed. M. Benzerath, A. Schmid and J. Guillet; Lectio Divina 112; Paris: Éditions du Cerf, 1982), pp. 159–66.

Perrot, C., 'Emmaus oder die Begegnung mit dem Herrn', *Theologie der Gegenwart* 26 (1983), 19–25.

Pesch, R., 'Eine alttestamentische Ausführungsformel in Matthäus-Evangelium. Redaktionsgeschichtliche und exegetische Beobachtungen', *Biblische Zeitschrift* 10 (1966), 220–45; 11 (1967), 79–95.

Pesch, R., 'Der Schluss der vormarkinischen Passionsgeschichte und des Markus-evangeliums: Mk 15, 42 – 16, 8' in *L'Évangile de Marc. Tradition et rédaction* (ed. M. Sabbe; Bibliotheca Ephemeridum Theologicarum Lovaniensium 34; Louvain: Leuven University Press, 1974), pp. 365–409.

Pesch, R., 'Das "leere Grab" und der Glaube an Jesu Auferstehung', *Internationale Katholische Zeitschrift/Communio* 11 (1982), 6–20.

Peters, T., 'The Use of Analogy in Historical Method', *The Catholic Biblical Quarterly* 35 (1973), 475–82.

Petersen, N. R., 'When is the End not the End? Literary Reflections on the Ending of Mark's Narrative', *Interpretation* 34 (1980), 151–66.

Pinnock, C. H., 'The Incredible Resurrection: A Mandate for Faith', *Christ Today* 23 (1979), 722–7.

Plevnik, J., '"The Eleven and Those with Them" According to Luke', *The Catholic Biblical Quarterly* 40 (1978), 205–11.

Ponthot, J., 'Gospel Traditions about Christ's Resurrection. Theological Perspectives and Problems of Historicity', *Lumen Vitae* 21 (1966), 66–90, 205–24.

Pousset, E., 'La résurrection', *Nouvelle Revue Théologique* 91 (1969), 1009–44.

Pousset, E., 'Résurrection de Jésus et message pascal', *Nouvelle Revue Théologique* 94 (1972). 95–107.

Pousset, E., 'Croire en la Résurrection', *Nouvelle Revue Théologique* 96 (1974), 147–66, 366–88.

Pousset, E., 'Aspekte der Auferstehungswirklichkeit', *Theologie der Gegenwart* 18 (1975), 29–35.

Quinn, P. L., 'Some Problems about Resurrection', *Religious Studies* 14 (1978), 343–60.

Radermakers, J., 'On Preaching the Risen Christ', *Lumen Vitae* 28 (1973), 267–80.

Ragozzino, G., 'Extra-biblical belief in resurrection', *Theology Digest* 26 (1978), 150–2.

Rahner, K., 'Encounter with the Risen Christ' in *Theological Investigations* VII (New York: Herder and Herder/London: Darton, Longman and Todd, 1971), pp. 169–76.

Rahner, K., 'Experiencing Easter', *ibid.*, pp. 159–68.

Recker, R., 'Matthew 28: 18–20 interpreted from the point of view of the apostolate' in *Zending op weg naar de toekomst. Essays aangeboden aan Prof. Dr. J. Verkuyl* (Kampen: Kok, 1978), pp. 46–58.

Rengstorf, K. H., *Die Auferstehung Jesu. Form, Art and Sinn der urchristlichen Osterbotschaft* (4th ed.; Witten, Ruhr: Luther-Verlag, 1960).

Rengstorf, K. H., 'Old and New Testament Traces of a Formula of the Judaean Royal Ritual', *Novum Testamentum* 5 (1962), 229–44.

Riga, P., 'The Resurrection and Mystical Experience', *The Bible Today* no. 54 (April 1954), 351–6.

Riga, P., 'The Resurrection: Social and Political Implications', *Spiritual Life* 20 (1974), 69–77.

Rigaux, B., *Dieu l'a ressucité. Exégèse et théologie biblique* (Studii Biblici Franciscani Analecta 4; Gembloux: J. Duculot, 1973).

Rogers, C., 'The Great Commission', *Bibliotheca Sacra* 130 (519, 1973), 258–267.

Sabourin, L., 'The Resurrection of Jesus', *Biblical Theology Bulletin* 5 (1975), 262–93.

Sabourin, L., 'Easter in the Early Church', *Religious Studies Bulletin* 2 (1982), 23–32.

Schaberg, J., *The Father, the Son and the Holy Spirit: The Triadic Phrase in Matt 28:19b* (Society of Biblical Literature Dissertation Series 61; Chico, Cal.: Scholars Press, 1982).

Scheffczyk, L., 'Die Auferstehung Jesu: der Lebensgrund des Glaubens', *Internationale Katholische Zeitschrift/Communio* 11 (1982), 32–41.

Schenke, L., *Auferstehungsverkündigung und leeres Grab* (Stuttgarter Bibelstudien 33; Stuttgart: KBW Verlag, 1969).

Schieber, H., 'Konzentrik im Matthäusschluss. Ein form- und gattungskritischer Versuch zu Mt 28, 16–20', *Kairos* 19 (1977), 286–307.

Schieber, H., 'The Conclusion of Matthew's Gospel', *Theology Digest* 27 (1979), 155–8.

Schille, G., *Osterglaube* (Arbeiten zur Theologie, Heft 51; Stuttgart: Calwer Verlag, 1973).

Schillebeeckx, E., *Jesus – An Experiment in Christology* (New York: Crossroad Publishing Company/London: Collins, 1979).

Schlette, H. R., *Epiphany as History* (London: Sheed and Ward, 1969).

Schlier, H., *Das Ostergeheimnis* (Kriterien 41; Einsiedeln: Johannes Verlag, 1976).

Schmauch, W., *Orte der Offenbarung und der Offenbarungsort im Neuen Testament* (Göttingen: Vandenhoeck & Ruprecht, 1956).

Schmidt, P., 'De interpretatie van de verrijzenis: historische feitelijkheid en theologische waarheid', *Internationaal Katholiek Tijdschrift/Communio* 7 (1982), 1–15.

Schmied, A., 'Auferstehungsglaube ohne Ostererscheinungen?', *Theologie der Gegenwart* 17 (1974), 46–51.

Schmied, A., 'Ostererscheinungen – Ostererfahrung', *Theologie der Gegenwart* 19 (1976), 46–53.

Schmied, A., 'Auferstehungsglaube heute und die ursprüngliche Ostererfahrung', *Theologie der Gegenwart* 20 (1977), 43–50.

Schmied, A., 'Tod und Auferstehung Jesu', *Theologie der Gegenwart* 24 (1981), 51–7.

Schmitt, A., *Entrückung – Aufnahme – Himmelfahrt. Untersuchungen zu einem Vorstellungsbereich im Alten Testament* (Forschung zur Bibel 10; Stuttgart: Katholisches Bibelwerk, 1973).

Schmitt, J., 'Le récit de la résurrection dans l'évangile de Luc. Étude de critique littéraire', *Revue des Sciences Religieuses* 25 (1951), 119–37, 219–42.

Schmitt, J., 'Les formulations primitives du mystère pascal', *Biblica* 54 (1973), 272–80.

Schnackenburg, R., 'On the Expression "Jesus is risen (from the Dead)"', *Theology Digest* 18 (1970), 36–42.

Schnackenburg, R., and Pannenberg, W., *Ostern und der neuen Mensch* (Freiburg/Basel/Vienna: Herder, 1981).

Schnellbächer, E. L., 'Das Rätsel des *neaniskos* bei Markus', *Zeitschrift für die neutestamentlichen Wissenschaft* 73 (1982), 127–35.

Schnider, F., 'Die Himmelfahrt Jesu. Ende oder Anfang? Zum Verständnis des lukanischen Doppelwerkes' in *Kontinuität und Einheit. Festschrift für Franz Mussner* (ed. P. G. Müller and W. Stenger; Freiburg/Basel/Vienna: Herder, 1981), pp. 158–72.

Schnider, F., and Stenger, W., *Die Osterberichten der Evangelien* (Schriften zur Katechetik 13; Munich: Kösel-Verlag, 1970).

Schnider, F., and Stenger, W., 'Beobachtungen zur Struktur der Emmausperikope', *Biblische Zeitschrift* N.F. 16 (1972), 94–114.

Schoenberg, M., 'The Meaning of the Resurrection', *Worship* 36 (1963), 414–20.

Schoonenberg, P., 'Te veel verrijzenis-catechese?', *Verbum* 28 (1961), 414–19.

Schrenk, G., '*entellomai, entolē*' in *Theological Dictionary of the New Testament* II (ed. G. Kittel; Grand Rapids: Eerdmans/London: SCM Press, 1964), pp. 544–56.

Schubert, K., 'Resurrection in Pre-Christian Times', *Theology Digest* 12 (1964), 203–8.

Schubert, P., 'The Structure and Significance of Luke 24' in *Neutestamentliche Studien für Rudolf Bultmann* (ed. W. Eltester; Berlin: Alfred Töpelmann, 1954), pp. 165–86.

Schurr, V., 'Die Auferstehung Jesu Christi', *Theologie der Gegenwart* 8 (1965), 219–20.

Schweizer, E., 'Resurrection – Fact or Illusion?', *Horisons in Biblical Theology* 1 (1979), 137–59.

Schweizer, E., 'Resurrection in the New Testament', *Theology Digest* 27 (1979), 132–4.

Schweizer, E., 'Auferstehung. Wirklichkeit oder Illusion?', *Evangelische Theologie* 41 (1981), 2–19.

Scroggs, R., and Groffe, K. I., 'Baptism in Mark: Dying and Rising with Christ', *Journal of Biblical Literature* 92 (1973), 531–48.

Sebastian, T., 'Death and Resurrection in Jewish Apocalyptic', *Jeevadhara* 9 (50, 1979), 117–27.

Seidensticker, P., *Die Auferstehung Jesu in der Botschaft der Evangelien* (Stuttgarter Bibelstudien 26: Stuttgart: KBW Verlag, 1968).

Seidensticker, P., 'The Resurrection Seen from Antioch', *Theology Digest* 17 (1969), 104–8.

Selby, P., *Look for the Living: The Corporate Nature of Resurrection Faith* (Philadelphia: Fortress Press/London: SCM Press, 1976).

Sellin, G., '"Die Auferstehung ist schon geschehen." Zur Spiritualizierung apokalyptischer Terminologie im Neuen Testament', *Novum Testamentum* 25 (1983), 220–37.

Sieber, J. H., 'The Spirit as the "Promise of My Father" in Luke 24:49' in *Sin, Salvation and the Spirit* (ed. D. Durken; Collegeville, Minn.: The Liturgical Press, 1980), pp. 271–8.

Siegman, E. F., 'And by Rising He Restored Life', *Worship* 34 (1960), 386–95.

Sint, J., 'The Resurrection in the Primitive Community', *Theology Digest* 12 (1964), 33–9.

Smith, J. J., 'Resurrection Faith Today', *Theological Studies* 30 (1969), 393–419.

Smith, R. H., 'New and Old in Mark 16:1–8', *Concordia Theological Monthly* 43 (1972), 518–27.

Smyth, K., 'Matthew 28: Resurrection as Theophany', *Irish Theological Quarterly* 42 (1975), 259–71.

Snodgrass, K., 'Western Non-Interpolations', *Journal of Biblical Literature* 91 (1972), 369–79.

Stein, R. H., 'A Short Note on Mark XIV. 28 and XVI. 7', *New Testament Studies* 20 (1973–74), 445–52.

Stein, R. H., 'Was the Tomb Really Empty?', *Journal of the Evangelical Theological Society* 20 (1977), 23–29.

Steinseifer, B., 'Der Ort der Erscheinungen des Auferstandenen. Zur Frage alter galiläischer Ostertraditionen', *Zeitschrift für die neutestamentliche Wissenschaft* 62 (1972), 232–65.

Stempvoort, P. A. van, 'The Interpretation of the Ascension in Luke-Acts', *New Testament Studies* 5 (1958–59), 30–42.

Stock, A., 'Resurrection Appearances and the Disciples' Faith', *The Bible Today* 20 (November 1982), 354–7.

Stravinskas, M. J., 'The Emmaus Pericope: Its Sources, Theology and Meaning for Today', *BibleBhashyam* 3 (1977), 97–115.

Surgy, P. de (ed.), *The Resurrection and Modern Biblical Thought* (New York: Corpus Books, 1970).

Swain, L., 'The First Easter: What Really Happened?', *The Clergy Review* 59 (1974), 276–83.

Swanston, H., 'The Road to Emmaus', *The Clergy Review* 50 (1965), 506–23.

Synge, F. C., 'Mark 16, 1–8', *Journal of Theology for Southern Africa* 11 (1975), 71–3.

Talbert, C. H., *Literary Patterns, Theological Themes and the Genre of Luke-Acts* (Society of Biblical Literature Monograph Series 20; Missoula, Mont.: Scholars Press, 1974).

Taylor, V., *The Passion Narrative of St Luke. A Critical and Historical Investigation* (Society for New Testament Studies Monograph Series 19; Cambridge: University Press, 1972).

Teeple, H. M., 'The Historical Beginnings of the Resurrection Faith' in *Studies in New Testament and Early Christian Literature. Essays in Honor of A. P. Wikgren* (Leiden: Brill, 1972), pp. 107–20.

Thévenot, X., 'Emmaüs, une nouvelle Genèse? Une lecture psychoanalytique de Genèse 2 – 3 et Luc 24, 13–35', *Mélanges de Science Religieuse* 37 (1980), 3–18.

Thompson, W. G., 'An Historical Perspective in the Gospel of Matthew', *Journal of Biblical Literature* 93 (1974), 243–62.

Thrall, M. E., 'Resurrection Traditions and Christian Apologetic', *Thomist* 43 (1979), 197–216.

Tilborg, S. van, *The Jewish Leaders in Matthew* (Leiden: Brill, 1972).

Trilling, W., *Das wahre Israel. Studien zur Theologie des Matthäus-Evangelium* (Studien zum Alten und Neuen Testament 10; 3rd ed.; Munich: Kösel-Verlag, 1964).

Trilling, W., 'Die Auferstehung Jesu, Anfang der neuen Weltzeit (Mt 28, 1–8)' in *Christusverkündigung in den synoptischen Evangelien* (Biblische Handbibliothek IV; Munich: Kösel-Verlag, 1969), pp. 212–43.

Trocmé, E., *The Formation of the Gospel According to Mark* (trans. P. Gaughan: Philadelphia: The Westminster Press/London: SPCK. 1975).

Trompf, G. W., 'The First Resurrection Appearance and the Ending of Mark's Gospel', *New Testament Studies* 18 (1971–72), 308–30.

Trompf, G. W., 'The Markusschluss in Recent Research', *Australian Biblical Review* 21 (1973), 15–26.

Turner, G., 'Varieties of Resurrection', *New Blackfriars* 56 (661; 1975), 272–6.

Turner, G., 'He was Raised and has Appeared: Evidence and Faith', *New Blackfriars* 58 (683; 1977), 160–6.

Vanhoye, A., 'La fuite du jeune homme nu (Mc 14, 51–52)', *Biblica* 52 (1971), 401–6.

Veerkamp, T., 'Vom ersten Tag nach jenem Sabbat. Der Epilog des Markusevangeliums: 15, 33 – 16, 8', *Texte und Kontexte* no. 13 (1982), 5–34.

Vellanickal, M., 'Feast of the Resurrection (Jn 20: 1–18). Identity of the Risen Lord', *BibleBhashyam* 2 (1976), 91–4.

Vellanickal, M., 'Resurrection of Jesus in St John', *BibleBhashyam* 3 (1977), 131–54.

Vögtle, A., ' "Er ist auferstanden, er ist nicht hier" ', *Bibel und Leben* 7 (1966), 69–73.

Vögtle, A., 'Wie kam es zur Artikulierung des Osterglaubens?', *Bibel und Leben* 14 (1973), 231–44.

Vögtle, A., 'Wie kam es zur Artikulierung des Osterglaubens? (Schluss)', *Bibel und Leben* 15 (1974), 174–93.

Vögtle, A., and Pesch, R., *Wie kam es zum Osterglauben?* (Patmos-Paperback; Dusseldorf: Patmos, 1975).

Walker, N., 'After Three Days', *Novum Testamentum* 4 (1960), 261–2.

Walker, R., *Die Heilsgeschichte im ersten Evangelium* (Göttingen: Vandenhoeck & Ruprecht, 1967).

Walker, W. O., 'Postcrucifixion Appearances and Christian Origins', *Journal of Biblical Literature* 88 (1969), 157–65.

Walker, W. O., 'Christian Origins and Resurrection Faith', *Journal of Religion* 52 (1972), 41–55.

Walter, N., 'Eine vormatthäische Schilderung der Auferstehung Jesu', *New Testament Studies* 19 (1972–73), 415–29.

150   *The Resurrection Narratives of the Synoptic Gospels*

Walter, N., ' "Historischer Jesus" und Osterglaube. Ein Diskussionsbeitrag zur Christologie', *Theologische Literaturzeitung* 101 (1976), 321–8.

Walther, O. K., 'A Solemn One Way Trip Becomes a Joyous Roundtrip! A Study of the Structure of Luke 24:13–35', *Ashland Theological Bulletin* 14 (1981), 60–7.

Wanke, J., *Die Emmauserzählung. Eine redaktionsgeschichtliche Untersuchung zu Lk 24, 13–35* (Erfurter theologische Studien 31; Leipzig: St. Benno-Verlag, 1973).

Wanke, J., ' "... wie sie ihm beim Brotbrechen erkannten." Zur Auslegung der Emmauserzählung. Lk 24, 13–35', *Biblische Zeitschrift* 18 (1974), 180–92.

Wansbrough, H., 'The Resurrection', *The Way* 11 (1971), 324–30.

Wansbrough, H., 'The Resurrection II', *The Way* 12 (1972), 58–67.

Wansbrough, H., 'The Resurrection IV. The Risen Christ, Lord and Head of Creation', *The Way* 13 (1973), 148–54.

Wansbrough, H., 'The Resurrection V. Christ's Hour of Glorification', *ibid.*, 229–35.

Wansbrough, H., *Risen from the Dead* (Slough: St Paul Publications, 1978).

Watson, N. M., ' "The Cause of Jesus Continues?" An Investigation of the Intention of Willi Marxsen', *Australian Biblical Review* 25 (1977), 21–28.

Watte, P., Lombaers, H., and Jezierski, C., 'For a Catechetical Presentation of Christ's Resurrection: I. On the Adult Level; II. On the Adolescent Level', *Lumen Vitae* 21 (1966), 405–11, 412–22.

Weeden, T. J., *Mark – Traditions in Conflict* (Philadelphia: Fortress Press, 1971).

Weier, R., 'The Structure of Faith in Jesus' Resurrection', *Theology Digest* 21 (1973), 17–21.

Wenham, D., 'The Resurrection Narratives in Matthew's Gospel', *Tyndale Bulletin* 24 (1973), 21–54.

Wilson, S. G., *The Gentiles and the Gentile Mission in Luke-Acts* (Society for New Testament Studies Monograph Series 23; Cambridge: University Press, 1973).

Winden, H. W., *Wie kam und wie kommt es zum Osterglauben? Darstellung, Beurteilung und Weiterführung der durch Rudolf Pesch ausgelösten Diskussion* (Disputationes Theologicae 12; Frankfurt am Main/Berne: P. Lang, 1982).

Yamauchi, E. M., 'Easter – Myth, Hallucination, or History', *Christ Today* 18 (1974), 660–3, 728–32.

Zehrer, F., *Die Auferstehung Jesu nach den vier Evangelisten. Die Osterevangelien und ihre hauptsächliche Probleme* (Vienna: Mayer & Companie, 1980).

Zumstein, J., 'Matthieu 28: 16–20', *Revue de Théologie et de Philosophie* 22 (1972), 14–33.